Editor's Note

Jonathan Wilson, Editor

Journalism is on its last legs. Publishing wheezes on life support. Sales are down again. A second Dark Ages await. The prognostications of doom come louder and more panicky every day.

From the established newspapers and publishers, it's understandable. The drop off in newspaper sales over the past decade is, for those whose livelihoods depend on them, terrifying. The number of independent book shops in Britain has fallen by a factor of 15 over the past five years. Ottakars, Borders and Books Etc are no more. Other chains are ailing. Magazines are going out of business. Those of us in football journalism see colleagues laid off with horrifying regularity. Those who remain on staff do twice the work for half the pay of their predecessors of even a decade ago.

Yet here's the paradox: we live in a golden age. There has never been so much football journalism of such high standard as there is now. There have been more high-quality football books published in Britain this year than in whole decades of the twentieth century. That's not just a personal view, it's also the opinion of the doyen of British football-writing, Brian Glanville ("There are two sorts of football journalists," Paddy Barclay once said. "Those who have been influenced by Brian Glanville and those who should have been.") I had dinner with him shortly after his eightieth birthday last year and he said that these days he looks round almost every press box he goes to and sees at least half a dozen writers who would have been the best in the country in any other era.

And that's without even mentioning the blogs and websites of which there are thousands upon thousands. The vast majority are boring, repetitive, badly-written and angry and most are dedicated to the same handful of clubs; but there are several that are genuinely high excellent, whether because they're clever, funny, well-written, emotionally powerful, provocative or just different. And the beauty of the modern world is that the writers of the best ones are rapidly elevated. Take, for example, Michael Cox, the editor of zonalmarking. net, who went in 18 months from being an unknown setting up his own website to a mainstream voice with columns on the *Guardian*, ESPN and Betfair websites.

"Zonal Whoever", as Owen Coyle once dismissed him after Cox had suggested his claims of playing passing football were misleading, is an example of the positives of modern journalism. Everybody can be heard and those who stand out prosper. The system is more democratic than ever before. Even by the time I began writing professionally, in 1999, the old route of a journalist working his way up through a local paper to beat reporter on a national to correspondent or columnist didn't really apply. Now it's non-existent —and only partly because of the decline of local newspapers. Perhaps some of the craft of journalism has been lost as a result but the gain has been freshness and innovation and a great sense of opportunity.

And that in itself is unpopular among those already in journalism. It's probably less true of football than of other sports (cricket, certainly) but there is a hostility among certain members of the old guard towards those who write for websites, less because of who they are than what they represent. And that, of course, is a threat. They represent the new age and in the new age, there are no sinecures. There are no lifetime contracts and there is no possibility of a comfortable dotage, plodding along to a couple of games and a couple of press conferences a week. The competition is relentless. There is no respite, no possibility of a lazy week: a journalist has to prove himself with every story.

That may be a bad thing for journalists but for journalism, of course, it's excellent news. Or it would be in isolation. But as well as increasing access, making it possible for anybody with an internet connection to publish their writing, the internet has destroyed the payment model of the newspapers. For two centuries, readers were happy to pay the cover price and that, along with advertising, was enough to pay for paper, ink, printing, distribution and the staff. Since the advent of the internet, though, there is an expectation that content should be available for free and, particularly given the decline of the advertising market in a worldwide economic crisis, that has slashed revenue. It's never been easier to break into journalism; it's never been harder to make a living from it.

The internet — clearly — hasn't diminished the appetite for information; if anything it's done the opposite. Publishers talk of the extraordinary demand for readers to meet and interact with authors — at festivals, as one senior executive put it in a tone of bewilderment, "even the Sunday 9 am slots are full." The problem is that nobody has worked out how to monetise that. A decade ago, the assumption was that a solution would present itself. As yet, it hasn't. The Murdoch papers have gone behind a paywall but opinion is divided on whether that has been a success. In July this year, the *Mail's* website became the first to turn a profit through advertising revenues; the *Guardian's* online revenues went up by 16% last year (but the paper as a whole lost £44million). Those figures, perhaps, offer hope for the future, particularly as global economic conditions improve and the advertising market picks up. That may come too late for certain papers, though, if it comes at all: the internet publishing industry has existed for too long on promises of jam tomorrow.

A frankly ludicrous piece in the *Guardian* by David Leigh — who has, as he announced in an opening line of tellingly quaint metaphor, "survived more than 40 years at the coalface of British journalism (longer than a term of service in the ancient Roman army)" —proposed a £2 per month levy on broadband subscriptions to subsidise ailing newspapers. There is no logic to this, nor any chance of it happening. If newspapers are to be subsidised, why not other industries affected by the internet? Why not book shops, music producers, cinema chains, printers and pornographers? If everybody paid just an extra £50 a month we could probably keep the world exactly as it was in the early 1990s. In fact, why stop there? Why not destroy the printing presses and set monks to work copying manuscripts by candlelight while the news is distributed by fat men with big hats and bells?

Luddism is not the answer to any new technology. Industry and society evolve: stasis and subsidy can never be more than short-term strategies to delay the inevitable. Journalism is not dying, but it is changing and part of that change might be the death, or at least the weakening, of the big brands. That can already be seen in the way writers use social media to publicise themselves — it's an on-going process but increasingly readers follow particular writers they like or articles on particular topics that interest them. The sense of being a *Telegraph* reader or a *Mirror* reader is not as binding as it once was. It may even be that the increasing number of independent voices, the questioning of the big brands, helped bring about the current debate in Britain about media ethics as represented by the Leveson Inquiry.

This is a world in which power is increasingly being devolved from the media brands to the consumer. The reader has more choice than ever before. In the abstract, it's hard to see that as anything other than positive. The issue now is making the new world work for writers as well as readers, which is essential if the best writers are to keep writing and not to drift off to more lucrative fields. Paywalls are unpopular, but even they have an essentially democratic ethos: after all, which is preferable, financial control coming from a community of readers each paying a small fee each year or from three or four major advertisers?

Other payment models may be found, are still waiting to be found. *The Blizzard*, thanks to readers being responsible in what they pay and writers being prepared to receive not a flat fee but a share of revenue, has stumbled upon a payment structure that seems to work for us, for now — which isn't to say that it will work for everybody or that it will work for us forever.

Journalism stands on a new frontier. There is great opportunity but also jeopardy. It is all but inconceivable, to look at this from an English perspective, that all 10 national daily newspapers will survive the next decade. Smaller, niche publications, whether online or print, will spring up. Many will flash brightly and fade away; some will establish themselves. The future is uncertain, but it is also exciting. And while the appetite for news, analysis and opinion exists, journalism will never die. It'll just look a bit different.

December 2012

Contents

The Blizzard, Issue Seven

8

El Dorado

"A few steps, no more, and four
shots ring out."

The Ball and the Gun

After a political rival was murdered, the Colombian government set up the world's richest league

By Carl Worswick

It's 9 April 1948 and the clock strikes one.

Jorge Eliécer Gaitán puts down his pen, removes his tie and lifts himself from his desk. He is weary and his stomach groans.

A long morning of meetings concluded, Gaitán withdraws from his work and gazes out from the office window.

Below, on one of the main high streets in the Colombian capital city Bogotá, shoppers throng.

Dr Gaitán's office is on the third floor of the Agustín Nieto building, which hulks over Calle 7 in downtown Bogotá. It's a cold, grey monolith, devoid of any architectural creativity. Obscured in its shadows shuffles a man, his hands tucked into his coat.

Behind Gaitán the office stirs and his friends prepare to leave. As he puts on his coat and fixes his hat, Gaitán checks his afternoon schedule. There are more meetings, starting in an hour's time with a 21-year-old Cuban law student called Fidel Castro. But first lunch.

The Hotel Continental was a brisk five-minute stroll away, along Calle 7 and then right towards the mountains in the east. Lunch there wasn't cheap but this was a celebration.

Gaitán is on the cusp of a famous victory as defence lawyer for Lieutenant Jesús Maria Cortés. The previous day he'd put in a masterful performance in the trial's final session and every radio station and newspaper in Colombia was hailing his brilliance.

Exhausted but jubilant the five men leave office 406. At about five past one, with the others following a few metres behind, Gaitán and his trusted friend and colleague Plinio Mendoza Niera leave the building arm in arm and step out onto the busy high street. It's cold but the sun is out.

They turn north, unaware of the shadow that now shifts behind them. A few steps, no more, and four shots ring out. Gaitán slumps into his friend and then onto the pavement, his face ashen. Blood trickles from his back. Fifty minutes later Gaitán is pronounced dead at a nearby hospital.

Over the 10 years that followed, an estimated 300,000 Colombians would die in the aftershocks of the assassination. Gaitán was more than a mesmerising orator skilled in the practices of the law, he was also a hugely popular politician and a shoo-in for the 1950 general election as left-wing leader of the Liberal Party.

Seismic historical events are never straightforward. They are laced with theory, counter-theory and outrageous conspiracy theories. Sixty years on from Gaitán's death, nobody is sure of the whos and whys.

Officially the killer was identified as 26-year-old schizophrenic, disgruntled at the Liberal leader's refusal to give him a job. Few believe it. Others, like Gaitán's daughter Gloria, point the finger at the CIA. Less credible versions claim it was Fidel Castro acting as a Soviet agent or militant Catholic priests angered by Gaitán's atheism.

Whatever the reason, the legacy of bloodshed, the human cost, was appalling. This was the period of *La Violencia* but the wave of death and despair wasn't the only result of the murder. It also led to the creation of the very first professional national football league in Colombia.

Football had, of course, existed in Colombia for many years before 1948. Debate still rages as to where the real birthplace of football in Colombia is but Barranquilla on the north Caribbean coast has perhaps the greatest claim. Its argument, at least, is the most vociferous.

Their story goes that the game was brought to Colombia by English sailors, railway workers and engineers just before the turn of the 20th century. Matches were at first sporadic and informal, arranged when sailors were in dock. Gradually local onlookers employed by the Colombia Railway Company became involved and on 6 August 1904, the first

official game took place. The English influence was obvious, one team wearing red and white stripes with blue shorts, the other side in halved shirts, the top white, the lower part red.

It provided the incentive for the first discussions about football and this, combined with the trickle of rich Colombians returning from studying in England, led to the formulation of a set of English FA-style rules as a basis for play.

The city of Santa Marta, two hours along the coast from Barranquilla, contests this theory. Although they record the first official game to have taken place in 1909, they argue football was played long before this — on the beach and among workers from the nearby United Fruit Company.

A few years later around 2,000 of those workers would be massacred by the Colombian army for going on strike. Their struggle was semi-fictionalised by a local writer, Gabriel García Márquez, in his masterpiece *One Hundred Years of Solitude*, but in the real world it was a young radical lawyer that took up their case. And with it Jorge Eliécer Gaitán became a household name.

But whether Barranquilla or Santa Marta, it was by the Caribbean that football found its most enthusiastic devotees and it soon became the coast's number one sport. Even today Colombia's World Cup 2014 qualifiers are played in the national stadium not in the capital Bogotá but in Barranquilla, a nod to the feverish support there and the historical roots of the game.

As clubs sprouted across the country in the twenties and thirties, football developed very slowly. While Argentina, Brazil, Chile and Uruguay began contesting international tournaments like the first Copa América in 1916, it was only in 1924 that Colombia formed a national governing football association – Asociación Colombiana de Fútbol, later known as Adefútbol. Its headquarters were in Barranquilla.

And yet problems persisted. Hamstrung by the peculiar topography of Colombia, football was confined to local league competitions under the heavy-handed authority of Adefútbol. It wasn't long before discontent with the latter's shoddy leadership and lack of organisation brought regional leagues into direct conflict with the ruling order.

It was a dialectical struggle that continued throughout the 1930s and 40s. The regional leagues were disobedient and provocative, Adefútbol authoritarian and dismissive in their response. With each party acting from self-interest, by the mid-1940s direct confrontation had become commonplace. And still there was no national league.

In the background raged another debate, that of amateurism versus professionalism. It's a discussion that most football associations across the globe have had to endure and in Alfonso Senior and Humberto Salcedo, Colombia found two very convincing voices in favour of a professional and national league structure.

In 1936 Colombia were accepted as a member of South American football's governing body, Conmebol. Of the present 10 members, only Venezuela joined later. Colombia made their Copa América debut in 1945 but performed poorly, winning just one of their six games. Senior and Salcedo saw professionalism as the key to improving the quality of football in Colombia and the Copa disaster prompted the first serious talks on how to restructure the regional leagues.

Senior and Salcedo had little initial success but on 9 April 1948, the pendulum took an incredible swing in their favour.

Guillermo Ruiz Bonilla is Colombia's most respected football historian. His house is a shrine to football, with three rooms stacked with documents, photos, videos, shirts, balls and books. He argues that the government saw football as the only way to mitigate the social unrest that Gaitán's death unleashed. "Before the creation of the league, the strongest regional leagues were those in the departments of Antioquia, Valle, Atlántico and a few others,'" he said. "These leagues were talking and working towards professionalism.

"But with the death of Gaitán in April 1948 and with the influence of the Mariano Ospina Pérez government, direct support from the president was given to the idea of a national professional league. This was essential. In just four months — May, June, July and August — a league was created and in all parts of the country football was seen as the solution to help alleviate the huge problems the country was facing."

Ruiz Bonilla argues that football's mass popular appeal made it a potent weapon in the government's fight to maintain law and order: "That's clear. Football was the only thing that the government could think of to control and calm the population after the death of Gaitán. There was nothing else that came close, except maybe horse-racing.

"Alfonso Senior and Humberto Salcedo were instrumental in the start of professional football. Years later Senior told me: 'If Gaitán's death hadn't happened, the start of the league in Colombia would have been delayed by years. Gaitán's murder was what triggered professional football in Colombia.'"

The project was born in Barranquilla on 26 June 1948. It wasn't without its problems, not least because of the resistance of the regional leagues who were set to lose jurisdiction over their teams. And with it, of course, money. The discussions were heated — club representatives stormed out of meetings and insults were traded — but, on July 7 agreement was reached. Professionalism had won.

"In the end the situation was resolved when Dimayor [the professional league] agreed to pay money, initially 3% of gate receipts, to the regional leagues," Ruiz Bonilla explained. "They also had to affiliate to Adefútbol, the body responsible for governing football in Colombia."

On August 11 at 11 am, 126 days after Gaitán was shot, the league began. A morning kick-off was chosen to fit with the established practice of Saturday afternoon horse-racing. Both events in the same stadium: a feast of sporting distraction.

The Bogotá side Millonarios began the season as overwhelming favourites. The club was only two years old, but had been founded by a group of wealthy and well-connected businessmen. One of those was Manuel Briceño Pardo, a lawyer who would later become mayor of Bogotá. Like most of the founding fathers of Millonarios, Pardo was also a prominent Conservative Party member and he understood perfectly the potential football had to connect to the masses. Initially Millonarios played in all white but Pardo moved quickly to reinforce the club's links to the Conservatives by changing its colours to blue.

But despite Millonarios's superior wealth and power it was their capital city rivals Santa Fe who won the first Colombian championship, pipping the Barranquilla side Junior to the title by four points. Millonarios finished fourth.

Undeterred, Millonarios kept on buying players. Under the watchful eye of their wily club president Alfonso Senior, new signings were lured by under-the-table sweeteners. In early 1949 the Argentinian Carlos 'Cacho' Aldabe was signed and appointed player-manager. "El Cacho was a friend of the great Argentinan player Adolfo Pedernera," Ruiz Bonilla said. "Soon after he joined Millonarios he approached Senior with the idea of bringing Pedernera to Colombia."

At the time Pedernera was arguably the world's best player, the star man in River Plate's fabled La Máquina side. He was, in the words of Uruguayan writer Eduardo Galeano, "the axis of River's La Máquina... generating play, threading passes through the eye of a needle, changing gear, surprising opponents with his bite."

It was a swoop so audacious, so ambitious, as to be almost unthinkable. But in Argentina in the mid-to-late-forties something peculiar was taking place. Invigorated by the election of a general in 1946, Argentina's working classes were flexing their muscles and demanding change. What's more, they were being listened to. This rise of union and worker militancy encroached into football and by 1948 the players' union, Futbolistas Argentinos Agremiados, was at war with the football authorities. Battle lines were drawn in April as the players threatened to strike to achieve three key demands: freedom of contract, a minimum wage and recognition of their union.

At the eleventh hour the authorities buckled and agreed to recognise the union. It was enough temporarily to release some steam but, despite attempted government arbitration, by November players were on strike. Stadiums fell empty and Senior watched on with an opportunist's eye. In March 1949, he would be handed the means to execute his daring raid.

Relations between Adefútbol and Dimayor had reached breaking point. On March 15, Adefútbol could take no more and disaffiliated Dimayor. It was a dispute that would only be resolved in 1971 but for Senior that was an opportunity. Dimayor were not only cast adrift from Adefútbol but also from Fifa. They were isolated to organise football as they wished. Tensions rose further when Adefútbol sent a team to the 1949 Copa América in Rio de Janeiro. The Barranquilla-based federation turned to the local side Junior to represent Colombia in Brazil. Colombia flopped to a last-placed finish

and, if the embarrassment of the players wasn't enough, Dimayor responded by banning Junior for the following season.

The Argentinian players' strike and Dimayor's disaffiliation were two quirks of history that coincided. Senior, unshackled from the usual Fifa restrictions, sent Cacho to find Pedernera in Argentina. "Senior was really afraid of giving Cacho the money," Ruiz Bonilla said. "He didn't trust him and thought that he may run away never to be seen again."

Cacho left Bogotá for Buenos Aires with a suitcase stuffed with US$5,000, an astronomical fee for the time. When he met Pedernera, the striker was well aware that he might never play football again. He was 30 and, with no end to the strike in sight, Cacho's proposition was attractive.

Pedernera named his terms — he accepted the $5,000 signing-on fee and asked for a monthly salary of $200. They were big figures that Cacho feared were beyond the reach of Millonarios, despite their name. He sent a telegram to Senior explaining Pedernera's conditions and received an immediate response: "Bring him."

Pedernera's club Huracán were never consulted and never received a transfer fee. Such details were considered unnecessary Fifa red tape. Why pay a club a fee when that cash could instead go directly to the player, enhancing his labour conditions?

The second Colombian football league was already five rounds old when Pedernera arrived at El Dorado airport on 10 June 1949. His move was condemned as a scandal in Argentina but he was greeted by hordes of fans in Bogotá. The following day he was unveiled at Millonarios's El Campín stadium. The Blues were playing the Medellín side Atlético Municipal but Pedernera was badly out of shape, having lost nine kilograms during the long months of the strike.

Still, while he couldn't play, his presentation was a monumental moment in the history of Colombian football and 15,000 fans turned up for his welcome. Senior, who had previously promised the other club directors he would foot the bill if Pedernera's stint didn't work out, saw $17,000 taken at the turnstiles. Pedernera's yearly salary was covered in ninety minutes.

Millonarios ran out 6-0 winners on Pedernera's debut. Expectation and excitement reverberated around the ground. El Dorado —the Golden Age — had begun.

Pedernera made his debut against Deportes Caldas on 26 June 1949. He didn't score but he was behind every attacking move. It was as if a Picasso had found its place in a high-school art exhibition. Millonarios won 3-0 and another $17,000 dropped into the accounts. Senior basked in the glory but he wasn't satisfied. And neither was Pedernera.

After a few games the gulf in class between Pedernera and his teammates was obvious. Pedernera requested a meeting with Senior to suggest the signing of more players. He asked specifically for some strikers — "without goals, we're not going to win anything."

Senior suggested Pedernera return to Argentina and search out the very best.

He did just that and, in August, the former River midfielder Néstor 'Raul' Rossi arrived together with a 23-year-old forward called Alfredo Di Stéfano. If Pedernera was the grandmaster, Di Stéfano was his apprentice. Many players would arrive in Colombia over the following three years from all across the globe, but none would make quite such an impression as 'La Saeta Rubia', the Blond Arrow.

On his debut he netted a hat-trick in a 5-0 win. That season Pedernera, Rossi and Di Stéfano helped Millonarios average almost four goals a game as they brought the 1949 title to the blue half of Bogotá for the first time.

As Colombians swarmed to pack stadiums and watch football of a calibre they had never seen before, elsewhere there was outcry at what was perceived as an act of piracy.

Efraín 'El Caimán' Sánchez is one of Colombia's greatest ever goalkeepers. In 1948 he became the first Colombian to play in Argentina after being scouted at the 1947 Copa América in Guayaquil, Ecuador. He witnessed first-hand the mass exodus of Argentinian players and the subsequent birth of Colombian football's golden age.

I met him in Bogotá's Museo Nacional where he gave a talk about his experiences playing for Colombia during the 1962 World Cup final. Our interview in the museum's leafy garden café was constantly interrupted by fans eager for photos, autographs or just the chance to shake his giant hand.

"René Pontoni, Argentina's main striker, approached me and asked me whether I'd like to play in Argentina," Sánchez said. "I was really excited — at the time Argentinian football was the mecca of world football — but I had already made a verbal contract with the Mexican team Oro de Guadalajara. I had to choose between Argentina and Mexico."

He chose Argentina and, at the age of 22, joined San Lorenzo. "San Lorenzo gave me my fame and in Argentina I became a star," he said. "It's also where I got my name, *El Caimán*. It was carnival time when I arrived in Buenos Aires and during my first interview for *La Critíca* they asked me where I was from and I told them Barranquilla. At the time there was a really famous song that was played everywhere that went something like '*se va Caimán, se va Caimán, se va para Barranquilla.*'" In the next day's newspaper the headlines said, 'They are bringing us El Caimán from Barranquilla.'"

Music was always important for El Caimán. One of his heroes was the great tango singer Carlos Gardel. But while music was an interest, football was his passion and it was another talismanic figure from the age that inspired him to take up football and become a goalkeeper. "As a child during the 1930s we used to form pitches in Barranquilla by throwing sand in the street,'" he said. "I remember from about the age of six playing one against one, kicking the ball from one makeshift goal to another. We made the footballs ourselves from sand, wood chippings and newspapers.

"I was 15 when I decided I wanted to be a goalkeeper and my life-long idol was always the Spanish goalkeeper Ricardo

Zamora. I collected a card of his from a sweet wrapper when I was a child and I remember watching him play for Spain during the 1934 World Cup. He was and still is my hero, him and Gardel."

El Caimán's first few months in Argentina were unhappy ones. He felt lonely and missed home but, ultimately, the experience made him stronger. "In Argentina I started to feel like a man, because it was really hard for me to adapt," he said. "After a while though I promised myself I would only cry if I had something serious to cry about and that way I became a star."

It's hard now to imagine this towering octogenarian once blubbering to himself but behind the proud veneer his tender and sensitive side is still apparent. Just two weeks after he made his debut for San Lorenzo against Gimnasio y Esgrima de la Plata. El Caimán was given a sharp reminder of home with the murder of Gaitán.

"I was in Buenos Aires when he was killed, it was a great shock," he said. "I read a lot about him, everybody was talking about Gaitán, just like they still are doing. The country changed when he was killed and Gaitán became a martyr. I saw lots of similarities between him and Perón. Both were very good speakers, very convincing with powerful voices that involved the crowd. I once went to a public talk with some musician friends. We were stood very far away from Perón but it was like he was a few metres away. He had the voice of a leader, complete charisma."

But however infectious Perón's charisma was, it couldn't save Argentinian football from strike action and when Pedernera departed, it left the country reeling. "It was like a bomb going off," El Caimán said. "Argentinians considered their football to be the best in the world and so to lose their stars hurt a lot."

One example of how Argentinians felt is given by a particularly lyrical and vitriolic attack on the Colombians in *La Epoca*. Upon learning that Deportivo Cali were poised to snatch three Argentinian players the paper published an editorial that said, "This latest case announces itself as a real hawk with a cannibal appetite. The question for us [the Argentinians] is, what we are going to do to safeguard our coveted pigeons... just how long will the suicidal zeal of the Colombians last? And we declare it a suicidal zeal because one day this will all collapse. Which castle of cards doesn't? The spectacle of football as business and not as sport can only give so much and so there will be many that will return with tears in their eyes and confessing to their dangerous adventure."

Bitter and angry words that at no point tried to relate to the frustration Argentina's stars were facing. As strike action continued and the authorities refused to give ground, just one year into his Argentinian career El Caimán left too. He claims his reasons were personal rather than economic but it must have been difficult to ignore the industrial strife and poisoned atmosphere of Argentina in the late 1940s. "I joined América de Cali in 1949," he said. "My mother was ill; she had a problem with her liver and so I returned home to be closer to her. The league had started in 1948 but it was in 1949 that all the big players began arriving from Argentina, Brazil, Peru, Paraguay, from all over the world."

Millonarios may have grabbed the initiative in El Dorado with Senior's daring raids but other clubs weren't far behind. Deportivo Cali, a club that was always closely linked to the ruling elite of Colombia's third city, were one of the first teams to act. In 1949 Cali's directors agreed to send a small plane to Peru. When it returned, 14 players, several of whom were members of the national team, were on board.

The greatest of those was Valentino López, who made his debut halfway through the season and ended the campaign as third-highest goalscorer, scoring in every game in which he played. Cali became known as 'El Rodillo Negro', 'the Black Steamroller', and finished the season in second place, level on points with Millonarios.

Independiente Medellín also looked to Peru to bolster their squad. With their recruits, the entire Peru national team was based in Colombia. This sudden influx of talent into the Colombian league didn't go unnoticed and across the continent discontent was brewing. The Argentinians, who had perhaps suffered most, found allies in Paraguay and Peru. Their case was eventually taken to Fifa and on 25 October 1949 Colombia were expelled.

Dimayor responded in bombastic style. In the following day's newspapers the league organisers boasted that the expulsion didn't affect them, that they weren't a member of Fifa anyway and its clubs would "continue to contract national and foreign players."

By the 1950 season the level of poaching had reached fever pitch. Cali, who had fielded a five-man front line of Peruvians the previous season, lined up with five Argentinian forwards. The great Argentinian goalkeeper Julio Cozzi joined Millonarios to add defensive solidity to a team brimming with the attacking talents of Di Stéfano and Pedernera. Paraguayans arrived at Pereira and Boca Juniors de Cali. By the time of the 1950 World Cup the whole of the Paraguay national team was playing at one of the two clubs.

Junior, back in the league after their suspension, brought in Brazilians, including another of the stars of the age, the enigmatic and troubled Heleno de Freitas. To this day, fans of a certain age remember de Freitas as an idol. "For me, he was the greatest player ever to play in Colombia," says Gustavo Hernandez, who owns a fish restaurant in Barranquilla. "I was just a little boy when he was playing for Junior but he made me fall in love with football. There was nothing he couldn't do. Sadly he had many psychological problems and it eventually killed him. He was a massive gambler, an ex-lover of Eva Perón and people say there wasn't a prostitute in Barranquilla he hadn't had sex with. I think only George Best can compare to Freitas."

The inner demons eventually became too much. At the age of 39, he died in a mental asylum back in Brazil. By then, he weighed just 30 kg and had only one tooth. With the exception of Atlético Nacional de Medellin — who were known as Atlético Municipal until 1950 — every Colombian team had international stars. Having syphoned off most of South America's top talent, it wasn't long before some clubs started to look further afield. Santa Fe led the charge under the

command of Luis Robledo. The son of a millionaire cattle farmer, Robledo had studied in England at Cambridge where he had started following Arsenal.

When he returned to Colombia he helped set up Independiente Santa Fe, copying the Arsenal strip of red shirts with white sleeves. Those were the colours of the Colombian Liberal Party but, initially at least, there was no political connection between the two. Robledo began ploughing his money into Santa Fe and in René Pontoni and Angel Perucca he had already attracted two of Argentina's star players when he set his eyes on England.

In the summer of 1950, England entered the World Cup for the first time. It would prove to be a disaster, forever remembered for the shock 1-0 defeat against the US and England's embarrassing first-round exit. But one of their main players wasn't in Brazil for the finals and was instead being dragged around the US on a pre-season tour with Manchester United. Pockets were being lined but not those of the left-winger Charlie Mitten.

Matt Busby's Manchester United played 12 games across the States that summer to sell-out crowds, but Mitten's wage remained stuck on £12 a week. And then came the call. It was from England's Neil Franklin, considered by Tom Finney to be the finest centre-half he ever played against. Franklin was England's number one defender but like Mitten he wasn't part of the England World Cup set-up. He had told the English FA he wanted to be excused duties to care for his wife who was about to give birth. But it was revealed that he was actually in

Colombia with his Stoke City team-mate George Mountford.

Robledo had approached them both after learning of the antiquated transfer policy of English clubs. As in Argentina, English players had no freedom of contract. It was a burning issue that Robledo sought to exploit. The two players were enticed to Colombia with a £5,000-a-year contract, £35 win bonus and £5,000 signing-on fee. It was almost 10 times the British maximum wage.

Mountford and Franklin were slated by the class-ridden British media and establishment as greedy and insolent working-class mercenaries. But Robledo's work wasn't finished and after signing the two stars he asked Franklin to find him the best left-winger in the world. It was to Mitten he turned. The offer was the same and, for the frustrated 29 year old, it was a chance too good to let go. When the call arrived, Mitten was in his hotel room on Times Square the night before the Manchester United squad was scheduled to go back across the Atlantic on the Queen Mary. Pondering his future and unable to sleep, he approached his manager that same night. Busby told him straight, "You'd better go, or you'll die wondering."

Busby's apparent blessing combined with a lack of financial security for English players made up Mitten's mind. He flew to Bogotá the next day and signed to become El Dorado's latest import. In the Colombian daily newspaper *El Tiempo*, his every move was traced. Looking through the archives today, there's genuine excitement and curiosity from local journalists that players from the home of football were prepared to

travel halfway across the globe to play in Colombia. It was confirmation, perhaps, of the fact that the Colombian league had become the best in the world.

But less than a week after Mitten arrived, Franklin left. He'd played just six games and had earned rave reviews, but the culture shock and the simmering political tensions were too much. Gaitán's death had had a major impact on the country. In 1950 the Liberals boycotted the elections, organised themselves into guerrilla units and took up arms. They were confronted by the brutality of the ultra right-wing Conservative president Laureano Gómez who had assumed dictatorial powers in the absence of a Liberal challenge. An estimated 50,000 people died in 1950, something surely not lost on the English players.

A few years before Mitten's death in 2009, the writer Richard Adamson interviewed the player for his biography, *Bogotá Bandit*. In it, Mitten speaks of his first impressions of life in Colombia: "We found that the country had a huge social divide: there was the great mass of poor people and above them a tremendously wealthy millionaire elite, mostly descended from the Spanish conquistadors, who in fact owned the country. And here we were, English footballers, pioneers — that's how we regarded ourselves — the first rebels against a restrictive and archaic system which treated its principal characters as second-class citizens, mixing freely with this upper class.

"We very quickly found that we were accepted into the inner circles of Colombian social life. As a professional footballer, I rubbed shoulders with oil barons, wealthy landowners and cattle ranchers and their cohorts."

Mitten's time is recorded in Adamson's book with an unconvincing positive spin. He talks enthusiastically of his experiences and an appreciation of the new-found financial security the Colombian adventure offered him. He was also given the opportunity to play alongside the great Di Stéfano in a propaganda-ridden showcase match the Colombian FA had organised against newly crowned world champions Uruguay.

But when Mountford departed Mitten was left alone. The swirling mess of violence and political instability was no place for him or his three young children and after a year he left too. Real Madrid came calling but he instead returned to England as an outcast. Busby had turned on him and the English FA banned him for six months. He later joined Fulham but he was the never the same player again.

When George Eastham famously ended the retain-and-transfer contract in 1963, one of the parties he filed against was his ex-manager at Newcastle for conspiring to keep him at the club. That manager was Charlie Mitten.

England may remember Mitten for his chequered career and questionable stance on footballers' rights, but in Colombia he left a more positive legacy. El Caimán took another sip of coffee. He waited a few seconds to consider my question and then nodded. "Yeah, Charlie Mitten was the best left-winger that was playing in Colombia during El Dorado,"

he said. "He was an extraordinary talent, so quick and very strong."

The historian Ruiz Bonilla agrees. He describes Mitten as a "crack," a Colombian expression reserved for only the finest players. "Mountford and Franklin didn't last long in Colombia," he said. "Franklin was strong, very technical but a little slow. But Mitten was a great talent. At Millonarios there were also a Irish player Billy Higgins and a Scotsman Robert Flawell. They were part of the same team as Pedernera and Di Stéfano. But later three more English players turned up, supposedly to play at Millonarios. Pedernera was furious and went to speak to Alfonso Senior about it. 'A quick word Don Alfonso, I want to know something — are we a team of Englishmen or Argentinians? Because, if these English guys play for Millonarios, I'm off.'" Pedernera's threat changed the directors' minds and the three other English players spent a week in Colombia before returning to England. They never played a game.

In October 1950 Billy Higgins also walked. He claimed he'd been lied to by the Millonarios directors and instead of the promised £135 monthly salary his Colombian adventure earned him just £28. But, central to the ex-Everton striker's decision to return to England was the hostility he encountered from the Argentinians in the squad. "The Argentinian players boycotted me and made me play as a reserve," he told the press in Southampton on his return. "The Argentinians at Millonarios have been acting like this for some time because they understood that the English were going to take their places in the team."

Sour grapes from a player who sacrificed so much on a move that didn't work out perhaps, but Pedernera's appointment as Millonarios player-manager in the same month as Higgins' departure must surely have played a part in hastening his exit.

The largely unhappy time served by the five British players that gambled their careers on El Dorado in little more than a footnote in English football history. But how different that could have been if other names had joined them. Mitten claimed that Stanley Matthews had been approached to play in Colombia and had considered it before deciding that at 35 he was too old. And while camped in Brazil for the 1950 World Cup finals Walter Winterbottom complained to *El Tiempo* that his team was constantly being distracted by Colombians trying to tempt players to switch to play in the pirate league: "Two of my players have been constantly chased by Colombian representatives, but their answers have always been the same: No, No."

In the summer of 1950 *El Tiempo's* pages were awash with transfer news, with barely a day passing without a new star player being unveiled. In July it was reported that Santa Fe had sent a representative to Brazil to sound out the England manager himself as head of their youth development. Their offer was described as "flattering".

Winterbottom's response was never followed up and his academic, school master-like approach to coaching would have been a strong departure from the existing methods employed in the fledgling league. But Santa Fe's approach was perhaps made in response to another set of disciplinarian

Englishmen that arrived in May 1950 and went on to make quite an impression. In 1948 when the league was hastily convened, little consideration had been given to the question of referees. The ruinous officiating that followed this oversight besmirched the opening two championships and match reports were littered with complaints about referees being ill-equipped to cope on the stage afforded them. If disrespect for authority and rule was absent on the football field, what consequences would this have on wider society?

It was with this in mind that Colombian football chiefs decided to take action and in May 1950 six English referees arrived on one-year contracts. At first they were derided. Adverts appeared in newspapers calling for foreign referees to return home and they were largely seen as too old and too divorced from Colombian sensibilities properly to understand the Latin game.

But gradually attitudes shifted and one, Tom Pounder, even entered Colombian history books as the first referee to score a goal. It was a crucial one too, having an influence on the outcome of the 1950 championship. Millonarios had started the season as strong favourites and coasted through the opening stages winning 11 of their first 12 games. But with all the wheeling and dealing throughout the season their form slipped away and when they met lowly Universidad, points were desperately needed to maintain their challenge. With four minutes left the score was 0-0 when a shot hit Pounder and was deflected into the goal. Players besieged the Englishman and the game was held up for several minutes. But the goal stood and Pounder was later found locked in his changing room having been assaulted. Millonarios ended up throwing away the title that season, finishing two points behind the surprise package Deportes Caldas.

Great teams rarely click straightaway and the fine tuning of Millonarios would involve another poaching mission in Argentina for it truly to flourish. In came Hugo Reyes, Antonio Baez and Reinaldo Mourin: Millonarios were complete. For the next three years they would be the dominant force not just in Colombian football, but as Real Madrid would soon find out, in world football too.

As the 1951 championship expanded to 18 teams, the flood of foreign talent hit its peak. Of the 440 registered players for the new season, only 153 (35%) were Colombian. Of the rest there were 133 Argentinians, 49 Peruvians, 28 Uruguayans, 24 Paraguayans, 18 Hungarians, 13 Costa Ricans, 9 Brazilians, 2 Englishmen, 2 Chileans, 2 Ecuadoreans, a Panamanian, an Italian, a Spaniard, a Czechoslovakian, a Romanian, a Yugoslavian and an Austrian.

But as many Colombian teams clambered to scrape together the finest talent in South America, there were other directors who simply wished to entice fans with the exotic and unknown. For every star signing like that of Eusebio Tejera who joined Cúcuta a few months after winning the 1950 World Cup with Uruguay, there were others who arrived whom nobody had heard of. "Spectators didn't have the communication access like they do now," the radio journalist Hernán Peláez explained. "People were seduced by the exotic foreign names. For example, I remember when the editor

of a newspaper was told somebody called Micara was going to arrive in Cali. Everybody assumed that this was a footballer and it was reported in the paper that Cali were about to sign a new player. Actually, he wasn't a footballer at all, he was a priest!"

The techniques to sign players grew ever more sophisticated. Money talked big but Argentinian and Brazilian teams were beginning to take measures to protect their players from Colombia's poaching. "Piracy is absolutely right, the perfect word," Peláez said. "One of the ex-bosses at Junior, Mario Abello, who's dead now, told me how it was possible to bring over players like Gérson dos Santos to Junior, a player who'd played for Brazil and was a star at Botafoga. He told me very plainly that they used to meet in Caracas because if Junior representatives went from Colombia directly to the Engenhão [Botafoga's stadium] everybody would know what was going on — that he was going to sign their players. So one of Junior's men was sent to Venezuela with $20,000; this was the price at the time. Gérson then went back to Brazil and then a few days later he appeared in Colombia. This was the strategy that was used to bring players to Colombia. Players were bought with the most incredible tricks."

But it wasn't just vigilante club directors that were involved in the piracy; the Colombian government itself was actively supporting these raids. Argentina didn't enter the 1950 World Cup finals because of a row between their football federation and that of the host country Brazil. But it's worth considering another factor. By 1950 Argentina's star players, like Di Stéfano, were no longer playing for Argentina — they had Colombian citizenship.

Alfonso Senior, speaking before his death in 2004 for a government-sponsored series of short documentaries, described how the government helped smooth the way for many of the transfers: "The government helped clubs bring players to Colombia. They gave them visas the moment they stepped into the airport in Bogotá. The government saw that football was a harmless way of calming people, of providing fun for people every Sunday."

Harmless fun in a country in which, in the two years that followed, 200,000 people would be slaughtered. And it wasn't just the relaxing of bureaucratic restrictions that the government were helping with. Funds were also provided, officially in the form of prize money and the relaxing of the exchange rate but also through back-door channels, as the league was given financial and logistical muscle.

Still Colombia swam alone in the wilderness of world football. No foreign clubs could organise games against them — at the time a rich source of income — and players were banned from representing their country. But that was accepted as a minor inconvenience compared to a level of play never seen in Colombia before.

Its protagonist was Millonarios and in 1951 they found expression in a type of football that married the technical with the artistic. Not only did Millonarios blast their way to the title with 28 wins from 34, they did it with a style that became known as *La Ballet Azul*, the Blue Ballet.

It was a system that had its roots in River Plate's fabled *La Máquina* side, for which Pedernera had played a starring role in. Like most sides of the age, River employed the 2-3-5 formation but they refused to accept that each player had a designated and fixed role. "Some players would enter, some would leave, all would attack, all would defend," said the River coach Carlos Peucelle. "On the blackboard and on the pitch our tactical system wasn't the traditional 1-2-3-5. It was 1-10."

Pedernera tried to replicate the style at Millonarios. He was helped by having some of the finest players in the continent at his disposal but it was the Argentinian's insistence on fluidity and flexibility that the opposition found so hard to deal with. It gave the team an almost unbeatable edge and to spectators this new style appeared almost as dance. As Millonarios waltzed their way to the 1951 title, fans swarmed to the stadiums. But the rivalry between Santa Fe and Millonarios was not the only red against blue rivalry in Colombia; as Liberals fought Conservatives, the level of violence increased until Colombia was in a state of civil war. For 90 minutes every weekend football acted as tranquiliser.

"The stadiums were completely full, especially for the *clasicos* and it was this that gave every player strength," El Caimán recalled. "Whoever scored became an instant hero with the fans. I still remember the noise of the crowd, it was a great motivation for every one of us. This was a new type of football in Colombia that had stars from everywhere. But we couldn't ignore the violence elsewhere in Colombia. For example I remember once that we went for some beers after a game. We were sat in this bar drinking when a man walked by and shouted 'Long live the Conservatives! Spit if you aren't with me!

"We knew that everybody was divided into Liberals and Conservatives, that it was war and it was a really dangerous time. So I kept quiet but one of my friends, one of the directors, jumped up and shouted, 'Long live the great Liberal party!' So the Conservative took out his gun and my friend jumped up, ran out of the room and leapt through the bar window — we were on the second floor! The Conservative came up to me with his gun and questioned why I was here. I told him I was just a football player. But he then asked me: which colour are you, Liberal or Conservative. I was panicking, because I knew that a wrong answer and he would have shot me. But then, very luckily, one of his friends must have recognised me because he told him to put his gun away, this was El Caimán and he's one of us."

For players like El Caimán, the thought of El Dorado brings back mixed feelings. He remembers fondly the atmosphere in the stadium and the great players he played alongside but being ostracised from the football community hurt. In March 1951, the first talks on resolving the crisis began but they stuttered for five months without any progress. Despite a special Fifa commission being set up, the countries most affected demanded huge sums of compensation for the players the pirate league had illegally contracted. It was something Dimayor and its members refused to consider and so disgruntled football organisations instead took to lobbying their respective governments to put direct pressure on the Colombian president Laureano Gómez.

Finally, in August 1951 an agreement was struck. The wave of opposition from all corners had caused Dimayor to crack and they agreed to a deal. Players would remain in Colombia if their original parent club agreed they could do so, but if not, they would return and a fee would be paid to the Colombians.

When Fifa met in October 1951, they lifted Colombia's suspension and 11 years later Colombia made their debut at the World Cup finals in Chile. But while the agreement, known as the Lima Pact, sounded the death knell for El Dorado, a cunning clause was inserted into the seven-point plan by the Colombians — that players would only return after October 1954.

While clubs were barred from bringing in more stars without proper transfer agreements along Fifa lines, current players could remain in Colombia for a further three years. Millonarios unsurprisingly went on to claim the 1952 and 1953 titles but, while the Blue Ballet had won many admirers at home, Senior looked to Europe to broaden the team's popularity.

In early 1952 Real Madrid organised a small tournament to mark their fiftieth anniversary, inviting River Plate and the Swedish champions IFK Norrköping to Spain. This puzzled the Millonarios president: why had Santiago Bernabéu chosen River and not Millonarios as the representatives of South America? Senior was friends with Guillermo Valencia, a keen football fan who worked in the Spanish embassy, and asked him to remind the Real president that River's *La Máquina* was no more and that South America's greatest team was now in Colombia.

Bernabéu sent a scout to watch Millonarios play and he returned so impressed that Real invited the Colombian club to replace River. As a Franco sympathiser, Bernabéu had similar political beliefs to the Conservative Senior and both were eager to use football as a way to portray an image of normality despite the horrors that were plaguing their respective countries.

Millonarios and Real met in the final of the Campeonato Bodas de Oro on 30 March 1952 and, after a sumptuous performance from Di Stéfano, the Colombians ran out 4-2 winners. Millonarios had turned professional only four years prior but they had now conquered Europe. Their trip to Spain had drawn many admirers and, after the final, Bernabéu approached Senior about signing their star man, Di Stéfano. A gentleman's agreement was struck but after the team returned to Colombia, Di Stéfano was invited back to Spain by Real's arch-rivals Barcelona.

He spent an all-expenses-paid week on the Costa del Sol where a couple of exhibition games were enough to convince the Catalan giants to sign him. Unlike Real they had no contacts with Millonarios and so they appointed a negotiator, Ramón Trías Fargas, to fly to Argentina to talk with River, who also claimed rights to his contract. A deal was reached.

Barça then sent one of their top men to Caracas to meet with Millonarios representatives. They were unable to agree a price with the Colombians and the Barça president Martí Carreto returned to Spain frustrated. When news got out that Barça were trying to sign

Di Stéfano, Bernabéu was furious. He immediately rang Senior to ask what had happened to their informal agreement.

What followed was one of the messiest and most complicated transfer wrangles in the history of football. Four clubs fighting over one player with interference from General Franco, suspicions that a Santa Fe-supporting representative had sabotaged the Barça deal and a ridiculous compromise idea by the Spanish federation for Di Stéfano to play alternate seasons for Real and Barça.

Eventually, Real emerged victorious and on 24 July 1953 they announced Di Stéfano's transfer. He made his debut two months later and would go on to play a leading role in shifting the balance of power in Spanish football to Madrid.

The transfer would signal the end of El Dorado but the final season of the pirate league would again belong to Millonarios. In 28 games they conceded just 13 goals and recorded a 6-0 win over their rivals Santa Fe as they romped to the title. Their reputation had spread fast as they beat Real, Hungary and the world champions Uruguay. But by 1952 it wasn't just the sporting world that was interested in *La Ballet Azul*.

That summer, a sweaty and bearded Argentinian doctor rolled up on his motorbike outside El Campín, the stadium shared by Bogotá giants Santa Fe and Millonarios. The 25 year old had been tending to patients in the Colombian Amazonian town of Leticia alongside his friend Alberto when the local football team, Independiente Sporting, signed him as player-coach. In his free time, despite his chronic asthma, he guided the side to the local championship final in which they lost on penalties.

Alberto, also a doctor, noted in his diaries, "During our trip we used football a lot to get into contact with the people." Hearing about Millonarios and the Argentinian contingent of Pedernera, Rossi and Di Stéfano, the two set off for the Colombian capital. They met Di Stéfano in a downtown restaurant not far from where Gaitén had been assassinated five years earlier and *La Saeta Rubia* gave the two doctors free tickets to a Millonarios game.

This little known meeting brought together two of the twentieth century's icons: Di Stéfano would go on to become perhaps Real Madrid's greatest player, while the doctor-cum-footballer-cum-revolutionary Che Guevara later headed to Cuba, overthrew a dictatorship and became a poster boy for the left and counter-culture.

Guevara was lucky: he caught Millonarios and El Dorado in their pomp. A year later, the Dimayor's project was falling apart. Faced with the impending loss of swathes of players under the terms of the Lima Pact, teams chose to cash in, grabbing whatever fee they could.

Players left en masse. Star names like Julio Cozzi and Néstor Rossi returned to their former teams in Argentina while others, such as the Uruguayan Ramón Villaverde and Santa Fe's Héctor Rial followed Di Stéfano to Spain.

The government knew the game was up and lost interest in supporting football. Finances were pulled and teams disappeared under the weight of mounting debt. In comparison to the 18 clubs that contested the 1951 title, just 10 registered for the season three years later. Even then, the 1954 championship saw 11 games cancelled at the last minute due to lack of players and funds.

Millonarios, domineering a year previously, were forced to field a mixture of youth players and unknown journeymen. In 1957 they finished bottom of the league. Other clubs were so drowned in debt that just finding 11 players became difficult. Predictably, stadiums fell empty.

However, despite this, Colombian players like El Caimán found heart amid the league's collapse. A return to Fifa and the chance to play in a World Cup outweighed the false glow of El Dorado. "During El Dorado we were excluded from the football community and people treated us as pirates," he said. "When we were invited back into Fifa we were delighted, but it was only later when I led the team out in Chile in 1962 that I realised how important that was. Nothing is worth more than the honour of representing your country in a World Cup."

Football could no longer sustain the mirage of normality. The mask had slipped from the face of Colombia and, according to the historian Guillermo Ruiz, a surge of violence swept the nation. "When El Dorado came to an end in 1954 there was an big increase in murders," he said. "It was terrible: without football, violence exploded. In the second half of the fifties when many teams fell into a massive financial mess, attendances collapsed and violence rose. There was a direct connection. In a way

I suppose you could say football saved lives in the years after Gaitán's death."

El Dorado had propelled Colombian football to the forefront of the world game. It had attracted stars, revolutionaries and controversy but following its demise Colombian football would spend the next 30 years enduring financial meltdown, pitiful match attendances and a poor quality of play. Its next moment in the sun would come in the 1980s with the boom of the drug cartels, when the fortunes of the Colombian league would again be manipulated by corrupt and unscrupulous powers. It would be awash with controversy, violence and death and be ostracised from the football community once more. But it would again attract stars and win prizes.

Unfortunately, for the first 60 years of professional football in Colombia, success on the pitch has involved paying a very heavy price off it.

Colombia's El Dorado league was a glimpse into the future, a world of imports lured from across the globe by vast wages. Yet the players (and referees) who arrived in Colombia in the late forties and early fifties found a country being torn apart by civil war and infrastructure lagging some way behind the quality of football being played. Pitches were poor, stadiums rudimentary and press coverage appealingly haphazard.

It's a fascinating period and one that given the status of the players involved, remains relatively unresearched. The photographs in this essay came not from an agency but were unearthed by Carl Worswick and the Septima Agency after a trawl through numerous museums in Bogotá. The captioning of photographs is often problematic (El Gráfico in Argentina recently discovered a previously unseen photograph of Diego Maradona performing a nutmeg on his debut, lost for 35 years because it had been filed under the name of the embarrassed defender rather than a teenager nobody had heard of), but it seems to have been particularly so in the Colombia of six decades ago. By cross-referencing with other sources we've tried to identify players but some, unfortunately, remain as they were captioned then: 'unknown Brazilian' or 'Millonarios defender'.

In a sense, it doesn't matter; even if we can't work out who every player is, the shots give a sense of the strange mixture of chaos and excitement, of the energy and sheer weirdness that made up El Dorado.

Circa 1950. Estadio Nemesio Camacho, El Campín, Bogotá. The Santa Fe players Neil Franklin and 'Chonto' Gaviria.

1951. Atlético Minicipal (later known as At. Nacional). Estadio Alfonso López, Ciudad Universitaria. Echeverry, Mesa, Rafael Serna (scorer of the first ever goal in Colombian professional football), 'Pildorita' Cardona, 'Manco' Gutiérrez, Osorio and 'Turrón' Álvarez.

1951. Estadio López Pumarejo, Ciudad Universitaria. The Millonarios players Antonio Báez, Alfredo di Stéfano and Adolfo Pedernera.

1949. Estadio Nemesio Camacho, El Campín, Bogotá. Millonarios v Sporting de Barranquilla, the match in which Adolfo Perdernera was presented for the first time. The bull-fi ghter Miguel Domínguin is a special invited guest.

The Argentinian goalkeeper Julio Cozzi playing for Millonarios.

1953. Estadio Nemesio Camacho, El Campín, Bogotá. From right to left: Francisco 'Cobo' Zuluaga (the Millonarios captain), Ramón Hoyos Vallejo (a soldier and five-times cycling champion of Colombia), Efrain 'El Caiman' Sánchez (the Santa Fe captain). Extreme left: Guillermo Cubillos Moreno, photographer.

1949. Estadio Nemesio Camacho, El Campín, Bogotá. Millonarios v Santa Fe. In goal, Julio Gaviria Zapata 'Chontafé' with Neil Franklin looking on.

1950. Estadio Nemesio Camacho, El Campín, Bogotá. Millonarios v Deportes Caldas. Vytautas Kriščiūnas punches the ball away under pressure from Pedernera.

A director from the confectionary company Caramelos Mara-Mar with the Santa Fe player Fernández.

1950. Estadio Nemesio Camacho, El Campín, Bogotá. The Santa Fe players Neil Franklin and George Mountford talking with three English officials.

1951. The reinauguration of Estadio El Campín, Bogotá. Alfredo Di Stéfano talking to the radio journalist Jesús Álvarez Botero from la Voz de Colombia.

Unknown Brazillian goalkeeper.

All images Carlos Cubillos/colecciónmuseodebogotá

The Blond Giant

Among the influx of foreign players to El Dorado was the Lithuanian goalkeeper, Vytautas Kriščiūnas.

By Stany Sirutis

If anyone had been expecting to see another dark-haired man with a carefully-trimmed moustache, the blond, 1.90m Vytautas Kriščiūnas must have come as a shock when he finally arrived in Manizales. A few days earlier, when the press announced that the local team, Deportes Caldas, had signed three Argentinian stars there had been no mention of his size, his broad shoulders or his muscular appearance.

Kriščiūnas was certainly not another *Argentino*. Born in Lithuania in 1925, he had come to South America during the war with his parents. Soon after settling in Buenos Aires, the young Vytautas started training as a goalkeeper with the second-division side Quilmes. By 1944, at the age of 19, he'd made his professional debut and, two years later, he was the first-choice goalkeeper for the team.

When Quilmes achieved promotion to the top tier in 1949, the Lithuanian was no longer the fixture in goal that he had been and was looking to change clubs. He signed for the first-division side Platense but never made an official start for them — no great surprise given Julio Cozzi, Argentina's number one, was ahead of him.

Meanwhile, in Colombia, Deportes Caldas's manager, Alfredo Cuezzo, was worried and had threatened to quit. His team were playing well but they weren't winning matches consistently. In July 1949, they had a lot of work ahead of them if they were to match the third place they'd achieved the previous year. Nonetheless, he'd been confirmed in his position by the team's authorities who'd said they would rather liquidate the club than go on without him. Even the fans had asked him to continue.

He took a flight to Buenos Aires, his second trip of the year, but brought back only the hope that his people in the south would continue to work on signing the players he needed. Weeks later, the sport pages were abuzz with the arrival of Alfredo Di Stéfano in Bogotá. In Manizales, news of their own reinforcements was greeted with much enthusiasm by press and fans alike.

There were delays and paperwork but there was an expectation that the new players would arrive and be ready in time for the home game against Deportivo Cali, but no description of their appearance. The day after the match, two of them arrived: Segundo Tesori, a stylish inside-forward of Italian descent, with a Clark Gable moustache; and Vytautas Kriščiūnas, the robust Lithuanian who would surpass everyone's expectations.

Traditionally, Colombians hold foreigners, particularly Europeans, in high regard and look upon them with a certain respect. Since the time of Carlos Gardel, the glamorous tango crooner who'd featured in several films and died in a plane crash in Medellín in 1935, there was a clear admiration for Argentinians. Anyone coming over from the River Plate would find an open door in the country.

Manizales in 1949 was certainly nothing like Buenos Aires, where the Lithuanian had left his parents and his girlfriend. Despite the welcoming nature of its people and its reputation as a city of culture, it had nothing like the grandeur of the big avenues, the obelisk and the imposing buildings of the Argentinian capital with its three million inhabitants. Indeed, just over 100,000 people lived there.

Up in the midst of green mountains, at 2100m above sea level, and with the impressive snow peak of El Ruiz volcano in the distance, the city had grown around the country's coffee industry. Most activity revolved around the city centre and its few multi-storey buildings. The cathedral dominated the main square from which a sprawl of houses stretched out along the mountain top.

Colombia itself is very different to the mostly flat Lithuania. Just days after his arrival, the team travelled to Medellín, Colombia's self-styled "Mountain Capital" where he would make his first appearance, taking the place of Delio 'The Witch' Londoño, Caldas's regular No 1. "The Lithuanian revealed himself as quite the goalkeeper," a correspondent for Bogota's *El Tiempo* wrote of Kriščiūnas's performance in a 6-0 away win at Deportivo Municipal. He'd made

the perfect start and, as if the city weren't already primed to make heroes of the new arrivals, the local paper *La Patria* built them up even more in the days leading up to next match in Manizales, against the defending champions Santa Fe.

The players read the papers on a regular basis. They looked for mentions of their names and pictures of themselves to cut out and send home or store away as keepsakes. Deportes Caldas had eight foreigners already, five of them from Argentina.

Days before the next encounter, disturbing news arrived from Bogota: a shootout in Congress after a dispute between rival politicians ended with one representative dead and a couple more injured. Calls for calm and claims that there were personal motives involved in the quarrel dominated the front page of *La Patria*. Surprisingly, there was also a smaller headline that read, "There was more talk of football in Manizales than anything else." To be sure, while the Caldas department saw regular acts of political violence during *La Violencia*, the city itself, a Conservative stronghold, is regarded by locals as having been an oasis of peace at the time.

So the stage was set for the match against Santa Fe. This time, despite a man of the match performance from Kriščiūnas, and a standing ovation from the crowd after a fantastic save, the visitors were too much for Caldas and took a comprehensive 3-0 victory back to Bogota. There's a picture in *La Patria* of Kriščiūnas making a save, and, curiously, an artist's drawing of his face with a football and a pitch in the background. The caption states his name and states, "Best out of the 22." He's captured someone's imagination: this type of drawing is not seen elsewhere, nor is it done for any other player.

It's interesting to note how often the Lithuanian featured in the few pictures printed every Monday on the sports pages. Photographers at the time had limited options and typically stalked the goalmouths at each end for the perfect picture which in part explains his popularity. But his success also kept his file photo in print when *La Patria* previewed an upcoming home game. It's also remarkable how much trouble the press had in getting his name right. He would come to be known nationwide as 'Vytatutas', with an extra syllable, and was often also referred to as Victor Kriscuonas — Victor being the literal translation of his first name.

Leading up to the next match, at home to Medellín, *La Prensa* wondered whether there might be a curse behind Caldas's irregular form and occasional bad luck. It referred to a similar case in Argentina where Boca Juniors had supposedly been the victims of the alleged malediction. Curses and football in South America are a familiar theme but Kriščiūnas was the talisman Caldas needed to start winning consistently, and they won the game 2-1 with another solid performance by the keeper.

The following Sunday, the local derby (round 20 of 26) pitted Deportes Caldas, the team of high society, against Once Deportivo, who were associated with the working class. There was city-wide enthusiasm for the clash but no signs of it spilling over into politics. The game took place in a healthy atmosphere, with events on the pitch claiming centre stage. It was to be a close encounter and Kriščiūnas performed well once again in a 1-0 victory. The press talked about "his crowd" being satisfied with the performance and lauded his skills in going out for the ball. The town had quickly taken 'the Phenomenon' into its heart. Caldas, by then in fourth place, awaited the visit of the star-studded Los Millonarios.

Midweek, the local police uncovered a terrorist plot and confiscated a stockpile of small explosive devices. It was the Communists who were behind it, according to *La Patria*. Still, nothing could distract attention from the match, and, if Los Millonarios' players had any concerns about their safety, it did not show: they played the home side off the pitch and won 5-1. Kriščiūnas was again cheered by the crowd but there was little he or his team could do to stop the visitors.

While the would-be champions were too much for Deportes Caldas, the same could not be said for their remaining opposition. The following Sunday the team started a five-game winning streak to end the season in style and manage a fourth-place finish. In their last match, at home to Deportivo Pereira, Kriščiūnas was knocked unconscious after rushing out for a ball and colliding with another player early on in the game. With the alleged curse broken, he was replaced in goal by Londoño who played his last game for the club that day.

The Lithuanian regained consciousness that same afternoon and, days later, travelled back home to his loved ones. After spending a couple of months in Buenos Aires, he returned to Manizales for the challenge of the new season.

Unlike in Argentina, where the league was, and largely still is, mostly composed of teams from the greater Buenos Aires region, the Colombian championships have never been centred on the capital but have always been truly nationwide affairs. That meant a lot more plane travel and a host of different climates to deal with. For a team from the mountains, flying into the heat and humidity of the coastal city of Barranquilla, where Junior and Sporting play, remains a challenge even now. Wearing a goalkeeper's jersey in the mid-afternoon inferno of the Caribbean coast is unpleasant even with today's high-tech garments. The same goes for playing in Cúcuta in the north-east or against Deportivo Cali or América in the west. Kriščiūnas was a pale giant; for him, it must have been a great challenge to prove himself in conditions he'd never known and a great experience to see the diversity of the country's people and its cities.

The 1950 season saw Cuezzo's men get off to a decent start, collecting four wins and three draws from their first nine games. On the tenth match-day, they went to Bogota to play the league leaders Los Millonarios at El Campín. Reports in the capital suggested that, after winning the derby against Santa Fe, Los Millonarios had been treated to a series of cocktail parties in celebration and were still reeling from the drinks when Sunday came. That day, both teams gave uninspired performances and a brace by Alfredo Di Stéfano was enough for the home side to win. Caldas were five points behind and had let a good chance slip away.

Whether Los Millonarios became overconfident is hard to say. What's certain, on the other hand, is that Caldas bounced back the next week, taking Deportivo Muncipal apart 5-1 in Manizales. It was to be the start of an impressive streak that saw them take 13 wins out of 14 matches, led by solid performances by 'Vytatutas' and his defence, and the goal-scoring prowess of recent addition Julio 'Stuka' Avila.

With things going well, it became common for the players to enjoy a post-match drink or two in the company of Manizales's high society. There was pride in being seen alongside the stars of Deportes Caldas. "Some of them would womanise and take full advantage of their status," said Javier Giraldo Neira, a local radio journalist of national reputation. Kriščiūnas, though, Neira insisted, was more reserved.

By his second season, Kriščiūnas had moved out of the team quarters on Santander Avenue, where most of the squad lived, and into his own apartment in the centre of town. No doubt it was a privilege in keeping with a player of his status but it was perhaps also a sign that he was more at ease on his own.

A special report in *La Patria* during Caldas's run of success offers a window into their daily lives. Cuezzo had achieved the perfect mixture of discipline and camaraderie. We see Navarro and Tesori, both Argentinians, wearing elegant house coats while the rest of the players sport white shirts. Kriščiūnas, for his part, is the only one wearing braces. In a team made up of foreigners, he seems the most foreign of all. This is illustrated by an anecdote referred to in the article which shows the Lithuanian making a mess of his comeback to a friendly insult.

"Move over Egg-face!" Garrido, a Chilean, shouts at him.

"As you wish, Mirror-face! (?)" is his reply — which the journalist has himself punctuated with a question mark.

Regardless of how he fitted in, he was a competitor who kept showing up for the big matches and putting on man of the match displays. Caldas's streak ended with a 3-2 home defeat to Los Millonarios in what was more a battle than a football game, according to *La Patria's* scathing attack on the winners. A picture of Kriščiūnas showed him being restrained during one of the more serious scuffles, dwarfing the members of the military police and their rifles as he is held back. The paper asserts that, despite appearances, the Lithuanian had been on the receiving end of a punch and had later tried to calm down his fellow players.

Deportes Caldas would be crowned champions in the end, despite struggling towards the finish-line. A parade made up of "every youth and amateur sports team" followed by marching bands and a caravan of vehicles into the Plaza de Bolivar — the main square — suggested how much the triumph meant to city in general. After a speech from the regional governor, the exclusive Club Manizales held a cocktail party that went on long into the night.

Kriščiūnas never played again. He gave up football after returning to Buenos Aires for the close-season, taking up the family business, a carpentry workshop, at the request of his parents. He married his long-time girlfriend and settled down to start a family but died just a few years later. Daniel Victor, his son, told me his father had very fond memories of Colombia; he wonders whether his dad made the right decision in leaving the game. Indeed, his career could have gone much further. As it was, he did what so few have managed, and went out at the top. Ⓑ

CRISTIANO RONALDO:
SIGNED BY THE WORLD'S BEST GOALSCORER

ICONS FIRST DID A SIGNING WITH CRISTIANO IN 2005 WHEN HE WAS
ONLY 20 AND HAD JUST ARRIVED IN MANCHESTER.

TODAY HE IS THE BEST GOALSCORER IN THE WORLD
AND HE STILL ONLY SIGNS FOR US.

VIEW THE FULL RONALDO RANGE ONLY AT WWW.ICONS.COM

ICONS.com™
SIGNED BY THE WORLD'S BEST

40

Interview

"Please, don't pick me because I received a threat in my city, so I am afraid to play."

Ivica Osim

The great Bosnian coach reflects on the war, Japan and Alan Mullery's lack of fair play.

By Jonathan Wilson

It was midmorning when I first pressed the buzzer outside the apartment block where Ivica Osim now lives in Sarajevo. His wife answered and, apologetically, asked if I could come back at noon because he was still in bed. Osim sleeps a lot these days, exhausted by the stroke that ended his time as manager of Japan in 2007. He had been watching a Premier League game when he fell unconscious; when he came round, the first thing he said to his wife was to ask what the final score had been. She now protects him, sheltering him from the demands of a football world that still reveres him. In April 2011, for instance, he was appointed head of a committee to oversee Bosnian football while the issues that had led to the Bosnian federation being suspended from Fifa were resolved.

"Don't wear him out," she said, when I buzzed for him again. He looks old now, the skin sagging over a frame no longer as powerful as it was when he was one of Europe's most dynamic midfielders. There is an air of melancholy about him too, although perhaps less about his own mortality than about the conflicts that have ravaged his homeland, the constant setbacks and betrayals of life. Football, as well, he feels has changed, is less pure than it was. Yet beneath the frail exterior, his energy still shines through; he may be

disappointed with football but he has not fallen out of love with it.

Let's start with the crisis point, the 1990 World Cup, when you were coach of a great Yugoslavia team that included the likes of Dragan Stojković, Safet Sušić and Darko Pančev with the youthful talent of Robert Prosinečki, Dejan Savićević and Davor Šuker in the squad. Is it even possible to begin talking about that team and its promise given what was going on politically at the time?

The team was far, far better than the country. That generation was really young. I'm not sure it's good to talk about it because football is football and life is life. Football is a pretty game but it's not larger than life. I don't like to talk about this because it would be an illusion to make a lamentation about that generation of players and not to talk about what happened afterwards. Lots of people have been killed. The country was destroyed. It's not fair for me to talk about the players and not to talk about what happened next. Sometimes there are things that are more important than football. One thing is sure: if the players were in charge instead of the politicians nothing could ever be like this.

Were you under pressure to pick certain players?

Unfortunately it was the same thing then as now. Instead of all the other things, you had to be careful about the name, about religion, about the club, about the region of the country a player's from. You had to calculate everything. Everything is politics. Every club was politics and especially the national team was politics. Let an Englishman try to pick the national team of Britain and Ireland.... So you choose two from Scotland, three from England but nobody from Ireland, it would be a riot...

⊕ *Was there a quota system?*

Nothing happened overnight. You can't create these things in one night. The key players, they had been working on that for a long time so in the end it looked like the normal pattern of the things that had to happen.

⊕ *Having lost to West Germany you then beat Colombia and the UAE, but the last 16 victory over Spain was probably the best performance in that tournament...*

From my perspective, you see the result and you see a positive result so automatically you think it's the best game of the tournament. But also I think that game was the best because Spain were always a football force. It was important in showing that we had the same number of good individuals as Spain. And it was the sort of game in which players could make sure they stood out from the crowd. Stojković did that but even without that game he would have been a great player. But sometimes you need that kind of game so the players and the fans can see they have a good player.

⊕ *And then, despite being down to 10 men from the 30th minute after Refik*

Šabanadzović was sent off, you drew 0-0 with Argentina in the quarter-final, only to lose on penalties. You must think about what might have been...

That should have been the biggest game. It had everything to be the biggest game. It had all the attributes. But that game was played at the wrong time because we had a lot of other problems and the team could not concentrate. And when the players are not sure about their quality, it's really hard to play.

⊕ *What do you mean by "the wrong time"?*

I had a case with one player who said a few hours before the game, "Please, don't pick me because I received a threat in my city, so I am afraid to play for the national team." That was Srečko Katanec, who was a really, really important player for us. He was afraid to walk around in Ljubljana because of threats. I can understand that's not a nice position. How can he play? If he goes to play in Italy and his family stays in Ljubljana then they are under threat. I can't persuade anybody not to think about that.

⊕ *Did you feel any pressure personally?*

The pressure was not on me. After the game you can feel the effects, what happened with football. You must end up in hospital, whether in 1990 or in 2007. Everybody ends up n the hospital.

⊕ *And then in 1992, what did you think of the decision to expel Yugoslavia from the European Championship?*

I wasn't disappointed by the decision not to let us compete at Euro 92. You have to expect these decisions in these circumstances. We put ourselves in a position that enabled Uefa to make that decision. But I felt like a lot of people couldn't wait to get rid of us, because we were such a dangerous side.

You felt people had a prejudice against Yugoslavia?

It's all politics and business as well, you have to understand. What can a team from Yugoslavia bring to the Euros? They can only cause problems, in terms of the game or in terms of riots. We were too dangerous for Europe in 1992.

Do you ask yourself what might have happened if there'd been no politics, no war, and Yugoslavia had been allowed to compete?

People often talk about the fact that Denmark came instead of us, so they wonder what would have happened if we had stayed in the tournament and they think that probably we would have won the European Championship. I don't know about that, but I think about the World Cup in 1990, what might have happened if we'd got past Argentina. Maybe I am optimistic, but in my private illusion I wonder what would have happened if Yugoslavia had played in the semi-final or the final, what would have happened in the country. Maybe there would have been no war if we'd won the World Cup. I don't think things would have changed in that way, but sometimes you dream about what might have happened. Things might have been better after the World Cup.

Is there any comparison, whether in terms of internal politics or the way the outside world looks at the country, *between the situation then and in Bosnia now?*

Thank God we are not in a situation like Yugoslavia was in 1990 and we're really lucky not to be in that kind of situation. I think back then things had gone too far and nobody or nothing could have prevented what happened in the next years. I would be happy if football could have changed that, but I don't think it was possible.

This Bosnia team seems highly promising, reaching play-offs for qualifying for both the 2010 World Cup and Euro 2012. How important was Ćiro Blažević in pulling together Bosniaks, Bosnian Croats and Bosnian Serbs?

We had a man who could bring peace between people who would be on opposite sides. And football doesn't always cause wars. Sometimes it brings peace. You can see how the city streets are when the national team plays. This is good for the politicians because they can see how important football is. It's not just in Bosnia — it's all around the world. If you win the games you have a peaceful time among the people. And we are people like that: when we have a good result, we spend more, we celebrate more.

He's very charismatic, somebody who's very good with words...

You can make philosophical arguments about tactics and football but when you talk with players and journalists, the most important thing is to choose your words when you talk about your rival. You can never talk in a way that makes your rival feel underestimated or overestimated.

If you talk in the wrong way, your rival could be motivated. After the game, people can see it was your words that motivated your rival. And that's a really delicate issue, because today you have to be careful about nearly everything. Anything can be manipulated. And it's really hard to avoid that kind of situation because, as I always say, everything is politics. A war can be started because of two words. Football is just like war because there is an enormous amount of money in the game.

◆ *You regret that?*

What would happen if England failed to qualify for a tournament and they had invested a huge amount of money in their football? There is an obligation for the players because they have to think about that also. I'm afraid that football will eat itself one day. Every step seems to lead towards that. Football now is money, money, money and I can't understand where that money comes from. It's gone too far. I don't believe that football was ever just a sport. From the early days, it was a professional way of thinking. In football nobody can do anything for free. If you make better biscuits than the next man you are more professional. Ordinary people cannot understand the figures involved. We are not excited by how Džeko is playing; we are waiting to see which club he will join next and what price he will be. Everybody forgets he is a normal guy, 1.90m [6'3"] tall, who plays good football.

◆ *And the present team, under Šušić, looks well set in qualifying for 2014...*

When you find yourself in the situation of the kind we are in now, when every point is like a house, it's not easy to play. Especially when you have that feeling that you're very close to something that you've chased for so long, you cannot pick holes. Now we are entering a period in which we need slowly to prepare the team, prepare the crowd to accept the fact that this team should not depend on one player. That's dangerous and we're sick of it. But now we have Džeko and also [Miralem] Pjanić who can raise us to the heavens. That's good but we have to make a collective that will thrive together. The path is there; the question is how long we can follow it.

Osim was born in Sarajevo and began his career there with Željezničar before moving, briefly, to the Netherlands and then France. Noted for his close control and dribbling ability, he also played 16 games for the Yugoslavia national side, including the final stages of the 1968 European Championship.

◆ *What are your memories of the 1968 semi-final and the 1-0 win over England?*

You can never play an easy game against England. They were the world champions at the time and the team that played us was almost the same team that played in the World Cup. We had to have respect for them. We thought that we were in a good position to play against England, even though they were a really interesting team and we were maybe not so dangerous.

It was a unique opportunity for us to see these players, even to touch them. The calmness of the way they played was the most impressive thing about them. They were fully focused on their plan, and that was something we didn't have. For them everything happens with the head, everything else is not so important. They did that all the time, changed the ball from wide to the middle. We had to be careful of that. They played a very good style. They all played with great heart and you had to be fully concentrated against them. They were great runners. You play against Stiles, Mullery, Bobby Charlton, and you thought they must be playing their twins as well, because it seemed there were such a lot of them, always more than us.

⊕ Was that down to fitness or organisation?

They were run from the bench. They always had individual quality, but that was the first time they started to use individuals. You can't say that Gerrard or Lampard don't have quality, but their first quality is their fluency, and it was the same situation then.

⊕ Dragan Džajić scored the winner and was hailed as one of the world greats by the English press after that game. How good was he?

He was a great individual, very hard to play against. It was not easy to control him. Džajić was a player who could always make it seem like you had one player more, and when you play against a team, an extra player is always important. He was always thinking ahead. I think maybe he was inspired by playing England, because he scored a goal in the English style, with his head. I think before that he never scored with his head. I think — I'm not sure; you'll have to be

careful about this because Džajić might read it and be angry, but he didn't score many goals with his head.

⊕ And that game is famous for Alan Mullery becoming the first England player to be sent off. What are your memories of that?

It was a big surprise, because Englishmen were famous for fair play at that time. In football, in games like that from time to time you forget yourself. Today it has gone too far as a business for fair play to matter. Even fair play is a business today. He made two or three fouls in a row: it was like in basketball — second mistake, third mistake and off he went. He was frustrated, probably because at 1-0 all we were doing was fighting to maintain the lead, keeping the ball away from the English players, trying to stop them getting a kick. And today everybody plays like that, just keeping the ball, stopping the opposition getting a kick.

Osim ended his playing career with Strasbourg in 1978 and returned to Sarajevo to manage Željezničar. After leaving Yugoslavia in 1992, he coached Panathinaikos and Sturm Graz before moving to Japan in 2003. There he became manager of JEF United and, in 2006, was appointed to replace Zico as national manager. He became hugely popular, a book of his sayings selling almost half a million copies.

⊕ How strong would you say Japanese football is?

They have a lot of complexes and they are trying to heal these complexes.

Unfortunately they are a really big nation but with a lot of complexes. They are not tall enough, and so you can't make a player look like Drogba or Crouch. You can't teach him to be two metres tall. They are not made from rubber so you can't stretch them to whatever you want. They have covered everything with full attention and they know they need that. They know everything they need, but they simply do not have that. They have an inferiority complex and also you can't buy tradition. In some ways they are the same as Arabic nations. They want to jump over something like the Arabs do. They want to buy the new stadium, buy the club, buy the coach, buy the tradition, and that simply can't be done.

Did you find it difficult to adapt?

The big problem for all coaches when they come to a different culture is that they want to copy what they left behind and that's not always possible. In Japan, you have to understand the way that they live their lives. There is always somebody above them and you always have to ask somebody because he always knows more than you. Their biggest problem is — and this was my feeling when I was working there — that there is no risk, there is no improvisation in Japan, and football can't exist without that. And also players were so afraid of the coaches that they didn't want to do anything on their own initiative. I had the feeling that players could go into the box, get in front of the goal and then stop and ask me what they should do: should I shoot at the goal or pass the ball away? On the other hand, it's very easy to work in Japan because the discipline is very strong. But maybe that isn't so good because it kills a coach. Inevitably

you start to lose ideas and authority. You don't want to provoke crises, but you need problems so you can create solutions. The most important thing in Japan is to make them think with their own heads, not with somebody else's.

But they have some football qualities other nations don't have. They are very determined when they play, they have a lot of aggression and these are important things in today's football. But maybe they need a little more imagination. They need a big player, a big name on the pitch to drive them forward. They need contact with big clubs like Manchester United.

How does a player like Hidetoshi Nakata, a real superstar, fit the culture you describe?

If you don't have a player like him in the team then you have to invent him. All teams need a player like David Beckham or Ronaldo, players like this. You must have a player like that in your team. They feel a lot of pressure because they are really responsible people, responsible in terms of their nation, their flag, their country. Their biggest problem is that they are the country of samurai and kamikaze, and that is a difficult history to live up to.

Did you enjoy your time there?

I didn't have enough time to enjoy my life in Japan. My responsibilities were very, very big, so I didn't have time to enjoy the country and the people. I made special preparations for every practice because they had an enormous number of journalists. They want to know everything, every detail. Why this? Why that? So I made special preparations for that. I had to explain even the smallest details. Somehow you have the feeling you're being underestimated by them with those kind of questions. You get the feeling that you have been provoked by them. Questions like why is this player playing and the other one not playing. And these are things that are very hard to explain to them. Football is a complex game. When you talk to the players you can't always tell them exactly what you feel, because that's a question of their personality and their character. You have to be careful with that.

On one occasion Osim shouted so vehemently at a translator he felt wasn't expressing his anger that he made him cry.

⊕ Did you find it hard to get your ideas across when you had to use a translator?

The first thing you have to do is teach the translator to think like you, and that's a really hard task. You can't really, because he is also Japanese. That's a real danger of the job. And if somebody doesn't translate properly, that can be really dangerous. You can make a simple joke and somebody can take it as a provocation or an insult. That's why you have to be really careful and not say everything you feel. And you can't have the atmosphere in a dressing-room without jokes.

They say if you tell people what's on your mind you are crazy, but I've always had a problem saying what I don't feel. I always say automatically what's in my head. And that's not good in life and football always to say what's on your mind. You can't tell the players directly that they have played at a low level. You have to think through

all the circumstances. And Japan is not easy because they are very proud people and when you say something that looks like criticism, they start to shake and to watch you with different eyes. But you can't go and work without criticising people. If you don't accept your mistakes you can't go forward. They have a problem with that, but that's how they act in Japan.

⊕ Do you think Japan can win the World Cup in the next 20-30 years?

The tradition, the history, the past they have... they have been a big world force in history. They have been rulers of Asia for years, and on that basis of their power, tradition, force, they have problems in football. And it's always buried somewhere, these factors. When I first arrived in Japan, I said to them that it would be a handicap for the World Cup to be without Japan because of the traditions. It's the same thing with England; a World Cup without England would be completely stupid. Japan is a big country, financially very wealthy, with a big tradition and history and it would be a handicap for the World Cup to be without Japan. They must be in the World Cup every time. It's a good thing for the World Cup to have a team like Japan with such a bright and long history and tradition. Maybe in a football way they maybe don't earn much by having Japan in the tournament, but in the other side it's a great plus. You get somebody who really, really likes football. It's a wealthy country, and a country that can always be relied on.

⊕ Can't you say the same of other countries?

It would be good also to have India, but the English made a historical mistake and left them cricket instead of football. I hope they choose football. They're a big market, them and China, but we have to wait for them. Things are moving rapidly in India. Money is the most important thing, of course, and they have money. They're moving very quickly, building the stadiums, making the teams, bringing in one good player to be the basis of the team.

You seem very disillusioned by modern football. Do you still like the game?

I can't say I don't have a passion for football. I was born and raised with football. I don't want to spoil my life because somebody today is earning more than I was when I was playing. Football is so much to me that when I don't have anything to do, I go to the playground and watch kids play football. Japanese journalists still call me to see what I think of games. It's still the group of players I chose when I was with Japan. Maybe they — coaches and journalists — send the DVDs to me to show me that I didn't do a good job... They let you think you are free, but day after day you have to think about what they are thinking. They [coaches and journalists] are here every 10 days.

And the modern game?

It's like when you play chess for money. When you play without money you just play, like Kasparov; when there is money on the table you are not so free. That's what we are seeing right now in the Champions League. You can see that they players are controlling each other and that they are scared of making mistakes and that's a sign that football has gone the wrong way. All tactics are the same just not to lose the game. Coaches are always afraid of losing their job and they pass that to their players and that is not the way to play. It's like some kind of disease. Everybody is afraid: coaches, fans, players, media, the chairman of the club.

Osim is 71 now, although as he shuffled across the stadium car-park in Zenica after Bosnia's 3-0 World Cup qualifying win over Lithuania in October, he looked older. But he still goes to games, he still thinks about football, he still points out to anybody who might have forgotten that he twice turned down offers to manage Real Madrid. And when a journalist stopped him to ask what he had thought of the game, of a Bosnia side managed by a player who was once his captain for Yugoslavia, as the lights of a television camera lit up his soft pink face, the pale eyes shone with passion. The delivery may not have the force it once had but the wisdom is there, the energy laced with caution. Osim may talk about wanting to be free of football, but it is has sustained him all his life and it is still sustaining him now. Ⓑ

Stroke is the third biggest killer and the leading cause of severe adult disability in the UK.

Please remember us with a gift in your will

Behind much of the Stroke Association's unique work are people just like you – people who want to do something powerful and lasting through their Will.

To find out more about leaving a gift in your Will please call us on **020 7566 1505** or email **legacy@stroke.org.uk**

stroke.org.uk

Registered as a Charity in England and Wales (No 211015) and in Scotland (SC037789). Also registered in Isle of Man (No 945) Jersey (NPO 369) and serving Northern Ireland.

Stroke
association

50

The Victorian Age

"What his prowess may be on the field does not really matter; it is enough for the audience that his true vocation is that of a comedian."

The First Columnist

How an early journalist for The Northern Echo *helped shape the modern game*

By Paul Brown

We've a lot to thank the Victorians for. They gave us the light-bulb, the telephone, the flushing toilet, and — perhaps most importantly — association football. Folk had been kicking balls around for hundreds of years, but the Victorians shaped the game, setting the rules, forming clubs and creating competitions. They established the Football Association, the FA Cup and the Football League. They built grounds, drew up fixture lists and introduced the offside rule. And, as the Victorians watched, played and embraced football, they wrote about it.

The world of Victorian football writers is a fascinating one, as you'll be aware if you've ever had cause to search through 19th-century newspaper archives for news of matches from the game's formative years. These often anonymous individuals were occasionally afforded pen names, such as Goal-Post, Full-Back or Spectator. In their columns, they added colour to the sports coverage in Britain's many regional newspapers and cast a proto-pundit's eye over the emerging game. These writers also played an important — and arguably vital — part in the development of football.

One particular writer has stood out as I've scrolled through the microfilm. Off-Side began writing for the *Northern Echo* newspaper in February 1885, immediately setting out his intention to be a fair-minded advocate for football. "The object of the writer will be raising the status of the game," he wrote in an introduction to his *Football Notes* columns. "A main feature of the notes will be their thorough independence. There will be no trucking to this club or to that; everyone will be treated alike. This is a most important point and the general public can depend on it being observed. The writer is not officially connected with any club, and will not sing the praises of one club at the expense of all the rest."

There's no record of Off-Side's real name and the *Northern Echo's* historian hasn't been able to identify him, but his pseudonym appeared in the paper every week for three seasons between 1885 and 1888. This short period was a particularly significant one in football history. The game was rapidly increasingly in popularity and was expanding across the country. New clubs were being formed, often by and for the working classes. Football was becoming the people's game. The FA Cup had been wrested out of the hands of the old guard of public school sides like Wanderers, Old Carthusians and Old Etonians, and new footballing powerbases had emerged in the West Midlands and in

Lancashire, with the likes of Aston Villa, Blackburn Rovers and Preston North End establishing themselves among a new generation of outstanding sides. This power shift led the Football Association to legalise professionalism in 1885 and would also lead to the formation of the Football League.

Despite this rapid growth, the coverage afforded to football by national newspapers in the mid-1880s was sparse. Horse-racing filled much of the sports columns while football vied for attention in the remaining space with the likes of rowing, pedestrianism and pigeon shooting. But appetite for football coverage was growing. Spectators were becoming supporters and developing strong affinities for their local teams. The *Times* and the *Daily News* covered selected FA Cup ties and international matches, and weeklies such as *Bell's Life in London* and the *Athletic News* provided more comprehensive coverage of other high-profile matches, but, in general, supporters had to rely on their regional papers for regular up-to-date coverage of their teams' fortunes.

The Darlington-based *Northern Echo*, which is still in circulation today, was at the time a halfpenny broadsheet with the sporting columns tucked away on the back page just above the shipping forecast. It was a local paper that was well-respected nationally and was rated by the Victorian historian EA Freeman as "the best paper in Europe". Certainly it had broad popular appeal. By placing commentary alongside reporting, the *Echo's* influential young editor WT Stead (who would later go down with the Titanic) had created a distinctive and

lively paper that, it was said, could appeal to pitmen and dukes alike.

Prior to 1885, the *Echo's* football coverage had been fairly rudimentary, typically consisting of nothing more than a brief summary of the region's results every Monday. Unlike papers in Blackburn, Birmingham or Glasgow, the *Echo* didn't publish a Saturday evening Football Special. However, results were received via telegraph after the final whistle and posted at the newspaper's offices so interested parties could go in person to find out how their team had fared.

Monday's match summaries were typically submitted by club secretaries and were brief and perfunctory — and quite often biased and unreliable. When more detailed reports appeared they were generally formal affairs lacking in colour. Teams played "plucky" games and players scored "clinking" goals, but there was little analysis or comment.

Off-Side changed that, introducing insight and opinion to the back page. In his new column he criticised poor tactics and training regimes, waded into rows between clubs and spectators and traded blows with correspondents who challenged his views. He campaigned against disorganisation in the game, including the lax rules of local associations and the tendency of clubs to pull out of matches at late notice. However, he turned his nose up at the creeping nuisance of professionalism, and shook his head when clubs and players pursued "the shekels".

"With to-day, the football season opens," he wrote on the opening morning of the 1885-86 season. "Saturday last practically heard the death knell of the cricketing season, and now the votaries of the popular winter game take the field and claim the attention of the public. All arrangements are completed, and to all lovers of the leather a more than ordinary programme is promised."

Off-Side's enthusiasm for the game was clear as he wrote about the "dash and power" of local sides including Darlington FC, Bishop Auckland Church Institute (winners of the 1886 Durham Association Challenge Cup), plus Middlesbrough, Sunderland and Newcastle East End (the club that later became Newcastle United).

He also looked further afield, covering FA Cup ties and other notable matches. In one early column he wrote about Blackburn's 2-0 FA Cup Final win over Queen's Park and noted how the English team had appropriated the Scots' pass-and-move approach. "The Blackburn Rovers beat them at their own game," he wrote. "The Scotch style of play, consisting chiefly of sharp, close passing and clever individual dodging is practised by the Rovers with a success which on Saturday humbled even Scotland itself."

Off-Side recognised that North East football was not yet at a standard comparable to that of other regions. While the big Midlands and Lancashire teams could attract gates of 5,000-plus, the North East sides could rarely attract more than a few hundred. He knew that there was potential, though, and that his local clubs could benefit from FA Cup ties and friendly matches against top sides. "The visits of a few more teams of the calibre of Aston Villa would have a stimulating effect upon football in the North," he wrote.

Off-Side clearly felt a duty to promote football and wrote positively of the games he witnessed. ("Where the play is so excellent all round, and where there are such faint signs of inferiority, any discriminating comment is difficult.") However, he was quite happy to hand out criticism whenever he felt it was deserved. "Darlington played quite up to their usual form," he wrote on one occasion, "which is to say, they played in no form at all."

Much of Off-Side's criticism was reserved for those clubs and administrators whose incompetence he felt inhibited the growth of the game. Clubs would be chastised for poor organisation and the problem of teams failing to turn up for fixtures became a regular theme. "This conduct cannot be too strongly condemned," he wrote, "and, as a punishment, means should be adopted for making the club in default pay the expenses which have been incurred."

Administrators, particularly the local Durham Football Association, received regular censure. "Football legislators are a queer set, and a capital type of the standstill, querulous old Tory," he wrote. "The Durham Association have sunk so low lately; it is questionable whether they could sink lower... The decisions given are unworthy of any body of representative gentlemen."

As his column became established, Off-Side began to occupy a position of some influence and was able to compel clubs and associations to account for their actions. He would criticise them in print, and demand answers — which he would publish in the following week.

Correspondence was a major feature of the column, which became a valuable forum for football discussion. Rules were debated, best practice was deliberated and arguments were settled, with Off-Side becoming an unofficial arbitrator of football-related disputes.

On one occasion he reported "strong feeling against the recorded result" of a match between Bishop Auckland Church Institute and Darlington, the latter having won 1-0, and published a letter submitted by a spectator detailing the grievance. "Dear Sir, I beg you will insert these remarks from an old football player," wrote the correspondent. "Firstly, the goal given Darlington by the referee was no goal, because Buckton was off-side when he kicked it... Secondly, Pallister headed a ball which was stopped by [Darlington goalkeeper] Wharton standing on the goal line, and he took the ball behind the line. I am sorry the Darlington umpire was so clannish. It was at least a drawn game, if not a win for the Institute."

"As a rule I look with little favour on the objections of a spectator," Off-Side responded. "They, of course, speak with no authority. But in this case the writer has much in his favour. He does not speak as the piqued supporter of a defeated team." Nevertheless, Off-Side went on to report that the Durham Association had thrown out an appeal from Bishop Auckland.

On another occasion, he dismissed Sunderland's claims of refereeing partiality following their defeat to Darlington in the Durham Association Cup. "They were outmatched in every way, and should have taken defeat in

better grace," he wrote. "It was felt by everyone on the field that the greatest partiality the umpire might have shown the Sunderland club could not have saved them from defeat. Above all, a club should keep clear of any objection that can savour of pettiness, or of a simple dislike of not receiving the lion's share of the cheering."

Such strong opinions didn't go unchallenged. After Off-Side accused the Church Institute team of cowardice, a correspondent calling himself Fairplay wrote, "As an old football player, I feel I cannot allow the remarks of your correspondent, 'Off-Side', whoever he may be, to be swallowed by the public without a protest."

The words "whoever he may be" could equally be applied to many of Off-Side's contemporaries, such as White Rose in the *Leeds Mercury*, the *Liverpool Mercury's* Spectator and Full Back in the *Hull Packet*, all of whom remain frustratingly unidentified. A rare exception is James Catton, who wrote about football using the pen name Tityrus. Catton worked for the *Nottingham Daily Guardian* during the 1880s and later edited the Manchester-based national paper *Athletic News*.

The influence wielded by local football writers was noted by their national contemporaries, with some disdain. *Bell's Life* launched an attack on "writers like 'White Rose' who do injury to the sport by casting imputations on those who have worked hard and unselfishly and fearlessly... safe under the shadow of a convenient *nom de plume*." Ironically, the Bell's Life correspondent remained anonymous.

The practice of writing under a pen name came from the letters columns, where readers would often engage in back and forth debate under 'newspaper signatures'. Most Victorian newspaper content was published without bylines and only a handful of writers were afforded credit by pseudonym. Football writers were most likely given pen names so that readers had a name to address their missives to.

Off-Side clearly received his fair share of missives. "I cannot adequately peruse the voluminous number of letters received," he wrote. "The postmen have had a heavy time, and the Postmaster-General has had to issue orders for the distribution of tonics to the unfortunate men." He refused to publish correspondence from supporters, players or officials who refused to be identified: "It would be foolish to attempt to deal with anonymous communications, and therefore they are weekly swept into the w.p.b."

As far as clues to Off-Side's identity go, we know that the *Echo* had a football team that in 1885 comprised Hodgson (goal), Brown and Hutchinson (backs), Martin, O'Hara and Appleby (half-backs), and Beswick, Johnson, Hazeldine, Stanley and Watson (forwards). It seems reasonable to suppose that the paper's football writers might have played for that team and that Off-Side could be one of those named in the line-up. In one column, he previewed an *Echo* team fixture in tongue-in-cheek style: "There is to be a great slaughter of the innocents. Full details on Monday. Newsagents will please send their orders early."

A recurring theme in the *Football Notes* column was "rough play", and Off-Side related tales of hacking, broken legs and the occasional "interchange of civilities" between players. "It cannot be too widely known that a referee, upon observing any foul play, may at once order off the field the player the player who indulges in such reprehensible practices," he wrote. "A large number of players are noted for their rough play, and it would be a decided gain to the popularity of football if they were suspended, not only for the season but for ever."

However, he defended the game from the criticism of a local magistrate, who claimed football was "becoming one of the greatest abominations of the nation." "There is no doubt that in football, as well as in every other sport worthy of the name, there is a certain amount of danger," Off-Side responded, "but whether football is becoming 'one of the greatest abominations of the nation' is open to much objection. If an 'abomination' stimulates the higher physical qualities of the youths of the nation, and provides pleasurable recreation every Saturday for countless thousands throughout the land, then I am willing to stick my flag in such an 'abomination'."

Then as now, match officials were placed under scrutiny and in general Off-Side was strongly supportive. On one occasion he reported that, following a contentious decision by one referee, "partisans attacked him with mud and stones". "This hostile demonstration cannot be too strongly condemned," wrote Off-Side.

He dismissed a protest against another referee, J Bastard of Middlesbrough (not to be confused with former referee and England international Segar Bastard of

London), writing, "Anyone who knows Mr Bastard — and I have met him many times upon the football field — knows that he is most painstaking and thoroughly impartial in giving his decisions."

Although there was relatively little tabloid-style tittle-tattle in Off-Side's columns, he did report rumours concerning club matters and player movements. The start of the 1886-87 season brought major transfer news, with the great Arthur Wharton moving from Darlington to Preston North End. "This is a great loss to Darlington," Off-Side commented, "There is not another man at the club who can keep goal with half his ability."

Conversely, Off-Side displayed a clear personal dislike for Darlington's other goalkeeper (and club secretary) Charles Samuel Craven. After Craven penned an article listing the attributes required by good goalkeepers, Off-Side commented, "The only particular in which he coincides with what a good goalkeeper should be is in height."

Other players also faced criticism. "It is a matter of grave remark that Smeddle [of North Skelton] bungles too often," Off-Side wrote. Some players had distinctive reasons for performing poorly: "[Darlington forward] Hope played badly towards the end of the game, owing, he diligently informed the spectators, to being at 'a jig all night'."

Humour played a key part in Off-Side's columns, and he was no stranger to sarcasm. "Sunderland!" he remarked of the region's most affluent side. "The great all-powerful Sunderland!! With their Scotchmen and special retainers!" On another occasion, he reported

rumours of a friendly match between the tiny St Paul's FC and the great Preston North End. "What is this I hear from Spennymoor, and of Spennymoor St Paul's FC of all the clubs in the world?" he wrote. "Preston North End! Spennymoor!! St Paul's!!! This is too awfully awful. How the mighty have fallen!"

When bad weather disrupted the fixture list he began his column with, "Football! The word sounds delightful with snow lying nearly a foot deep." Correspondents, too, brought humour to the column. An anonymous Port Clarence player wrote to Off-Side ahead of a big match: "Already the gloomy tidings of certain defeat have reached our ears, and we look forward to coming home with lengthy visages."

"What are footballers to make of the following?" Off-Side wrote in another column. "On Saturday Preston North End defeated the Bolton Wanderers by twelve goals to one. On Monday West Bromwich Albion defeated Preston North End by five goals to two. On Tuesday the Bolton Wanderers defeated West Bromwich Albion by two goals to one. Query — which is the best team?"

The increasing interest in football was reflected in the popularity of Off-Side's column. The *Echo* promoted *Football Notes* throughout the week and it was expanded in length and in frequency, being switched from weekly to twice-weekly. Football was important to a paper seeking to meet the needs of its many working-class readers. Off-Side celebrated "the increased interest which has been evoked by the game among the masses — it is always the masses. This has never been so marked in this district, and bids fair to increase rather than abate in future seasons."

"It is the same all over the country," he wrote. "The contagion — if one may be allowed to use the word – is growing... There are on every hand signs of the increased popularity of football... The cause for this is not far to seek, and that is the great encouragement given to the game by the local press."

Certainly, football's rapid growth had been fostered in the regions, and local newspapers and their football writers had played an important role. When, in April 1887, the *Times* published a leader reflecting upon "how immensely the game has grown in public favour in late years", it felt overdue and ill-informed. "Five-and-twenty years ago football was the game of schoolboys and of some clubs of hardy northerners," wrote the paper. "Now it is played with passionate zeal at the Universities." (Off-side wrote in his own column that he had gained "much amusement" from the *Times* article.) The national paper did get one thing right, though: "At every great centre of population football matches are among the most frequented of public entertainments." Every great centre of population had a local newspaper, and that was where the real story of football was being told.

A leader published in the *Northern Echo* painted a more accurate picture of the state of association game: "A few years since, football was almost confined to a particular class, and the games only proved of interest to the players and their own friends. Now, however, all classes are represented by the players, and the games afford amusement to countless thousands of spectators throughout the country... There can be no doubt that football is becoming very much of a business. Gate money is now a necessity to the game, but as it is now played, the charge for admission to the ground is more than justified, and the benefit clubs and players receive is far outweighed by the existence among us of a great and popular game."

Football's development in the regions continued in the months that followed. Later in 1887, the Aston Villa director William McGregor set out his plans to form the Football League, which, when it began in 1888, was made up exclusively of sides from the Midlands and the North West. But football in Off-Side's North East was developing rapidly, too. The very competitive Northern League was formed in Darlington in 1889, and in the following year Sunderland became the first North East side to join the Football League. They won it three times in their first five seasons, with their Scotchmen and special retainers.

Off-Side didn't get to report on Sunderland's triumphs, having left the *Echo* at the end of the 1887-88 season. "In concluding these notes it may be stated that in all that has appeared the true interests of football have been in view," he wrote. "There has been no trucking to this side or to that for the mere sake of popularity. That kind of thing has been left to others. There are some who condemn the action taken in these notes: time alone will prove who was right or wrong."

His successor, Observer, paid fond tribute to Off-Side's "conscientiousness and ability", adding: "I heartily trust that he may find in his new sphere across the 'herring pond' due scope for his talents, and that he may haul in the dainty shekels to his heart's (and his pocket's) content."

The "herring pond" reference suggested that Off-Side had emigrated over the Atlantic to North America. However, in July 1888, a new column entitled *Football Notes by Off-Side* appeared in the Wanganui Herald in New Zealand. Archives suggest Off-Side continued to write about football for various Kiwi newspapers for the next 20 years.

Stiffy the Goalkeeper

Lazy, drunken and corruptible, the first footballing hero of the stage could hardly have been less heroic

By John Harding

"I used to keep goal and was well-known to fame,
As the greatest goalkeeper and Stiffy's the name,
The man who made all centre-forwards sit up,
When we fought in a friendly, the League or the Cup..."

So sang Harry Weldon, aka Stiffy the Goalkeeper, the most famous fictional footballer of the period before the First World War. Stiffy was a nationwide success, but he was also a rarity. In Victorian and Edwardian England, footballers as fantasy figures hardly featured at all in print, on stage or on film, which might seem odd given the wild enthusiasm with which the game and its heroes were treated up and down the land.

Nationally, the working class had no fictional voice. Writers, even those journalists working on popular newspapers then feeding the burgeoning soccer appetite, were middle-class in origin or aspiration and the middle class had great difficulty in coming to terms with professional football. The governing body of the game, the Football Association, had agonised for some time before consenting, in 1885, to allow paid players to appear in its, until then, strictly amateur competitions.

The Football League, founded in 1888 to provide football clubs with a regular series of fixtures, and thus the principal 'employers" organisation, was run by men who preferred to exploit the suspicion, even the disgust, that professional players appeared to engender in official breasts. They were thus able to restrict professional players in terms of their pay and freedom of movement, almost as a condition for allowing them to exist at all.

Not surprisingly, the soccer professional struggled to attain respectability, being condemned for a variety of reasons ranging from the stain his calling inflicted on 'pure' amateur sport to the pernicious effect the paid game supposedly had on its wider working-class audience, leading them into indolence, gambling and alcoholism. Professional players could never be 'official' heroes of the realm. Soldiers and sailors, statesmen and explorers might be moulded into role models for the young but never men being paid to play a game. Unlike in the United States, where the pro-baseball player personified a variety of cultural and historical ideas close to the hearts of the American people, in Britain, the professional footballer remained marginalised and ignored in imaginative, creative terms, fit only for children's literature.

In parallel with the pro-football game, the music hall (that unruly offspring of the dramatic stage) also struggled for some time to be considered respectable in the eyes of officialdom. Its practitioners and stars were condemned in remarkably similar fashion to professional footballers: accused of encouraging, within the precincts of the halls, all forms of licentious activity while at the same time bringing the noble art of thespianism into disrepute. Just as pro-footballers were inferior versions of the amateur game, so music hall artists remained in the shadow of the 'legitimate' theatre.

For the professionals in the halls and in football grounds up and down the country, the consequences of these attitudes were fairly similar: arrogant treatment by management and agents, poor contractual arrangements and very little personal control over their professional lives. Perhaps it's no surprise, therefore, that it was in the music hall that football would first emerge as a suitable subject for truly popular entertainment in a show that would celebrate exactly those aspects of their respective worlds that caused the most official displeasure.

At the turn of the twentieth century Fred Karno was an impresario and writer just beginning to establish himself and his production company as a force in the entertainment world. Very early on, he had glimpsed the influence football could have on the success of a show. In 1905, he and his co-writer Fred Kitchen produced a knock-about sketch called "The Bailiff", which had inadvertently created an early football terrace chant. The main character had a catch-phrase, "Meredith, We're In!" which was taken up by the young apprentices and manual workers then thronging the terraces. The Meredith in question was Billy, probably the most talked about player in the history of the game up to that point.

At the height of his fame, having helped Manchester City to the FA Cup in 1904, Meredith had spectacularly fallen to earth following accusations of bribery. He was suspended for a year and a half, during which time he was sensationally transferred to Manchester United. His official disgrace, however, hardly dented his terrace reputation and his return to the field of play was, in late 1906, eagerly awaited in football-mad Manchester, if not the country at large.

It was at this moment that Karno and Kitchen chose to write "The Football Match" which opened at the Palace Theatre, Manchester, in December 1906 — just a few weeks before Meredith was due to run out at United's Bank Street ground for his return. Meredith's involvement in bribery and match-fixing had created an establishment anti-hero. The central theme of "The Football Match" would also be match-fixing and bribery and the principal character was destined to become one of the game's great fictional anti-heroes.

An early review of the Karno sketch sets the scene: "An attempt to bribe certain members to lose the match is afoot, and the attempt is watched by a detective, who bears no resemblance to any detective ever seen at Scotland Yard, and whose idea of finding out the delinquents is to watch the action closely from the fragrant precincts of the smoke-room. The chief person to be bribed is Stiffy, the goal-keeper, whose integrity, however, in spite of his many oddities of conduct, is proof against temptation. What his prowess may be on the field does not really matter; it is enough for the audience that his true vocation is that of a comedian and the extent of his fitness for the stage is demonstrated with ample effect by Mr Harry Weldon."

Harry Weldon was an up-and-coming music-hall comedian. Born in Liverpool and a staunch Evertonian, (the theatre critic Hannen Swaffer wrote that Weldon's creation of Stiffy the Goalkeeper was "inspired by his almost maniacal allegiance to the Everton Football Club") he could also play the game himself. He founded, organised and captained a team made up of Fred Karno employees, whose exploits against other music-hall sides raised almost £500 for charity in 1909 alone. Weldon even supplied the theatrical paper *Performer* with the team's record for the year: "23 matches played, 14 have been won, 2 drawn and 7 lost."

Weldon would befriend scores of professional players, including Billy Meredith and the majority of the two Manchester sides. He would boast that on the opening night of a one-man show in 1909 over forty football pros sent him telegrams of support. He later wrote, "Between the football pro and myself there has always been a bond of friendship in fair weather and in foul weather and my only ambition is to always remain 'one of the lads'."

He was a particularly good friend of Jimmy Crabtree, the ex-Aston Villa player who would appear on stage in the first version of "The Football Match". "Two years prior to his death he presented me with his English Cup medal obtained when Villa won the Cup in 1897," Weldon wrote just after Crabtree died from the effects of alcohol abuse in 1908. "I shall never forget his words as he handed it to me at his hotel in Aston. 'Harry, lad,' he said, 'I'm giving thee this medal on one condition; that is, that tha' never parts with it to anybody but me.' The medal still hangs on my watch chain. Where I go, it goes." As he developed his Stiffy character, Weldon would slowly acquire more discarded artefacts from his soccer pals: on stage he would wear the giant goalkeeper 'Fatty' Foulkes's shorts, a shirt once worn by Preston North End legend John Goodall and boots that had been given to him by Billy Meredith himself.

But what was so unique about Stiffy? According to one of Weldon's biographers, "There isn't anything funny about a goalkeeper at a Cup tie or league match — at least, I never met anybody who thought there was until I met 'Stiffy'."

Perhaps the key to the character was just that — he was a goalkeeper, a position already noted for being occupied by eccentrics. Indeed, Sheffield United and Chelsea's Fatty Foulke, could easily have been a Karno creation. He was, in an almost literal way, larger than life: weighing 15 stones when he signed for Sheffield United, he had managed to put on an extra seven stones before he moved to Chelsea in 1906. He even had his own a catch-phrase: "I don't mind what they call me as long as they don't call me late for lunch." Foulke wasn't the only keeper regarded as an eccentric: LR

Roose, Harry Trainer, Albert Iremonger — all were considered a little bit odd. There was also Jack Hillman, a former Manchester City keeper of considerable bulk, who had been embroiled in the Billy Meredith scandal and who had himself been banned for a season in 1900 for accepting bribes.

In football, a goalkeeper can be a hero, but he is also much more at the mercy of fate than any other player. Before the First World War, keeping goal could be a high-risk job, subject to man-handling and serious injury. Weldon played on the bathos of such a position, the sweet sorrow involved. A critic at the time wrote, "The first time I saw Stiffy I laughed until my sides ached. Harry Weldon was new to the stage in those days but he created a character that was pathetically ludicrous. Poor Stiffy, the forlorn hope — ill-used and abused, and yet the saviour of his side..."

While a gifted comic, Weldon was careful not to give the impression that he was mocking Stiffy or the football world in which he existed. "Stiffy was a character study – full of burlesque, perhaps, but never satirical," Swaffer wrote. "A lesser comedian than Harry Weldon would have failed to have realised the character and, instead of applauding, the gods would have hissed. That was the beginning of Weldon's popularity."

Weldon's knowledge of the game, his keen eye for the quirks and habits of professionals, lent his interpretation an insiders' perspective that was well appreciated by players who were among Stiffy's greatest fans, filling the front rows at every performance and eager to make guest appearances on stage.

Yet Stiffy was hardly a portrait of the best that professionalism could offer. He was clearly a 'dud' player and his training consisting largely of drinking and eating. Indeed, drink was very much in evidence in "The Football Match" and there was certainly no sense of shame about it: the reviewer for *Smith's Liverpool Weekly* wrote in February 1907, "See Stiffy the marvellous goalkeeper train, bar-bell in right hand and jar of beer in left. Three up and three down with bar-bell and then some beer. How well he finishes a 50 yard sprint with the beer in sight."

The rest of the pro-players in the play were depicted as rough diamonds. Laughs were derived from their social awkwardness in the company of directors and financial backers, their capacity to drink and eat huge quantities, not to mention their skill at breaking training curfews. Their wives, meanwhile, were presented as heavy drinkers and sexual predators — nothing new there.

What's more intriguing is that Stiffy's morals were more than a little unclear. In the pre-First World War version of the show, the *Birmingham Daily Post* reviewer wrote, "Harry Weldon as Stiffy the goalkeeper, ultimately sells the match for a gallon of beer," while the *Sheffield Telegraph* wrote, "Stiffy betrays his side and loses the match through his bad goalkeeping..." Later reviews, however, suggest his integrity, "in spite of his many oddities of conduct" remained proof against temptation.

What is certain, however, is that Weldon, through his burlesque character, was calling into question the nature of success, the desire to win at all costs. As one of Weldon's obituarists wrote in

1930, "He was one of the most inveterate of anti-romanticists, for no hero's glory was safe from his tarnishing." "Stiffy's Song" was set partly to the tune of Handel's "See The Conquering Hero Comes," but in contrast revealed his wonderfully anti-heroic qualities:

"Hark to the shouting, Stiffy is the man they're cheering
Stiffy is the best goalkeeper that ever let a ball go through
They said this morning that by a hundred goals they'd beat me
But they didn't know the man they had to deal with
'cos we only lost by forty-two."

The essence of the show's success, however, was that no matter how ludicrously it was depicted, it presented to the audience the world of the professional footballer as seen from within. Slapstick humour aside, this was a play about football and all its aspects. From the training quarters at the local public house (some professional teams still used pubs as headquarters) where the audience was treated to the spectacle of players going through their exercises, to the turnstiles outside where hundreds of extras from the Manchester streets were employed to create a sense of expectation, to the dressing-room prior to kick-off, and thence onto the pitch itself: no aspect of a typical Saturday football afternoon was excluded. A great deal of "eccentric acrobatics and comic tumbling" was exploited, but throughout the audience was being given, according to one reviewer, "an interesting peep into the immediate preliminaries of a match".

For this, Fred Karno must take all the accolades. "The Football Match" would establish him as the supreme music-hall producer. Prior to his success, the stage had appeared to be an unsuitable setting for a sport that gloried in spectacle, colour, noise and excitement. The early cinema was also poorly equipped to handle the ebb and flow of a game like soccer, but Karno surmounted all the technical difficulties with ease.

For "The Football Match", his biographer recalled, "Karno had a huge panoramic cloth made to go right round the back of the stage with a great crowd of spectators painted on it. Ordinarily, nothing on earth looks as lifeless as a painted crowd of people. It has been done frequently, and the effect was usually to kill the 'effect'… But mark where the cleverness of Karno came in. He engaged a big crowd of live 'supers' to stand in the foreground on a raked 'ground row', the big ones at the front and the little ones at the back standing higher up the rake than the tall ones. The perspective effect was perfect. The living spectators merged into the painted ones so artfully that the public didn't know that they were not alive. Further, to heighten the illusion, on the painted cloth he had loose arms that waved white handkerchiefs and threw little hats excitedly into the air when a goal was scored. This effect was gained by very powerful electric fans placed out of sight of the audience behind the 'ground row'. A football match was played on the stage and the enthusiasm of the crowd was indescribable. It was a Cup Final played twice nightly with matinees as well." There was even, apparently, a simulated rain storm to end act one, "which looked as though the actual wet afternoon outside had suddenly broken furiously through the roof."

The match itself, the climax to the piece, featured various popular former players, whose early appearance on stage set the overall tone of the evening. A reviewer for the theatrical paper *The Age* wrote, "In the composition of the teams, some one-time famous players were introduced, namely, Jimmy Crabtree and Billy Athersmith (late of Aston Villa), and Fred Spiksley (late of Sheffield Wednesday); when they appeared on stage with the referee announcing them by name, the applause was almost deafening but the function of this trio was not to give an exhibition of the game against the less experienced company of comedians, (the Middleton Pie-cans) who were playing their own game for the audience; they added a touch of realism, and served to give the play just a suspicion of definite form. Goals were scored, and easily; but the chances against the Pie-cans, one may take it, are nullified by an arrangement, quite in keeping with the spirit of the piece, that no matter how many goals may be scored on either side the result shall be announced as a draw, no score."

Karno's "Football Match" with Stiffy as star thus saw a unique coming-together of two nascent professions to produce a memorable theatrical event. In fact, the links between the two professions were, for a time, quite strong. Both had emerged at around the same time, the 1880s, when music halls and football grounds were being rapidly constructed in great numbers. Their respective Unions (The Variety Artistes Federation (VAF) and the Association Football Players' Union (AFPU)) were formed within a few months of each other in 1906 and 1907, and only a year or so separated militant action on behalf of their specific aims. At

first, neither group was concerned about money; their grievances related rather to questions of status, both contractual and social, than with salary levels.

As the twentieth century began, however, both sets of performers experienced negative changes in their economic situation, as their pay and conditions deteriorated dramatically. In the music hall, casual agreements and engagements began to be replaced by contracts which quickly became the instrument both for disciplining and expressing 'ownership' of entertainers, who began to perceive proprietors' actions as 'aggressive policy'. They objected to the power of hall proprietors, "sitting in conclave over a glass and a cigar" considering them as a "huckster would merchandise", speaking of their "market price as a butcher would of cattle".

This is remarkably similar to the experience of professional footballers in relation to their situation vis-a-vis the transfer market. What's more, footballers at the top of the profession saw a dramatic fall in their salary levels in 1900, due to the institution of a £4 maximum wage, which they had found forced upon them by their employers, the Football League.

Both unions were also concerned with the well-being of the less-well-known individual artiste/player who struggled to make ends meet. In 1907, the VAF launched a campaign against certain theatre managers in order to get them to agree to better terms of employment as outlined in a charter. They also instituted a charitable fund, death benefits, legal assistance and pensions, all intended to encourage the "steady, sober and reliable performer". In fact, when "The Football Match" opened in Manchester in January 1907, the VAF had members outside the theatre demonstrating against music-hall managements whom it considered were "exploiting" performers. Within a month, pro footballers, led by Billy Meredith, had established the AFPU. It, too, pressed for profession-wide accident insurance, death benefits and legal assistance: it was an insistence on providing the latter to its members that saw the APFU come close to being banned entirely in 1909 following strike threats.

The two unions certainly supported one another from very early on. During the 1909 football dispute, music-hall artistes held charity football matches to raise funds for the Manchester United players (led by Billy Meredith) who had been locked out. Both Unions would hold summer sports meetings involving prominent stars to raise funds for themselves: the VAF held its first Federation Day at Crystal Palace in June 1907 where Harry Weldon competed in the 50-yard handicap. The AFPU held three very successful summer sports meetings a couple of years later, also to raise funds and was well-supported by their thespian comrades.

"The Football Match" kick-started various illustrious stage and screen careers, none more so than that of Charlie Chaplin who got his first big stage break in "The Football Match" in January 1908 when, at London's Coliseum, he played the villain who attempts to bribe Stiffy to throw the match. ["Are we alone?" asked Chaplin, "No," said Weldon. "Who's here?" asked Chaplin. "Me," said Weldon.] Chaplin later claimed he'd upstaged Weldon at one point and been severely reprimanded for

stealing laughs in the show. He wrote, "For the life of me I couldn't understand what it was all about. Karno had sent me out to 'get the laughs', and all I got for getting them was a clip on the ear."

Harry Weldon would play the character of Stiffy the Goalkeeper some 900 times for Karno up and down the country before incorporating the creation into his solo act and transforming him in later years into a boxer as well as a number of other characters. Weldon became one of the highest paid performers in variety but suffered the same fate as his sporting hero, Jimmy Crabtree, dying of drink-related problems in 1930. Fred Karno would go on to become one of the variety industry's greatest impresarios, earning himself millions before going bankrupt in the late 1920s.

As for Stiffy, he would re-emerge in the interwar years as a vehicle for another star comedian, Sandy Powell of "Can You Hear Me, Mother?" fame. Powell had admired Weldon immensely and was also a keen player for charity. In Powell's version, ex-football stars such as Chelsea's George 'Gatling Gun' Hilsden donned greasepaint and performed their soccer tricks. By 1931, however, the character and the sketch were unrecognisable from the Weldon version and commanded little of the original's nationwide success.

After "The Football Match", there would be little subsequent development of fictional football characters either on stage or in the cinema. Occasionally, a professional player might appear as a romantic lead, or revered hero, but nothing would be revealed of professional football life, the nature of the trade, its stresses and strains, certainly no examination of the players' roles in the lives of working people.

Why this should be so remains an enduring mystery, given the imaginative hold the game has had on the British psyche for more than a century since Stiffy trod the boards, proclaiming:

When Stiffy's between the sticks,
When Stiffy's between the sticks,
He can stop any kind of ball,
A football or a brandy ball,
And Vivian Woodward says, when I start
me monkey tricks
What's the good of trying to score
When Stiffy's between the sticks? Ⓑ

Out with a League Team

A journalist, writing in 1900, describes his experiences travelling the country reporting on Notts County

By Henry Leach

"What a jolly fine time you chaps must have, going away with the teams every other weekend!" This was a remark which was often addressed to me during one period of my journalistic career, when it became my humble duty to follow one First Division football team or another up and down the country in its peregrinations for points. Possibly the many who made it would have been less envious if they had experienced some of the discomforts of the business.

For instance, I have yet to learn that it is one of the pleasures of life to be forced to get out of a warm bed at 4.30am the Saturday before Christmas, to find there is no time to wait for breakfast, and then to trudge two miles through the blackness and a cold drizzling rain to a station where a two hundred miles' journey north is commenced, and to which you will return in the very small hours of the morning.

But, all the same, these little trips are somewhat interesting, especially if one is so young and enthusiastic that the results of league matches are considered of more importance than alliances between foreign powers. The genus professional footballer, when he goes abroad to meet the enemy, is a distinct study, and as most boys, especially those residing in a 'Socker'-infested neighbourhood, have the form of the league clubs weighed up to an ounce, and follow their doings with the closest watchfulness, it occurred to me that they would like to know what takes place as a rule when the teams go away. Few may find out in the ordinary way, for the players' saloon is sacred to all but the players and trainer, committee-men, and the football war correspondents who follow a club faithfully through the glories and disasters of a whole season's campaign.

And let me say here now that the experience has taught me that much injustice is done to the football pros, as a class, by those who know nothing about them. I am no believer in the limited company manner in which association football is carried on nowadays; but it is wholly unjust to visit the sins of the system upon the men who are the necessary result of it.

From what I have seen of them — and it is very much — they are a very steady and respectable class, and are very probably much better men than they would have been if they had not taken up football as a profession. Regular habits of life are compulsory, and that is a great thing; and I have never known a professional to take any less interest in the game or be any less loyal to his club or solicitous for its welfare than would have been the case if he had been an amateur and did not get well paid for his services. He does not think of his wages when he is on the field, but only of his side and of the victory which he hopes may come of it.

Well, then, the team, with one or two good reserves, is usually selected in good time during the week, and the secretary briefly notifies each man of the arrangements which have been made. His note runs something like this: "DEAR SIR — You have been selected to play in your usual position in next Saturday's match against Everton; kick-off at 2.30. To be ready for the 8.25 am train at the Midland station, you will please report yourself there at 8.15."

As a matter of fact, that train is not due to leave till 8.35, but the secretary is a good judge of human nature in the matter of catching early trains and it would never do for a single player to be late. Still, in time the player becomes educated to this little dodge and looks up the timetable on his own accord with the result that more than once have I seen an indispensable forward or goalkeeper rushing madly on to the platform, with his arms going about like the sails of a windmill, when the wheels had already begun to move. If the guard sympathises with football and realises the state of affairs, he will pull the train up, especially if it is a special, as it frequently is; but if his heart is stony those wheels roll on and there is distress in the players' saloon for a long time, while at the first stopping place execrations are heaped upon the head of that villainous guard.

On one journey we left a player behind in this way and the match we were going to was one of great importance, for it was generally considered that it would have a lot to do with settling whether our club should rise from the Second Division to the First. There was a reserve in the saloon but he was not a man to be depended upon; and the state of affairs was distinctly unpleasant.

A brilliant idea occurred to one of the committee-men. Our opponents were Manchester City, and our route to Manchester lay through Derby. At Derby there resided one of our regular first-team players, who had, for some reason or other, been dropped this particular week. What could be simpler than for one of the committee to drop out at Derby, secure this man, and hurry away with him to Manchester by the next train, which would land him there just in time?

But the idea didn't work out very well — at least, at first it didn't. The official got out and hurried to that man's quarters, only to find that, as he was under the impression he was having a holiday, he was not at home. Away went a telegram to the secretary: "Can't find him," and the secretary became despondent. But the official later on obtained a clue as to the man's whereabouts, and he wired again: "On his track." Up and down Derby he went from one place to another, and at last, only just in time to catch the very last train which was any good, he was enabled to wire: "Found him. Coming."

But at the Manchester end the coming seemed to be too long delayed. The minutes sped away, and the time for dressing came, and "He cometh not" was the sorrowful reflection of the secretary. The reserve was ordered to turn out, and the players had lined up before a big crowd, when there was a commotion on the rails. A way was made, and an official rushed on to the field and dragged off the unwilling reserve. The eleventh man had arrived, and, of course, if the game had begun with the reserve in the team, it would have had to go on with him, no changing after the start being allowed. The referee wouldn't wait while the eleventh man donned his football toggery, and so our side began with 10 men; but soon the other bounded on to the turf, and that day a quite brilliant 4-1 victory was accomplished.

The same team seemed to be in an even tighter fix than this on another occasion. I may as well say that it was Notts County. We were coming down South with the intention of getting two points out of Arsenal and the match was of no less importance than the other. The train stopped at Kettering and two or three of the men got out to stretch their legs. Long railway journeys are very wearisome to trained athletes. Suddenly, without any warning, without any blowing of the guard's whistle, the train began to move on. The secretary shouted out, and the players on the platform made a rush for the carriage-door, and, as it seemed, all got safely inside and congratulated themselves on being so close at hand. From a large party it is not difficult to miss one man and we had gone some little distance before a most hideous fact dawned upon us, which threatened to bring about an immediate and universal greying of hair. [George] Toone, the goal-keeper, many times international, whose place really could not be filled, was missing! The timetable was appealed to in vain for consolation. There was no other train from Kettering which could land him in London in time.

A council of war was held, and the inevitable was accepted with all the grace possible under the circumstances. A rearrangement of the team was decided upon and a half-back was ordered to go between the sticks. The outlook was gloomy and it was by no means a safe proceeding to attempt to open up any conversation with the secretary, even on such an innocent subject as the weather.

On reaching King's Cross the party filed across the road to a restaurant, where orders were given for steaks for fourteen. We hadn't been sat down more than 10 minutes waiting for those steaks to cook, when, in a manner peculiar to him, but which was certainly very tantalising in these times, Toone quietly walked in and sat down amongst us as if nothing had happened. Helped by a lot of luck, he had made a very good best of a very bad job. When he found that the train had left him at Kettering, he naturally cast his eyes about him for another, and there on the other side of the line he saw one waiting to go out. It was a train which was behind its time, and should have been on the other. It was promptly boarded, and that is why an extra steak had to be ordered at King's Cross and also, very likely, it was the reason why Woolwich Arsenal were beaten, for Toone, as if to make up for his morning's faults, played a very great game that afternoon.

But now let me say something about what goes on in the saloon in a general way and about the arrangements which are made for the comfort and well-being of the party.

Of course the saloon is always engaged, no matter whether the journey to be made is short or long. It is a detail that in the case of a party of such dimensions the railway company makes no extra charge for it. It is necessary that all the men should be together, and under the eye of the trainer and the secretary, who also acts as manager. The latter gets all the tickets (fare and a-quarter for the double journey) and distributes them, gratuitously of course, when the train is in motion. Each man usually has his bag with him; but, as a rule, the trainer, who always accompanies the team, is largely responsible for shirts and knickers and keeps them all in his own hamper. Another very important matter to which he attends is the commissariat, for in a large number of cases it is necessary to lunch in the train. Therefore the hamper is laden with goodly things — not fancy things, but good big joints of roast beef and loaves of bread, with a few pots of pickles, which have to be consumed very sparingly.

Nobody has such an appetite as your well-trained footballer, and about midday, very fidgety, and tired of doing nothing, his thoughts turn towards eating and fitting himself bodily for the fray before him.

Not till the trainer wills it, however, is his hunger to be appeased; but by-and-by this autocrat disappears into the little ante-chamber at the end of the saloon, a clatter of knives and forks is heard, and presently he emerges with a pile of crockery, which he follows up with the big lumps of beef, the loaves of bread, and all the other comestibles which in his wisdom he has provided for his crew. The secretary, or whoever is most skilful with the carvers, promptly commences to deal out the grub, and

by the time he gets to No. 7, No. 1 is clamouring for more!

Eventually, however, the hunger of all is appeased, and then, with a happy contentment and an optimism which is the normal result of a full stomach, the men discuss the coming encounter and the number of goals they will probably win by.

At best, however, these outward railway journeys are weary affairs, for there is so much anxiety as to what is going to happen. Coming home, either victorious or beaten, is ever so much easier. The saloon is strewn with the morning papers, all invariably open at the football page, on which is very likely to be printed the names of the opposing team. This naturally becomes the subject of keen discussion and it is a matter for all-round congratulation if from some cause or other the rivals are a little below strength.

The grown footballer is not infrequently a smoker, but on no account is he allowed to smoke in the saloon on the journey out. This rule is most strictly enforced, not so much perhaps on account of the injury it would do to the smoker himself, as on account of the contamination of the atmosphere which would ensue, for it is one of the first principles of the trainer that his men must breathe pure air. Now and again, however, you see a player get up and evince some curiosity as to what is in that little ante-chamber aforesaid. He looks about for a moment, and then, as if by accident, the door quietly closes. A couple of minutes later another player follows him, and as the door opens you get a sniff of tobacco which tells a tale of guilt and the little game is promptly stopped. No great harm, however, is done.

Things are usually so arranged that on the team's arrival at its destination there is but little time cut to waste, for nothing so much depresses the football player away from home, and discounts his side's chances of victory, as an aimless idling about for an hour or two before the match.

He knows he is in a hostile country, and that it would be foolish to expect either the admiration or the respect to which he is treated when he is on his own pitch. Instead of that, these foreign urchins make it their business to discover at the earliest possible moment all the weak points in his physique and the peculiarities of feature, and to communicate the results of their researches to each other in stage asides, which are audible to all, and most of all to the man criticised. An argument arises also as to the precise number of goals by which the home side will beat their visitors. As a rule the consensus of opinion inclines to six but sometimes double figures are favoured.

Some very big boys, who ought to know better but don't, occasionally follow the example of the youngsters in these matters; and, though it is all very wise and well to say that no man with any common sense would take notice of such folly, it all adds to that feeling of sojourning in a strange land, the ultimate result of which is a lost match.

Everybody knows that a good team stands more chance of winning at

home than it does away, and I should say, speaking without the book, that the average league XI — the "average" is important here — wins three matches at home for every one on foreign soil. Why? Certainly not because it is more familiar with its own ground than any other. Many people fancy this is the reason, but every league player whom I have sounded on the question denies it. And I agree with them. Except in such cases as Newcastle United, the ground of which the ancient Britons might have thought good for football but which the modern artist always dreams of in his worst nightmares, the playing patch of one League club is so like that of another that a forward pegging away at top speed scarcely ever notices any difference. Now and again, on a small ground, when he does look up, he is crossing the goal line just when he begins to think it is time to put in a long shot, but that is all. It is the morning's anxiety, the restlessness, and the lack of public sympathy which cause a visiting team to be beaten so often — and particularly the anxiety, because in the case of league clubs fighting for position everything depends upon the away matches.

In speculating upon the possible and probable results of its matches at the commencement of the season a club always takes it for granted that it is going to win its home matches. If it cannot do this it stands a poor chance away and it might as well 'put its shutters up' at once. An observation I have made which bears out what I have said is to the effect that, whether a team pulls the game out of the fire or not, it nearly always plays better in the second half away from home than it does in the first. So much for that point.

The footballer abroad has many anxious thoughts for those at home, as he plainly shows when he hurries up to a friend who has come with them, just before going on the field and hands him a big batch of addressed telegram forms, with the humble request that he will send half away at half-time with the score and the other at the finish.

Sometimes, if there are parents at home who look upon football as only less dangerous than standing with one's back to the muzzle of a hostile Maxim gun, a further request is also made that in the last telegram there shall be an indication that the sender's neck, arms and legs are still intact — in short, that all is well.

I particularly remember the case of a friend of mine, who was nonetheless playing, as amateurs sometimes do, in the ranks of a team which was otherwise wholly professional. A very good half-back he was, too, and he loved the game intensely. The club for which he played was located some thirty or forty miles away from his home, so that this journey had to be made for all home matches and it was an extra when his side had to go away. The 'governor' was very sorely set against this footballing and it was grudgingly that he waived his scruples at this point. Consequently, I received standing instructions from my friend always to send a telegram home at close with the result and the words, "All well". The said standing instruction was given to me because, as he said, he himself might forget sometimes, and it was nice to have somebody to depend upon — and blame. He said that if a match began at three o'clock, the 'governor' at home spent the time between half-past four and five in walking to and fro uneasily between the post-office and his home and it was with a great sense of relief that the brown envelope was at length delivered to him.

Woe was me! In an evil hour one Saturday afternoon, having a lot of extra matter to put upon the wires, I forgot the telegram to the dad and the reproaches cast upon me a week later almost made me quiver with repentance.

But I remember at least one occasion on which I had to send a sorrowful message to a player's home, though not to this player's home. It was from one of the most exciting cup ties I have seen. Aston Villa were then at the head of the league and without doubt a team of extraordinary brilliance. It is the usual thing for those who are learned in football history to say that the Preston North End team from 1887 to 1889 was the finest that ever stepped on to a field; that it was the forwards' pleasure to take the ball from one goal to another, passing it from one foot to the next, without ever letting it touch the ground; and so on. Certainly, I grant that a team containing such men as NJ Ross, a prince of backs, R Holmes, David Russell, John Goodall, Drummond, and a few of the others of such calibre was necessarily a fine one; but I doubt, if it could have been pitted against the Aston Villa XI of two or three years ago, whether it could have achieved victory. Preston North End taught us what combination could be, and, as the only club of that time who attained anything near perfection, they naturally asserted a great superiority over their rivals, and this superiority made us think at the time that they were a far more brilliant team than they really were. Aston Villa asserted the same superiority over teams which were ever so much stronger than the opponents of the North Enders, and in a day when combination and the science of football generally was made the closest study of by all clubs, high and low, and when the game had developed amazingly from what it was in the eighties, they yet toyed with most of the XIs pitted against them as if they were children.

This is a digression. The point I want to bring out is the strength of the Birmingham men this particular year and the utter hopelessness, as it seemed, of the task set Notts County when they were drawn against them in the first round of the English Cup competition. To make things worse, the match was to be played at the Villa ground. Notts were then at the head of the Second Division, and, therefore, nominally the seventeenth best club in the country. Actually I should say that they were about the fourth or fifth just then. They went into very special training for this match; but I cannot think that anyone connected with the club thought they had the remotest chance of winning. But they came very near it. The men were in the pink of condition and played beautifully and very early on in the game a free-kick taken by a full-back was placed in the right spot to an inch and was headed through the Villa goal. With a point in hand they played desperately and, though their famous opponents realised now that they had their work cut out and bent themselves to it with a will, they could make no headway. They were penned in their own half and as often as they tried to get away the Notts halves vetoed their attempts. Conspicuous among these halves was Charlie Bramley, who

had aforetime helped Notts to the pinnacle of fame, being one of the team that won the Cup. He was playing as steadily as a rock. Out from the Villa pack came the famous Crabtree, with the ball at his toes. Bramley rushed to meet him. Two legs shot towards each other at the same moment, and the next one Bramley lay on the ground with a compound fracture of the leg! I was standing near the touch line at the time, about 30 yards away and the crack smote my ears like the falling of a stack of timber. It rang out all over the ground. Notts's chances had gone!

The affair, of course, was purely accidental, and there was not a particle of roughness in the play which brought it about. Crabtree is a thorough gentleman-professional on the field and he was dreadfully cut up about it. A stretcher was brought into the arena. Bramley was laid upon it and a surgeon temporarily bound up the broken limb. He bore himself bravely and was in no spirit of bravado that he asked for a cigarette, and, obtaining it, proceeded to smoke it whilst still lying there! I asked him if there was anything he would like me to do for him. Yes, there was just one thing; would I wire his father to say that, though his leg was broken, he was all right? Then they carried him to a Birmingham hospital, where he lay for over a month. A broken leg is bad enough for anybody; but it is perhaps worse for a professional footballer not in the first blush of youth than to anybody else.

From that moment Bramley was dead to first-class football. Those who think there is no more sportsmanlike chivalry left in football may reflect upon the fact that Aston Villa, then the greatest possible attraction to the football world and a team run at tremendous expense, promptly offered to play their full team in a match, either at Birmingham or Nottingham, for Bramley's benefit, free of any charge whatsoever. Trent Bridge was chosen, and a substantial cheque for the beneficiary was the result.

As for this Cup tie, the Villa won, but only just; they soon equalised; and once looked as if they would never get the winning goal. The ghost of Bramley seemed to lead on those 10 men of Notts, and it was only at the very finish that the Villa won from a corner. It was the hardest match they had, though they went right through the competition and won the Cup. 20,000 people watched it, of whom 16,000 were supporters of the Birmingham men; but so much was sympathy with the visitors after their loss of Bramley, that I believe at the finish the crowd was just a trifle disappointed that its own side had won.

League teams inevitably play two games the same day. One is fought on the field and another commences in the dressing-room immediately afterwards.

A separate dressing-room is, of course, provided on every ground for each of the teams and the scene inside during the half-hour following the blowing of the 'Time' whistle is one full of animation, no matter whether victory or defeat has attended the efforts of the men. The only difference this makes is the point of view from which each man discusses — first, the referee; second, his colleagues; and third, the enemy.

If the result is a win, all are as good as good can be; and while the trainer, beaming with satisfaction, rubs away at the legs of the centre-forward, that worthy shouts across to a full-back who is scraping the mud from his face, to compliment him on an exceedingly neat piece of work, whereby single-handed he stopped a mad rush of the whole of the opposing forward line.

The full-back realises that the proper thing to do under the circumstances is to express to the company his admiration for the shot with which the centre-forward scored the winning goal, which was absolutely the very finest he had ever seen in his life. And so the merry prattle goes on, till all have been bathed and rubbed and tidied up, so that they are fit to go out into the outside world again.

All the timidity with which they moved amongst that throng of strangers before the battle-blast was blown has vanished now. They walk abroad through the streets of the enemy with a proud consciousness of superiority and pretend not to hear the remarks of the little boys, who have come to the conclusion that they are a much better lot than they at first supposed.

Under such happy circumstances as these it is the wont of the players of a league team to keep together, and the officials, too, form part of the company which wends its way to the big hotel of the place, where a very high tea is ordered. At each end of the table steams rises from large plates of chops and steaks, and during the meal yet a third game is played.

The outside-right, fully conscious that he did all that human man could do, but craftily fishing for a compliment, declares that he blames himself severely for not scoring when he received that lovely pass from Jones. There is a chorus of dissent, one and all declaring that the outside-right played the best game of his life. He blushingly protests, but all to no purpose; and then the goalkeeper recounts how he saved four hot shots in 30 seconds!

It is so different in defeat. Each man thinks there were 10 bad players in the team and one good one; but the conversation is not so free. It is deemed wisest to maintain an attitude of sullen reserve to everybody. The trainer is most talkative, and expresses his opinions very bluntly. He knew what was going to happen — in fact he told all his friends some days before that if they got off with a four-goal defeat they would be lucky! With a very angry candour he impresses upon each man, as his turn for rubbing comes, the necessity of an immediate reformation if he wishes to keep his place in the team and declares moreover that if he, the trainer, had his way, he would never play again. What did he tell him on Monday? How were his orders disobeyed on Tuesday? And where was that wretched player on Wednesday when the others were at practice? There is no great gathering in the hotel now. The secretary gives each man half-a-crown to go and get his tea 'somewhere', and in couples they slink out, and are seen no more till train time!

On the journey home events are discussed in a more philosophic manner. Officials do not reproach the men for the defeat. Rather do they seek to restore fallen spirits, with here a "Can't be helped," and there a "Never mind, lads — better luck next time."

If it is a long journey, a few of the men, tired out with anxiety and severe play, drop off into a slumber, and the remainder converse in low tones. Not surprising can it be that these healthy athletes can fall to sleep in the train by nine o'clock in the evening.

Once we had to go to a league match at Newcastle-upon-Tyne and the committee decided that we should start the same morning and not travel overnight. And a miserable morning it was, too, when we turned out at about four o'clock. I think it was after one when we got to our stopping place in the north. A very early kick-off had been arranged and there was only just time to get to the ground; and as soon as the match was over we had to bolt for the train again, and landed home at about four in the morning. That was rather stiff for twenty-four hours, yet nobody minded, for a draw was effected, and a point secured which had hardly been expected.

When the expense in such matters is not considered by the big clubs, it may seem a trifle strange to some of you that the travelling should not have been done the day before, so that the men would be fresh and vigorous on the day of the encounter. Surely it would seem that their chances of victory were very much discounted by that dreadful ride on that cold winter's morning, what time their opponents were sleeping peacefully in their beds in Newcastle.

Yes; but just then the committee were afflicted to a theory. It so happened that the preceding match away from home was at Blackpool, and in view of certain aspirations it was regarded as highly desirable that a win should be booked on that occasion. Consequently, the team was despatched at midday on Friday, arrived at the Lancashire watering-place early in the evening, and after a good meal took a pleasant walk along the front. They turned in early, and the order "Lights out" at 10 o'clock was implicitly obeyed. In the morning all were fresh as daisies; but in the afternoon they lost! It was a bitter pill to swallow. Various theories were propounded for the defeat, but the one most generally favoured by the committee was that the sleeping in strange beds had done it. It seemed to me a rather whimsical theory; but the players associated themselves with it at once, principally, I suspected, because it took all the blame from their own shoulders. That was why the next big journey was commenced when the rest of the world was asleep.

For joy and happiness on the part of the men and officials after a great match, two home-goings stand out in my mind before all others.

The first was in the initial round of the English Cup competition a few years ago, and we were drawn to play against Wolverhampton Wanderers away from home. The chances of pulling it off seemed very small indeed. The Wanderers were a much stronger team than ours then; they had the immense advantage of playing at home; the form of our men was unusually poor; and, worst of all, there was no money in the club till to put them through a special course of training. The simple fact of the matter was that the club was in very low water and it was realised that if it was to continue its existence something would have to be done. For "something"

could be substituted "win or draw at Wolverhampton", which would mean half-share in another Cup-tie "gate", always big ones. Consequently, a public fund was raised, and after some difficulty enough money was scraped together to provide the players with special training at a quiet and healthy country place.

It made a wonderful difference to them, and they seemed as fit as fiddles when they turned out at Wolverhampton. The first half of the game, however, went dead against them, and all chance of averting defeat seemed to have vanished when half-time arrived and the score was 2-0 in favour of the Wolverhampton men. Then, however, the training came in. Our men stayed right up to the finish — improved, in fact, as the time went on — whilst the other side fell to pieces. A goal came, and then the equaliser, but though we pressed desperately towards the close, and were very unlucky, no winning point could be secured. The match had, therefore, to be replayed on the following Wednesday.

What a journey home it was that night! Some thousand followers of the club had gone to see the match, and took with them flags of the colours of the club, for use in case the hoped result should come off. Those flags waved in the breeze outside the carriage windows all the way back, and at every stopping-place they were frantically shaken, to the accompaniment of vigorous cheering, that all the world might know there was life in the old dog yet.

Inside the players' saloon, the scene was pathetic. The achievement was too much to talk about and most of the players were occupied in building aerial castles and speculating upon what they would do with the Cup when they got it.

Two players would discuss an incident of the game in which they were jointly concerned; there would be expressions of mutual admiration and then a soft lingering shake of the hands.

Arrived home, a roaring welcome was accorded them and for 96 hours the cup of contentment was full. There was a melancholy sequel. On the following Wednesday the Wanderers came for the replayed match and won by four goals to three!

One time, however — and this is the other happy-home-going I alluded to — there was no after sorrow to mar the memory of the day. The victory, too, was of much more consequence than the other would have been — in fact, it was the consummation of a whole season's patient work, and the realisation of a three-years' dream.

Our team, having got to the top of the Second Division of the league, had earned its right to play against the bottom clubs of the First Division in the test matches and if it proved successful in them it would go up at the expense of one of the seniors. There were four of the test matches and things so eventuated that everything depended upon the last one.

We had to visit Burnley and either draw or win; and, since Burnley had previously drawn with us at home, our prospects of going up into the First Division looked anything but rosy at this stage. The anxiety on the outward journey was intense, and it was a relief to all when, early on this April evening, the game began.

It was fast and furious from start to finish. For excitement there has never been anything like these test matches; often they have meant life or death to the clubs concerned. Our men were promised 10/. each extra if they did what was wanted and right well they earned it. A goal was scored by them at an early stage of the game and, by magnificent defensive play, they retained this lead to the finish, winning by the narrowest of margins. But it was enough; the promotion had been secured, and there was joy in the camp.

The Burnley people were dismayed! They had counted upon an easy win for their pets, but they had lost; and now they would have to go down. It was horrible. In their anger all kinds of calumnies about our players were spread and threats of reports to the Association about breaches of rules were freely made use of. But, to their credit, be it said that their sportsmanlike instinct soon reasserted itself, and when we left Burnley station there were not a few there to give us a cheer — much as it cost them — and to congratulate us on a fine performance.

That was a journey home! Three or four years before, the club had lost its position among the elect just as Burnley had done that day. Now the football paradise had been regained. Many of the team belonged to it in its former days as one of the First League and on these the effect was greatest. They could not speak. They could only smile consent when you spoke to them of all the glory of the day. The international goalkeeper, hardened against emotion by many seasons' severe campaigns, declared himself to be happy at last; and the captain, David Calderhead, one of the best captains who ever stepped on to a field, echoed that sentiment.

At such times the hours of homeward travelling drag wearily, for the men and officials yearn for the plaudits of those at home who they know will be at the station to welcome them. As home is neared all become restive, and the railway companies are blamed because the carriage-windows are not wide enough for six great bodies to lean through at once.

At last the whistle shrieks, you hear the brake put on, the train slackens speed, and finally, amidst deafening cheers, runs into the station and finishes its day's work, for it is a special. This particular time it was long past midnight — somewhere about two o'clock, I think — when we got it; but there was a crowd of many hundreds of people on the platform waiting for us, and their cheers and waving of flags lasted many minutes. The players were carried away on shoulders, and outside were mounted on trucks and asked for speeches. Football madness was in the air, and it was nearly midnight before enthusiasts could sleep.

And now, I will draw down again the veil which I raised to show something of the ways and thoughts and feelings of the men who constitute a great league club of to-day. I could write many more of such columns; but I think I have already shown that the business is not so black as it is painted and that, even though a football player be paid for his services, he may still remain a gentleman and a sportsman. Just as there are black sheep in every fold, there are professional football players here and there who do the game no credit. But for the most part, as those who knew them best will agree, they are a respectable set of fellows and, as I said at the beginning, are in all probability better men than they would be if they did not play the game they love so well, and be paid for doing so.

Extracted from the book Goal-Post: Victorian Football, *edited by Paul Brown, published by Goal-Post (www. victorianfootball.co.uk).*

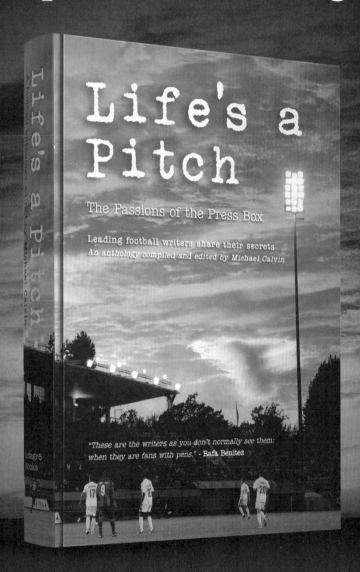

LONG BALL
DIRECT BALL
POSSESSION
FOOTBALL
COUNTER
ATTACKING
FOOTBALL
MAN—TO—MAN MARKING
ZONAL DEFENCE

81

Theory

"If at the start of the season a kid is
making 50 mistakes per game, and he's
still making 50 at the end, the conclusion
is he has no talent. Talent is the ability to
learn quickly."

Don Leo's Odyssey

From Amsterdam to Madrid to Guadalajara to Budapest, Leo Beenhakker has never stopped learning

By Joachim Barbier

He coached the Real Madrid of Butragueño and Hugo Sánchez. Managed the Netherlands at the time of Van Basten, Gullit and Rijkaard. Brought Zlatan Ibrahimović to Ajax. Qualified Trinidad and Tobago for a World Cup. And his travelling instincts carried him to a thousand more dugouts. Leo Beenhakker — until recently the sporting director of Újpest FC — has seen a lot in life, and in football, during his 40-year career.

Bow-legged, with a crooked smile and a passing resemblance to Nick Nolte, Leo Beenhakker reaches out for a handshake. "What on earth is so interesting about meeting a Dutch arsehole like me?" he asks. A lot, if truth be told. Before holing up in the summer of 2011 at Újpest — traditional giants who won their last Hungarian title an eternity ago — Don Leo dragged his old, battle-worn body to every corner of the globe. Successor to Rinus Michels, Johan Cruyff's contemporary and Guus Hiddink's predecessor, Beenhakker coached the biggest teams of the eighties and nineties and some of the biggest players. The Dutch adventurer then set sail. Mexico first of all, before Trinidad and Tobago, then Poland at Euro 2008 before he returned to the Netherlands with Feyenoord.

🔄 *What has driven you on during your career?*

I've always looked to go and discover something different. There's no point asking me where I have come from or where I am from originally. I don't know. All I know is I was born more or less in the port of Rotterdam. I spent my youth watching passing cargo ships from all over the world, hoping to jump on one of them so that I could leave and discover the world. I always had this taste for an adventure. I also understood that even though football's supposed to be a universal language, the perception of the message changes depending on the country you're in. Trinidadian players interpret your words in a totally different way to Polish players, for example. You realise very quickly the key question isn't what you say but what they hear. We're talking about the human element and that for me is the most exciting part. Imagine the cultural shock I had when I quit Trinidad after the 2006 World Cup to take charge of Poland. In two weeks, I went from a Caribbean Island full of Rastas who party in the street all night listening to Bob Marley to a totally depressing and rigid Eastern European country. And despite everything, I liked both.

🔄 *From your time with Poland, we recall above all the context surrounding the game against Germany at Euro 2008...*

I'd never known anything like it. The Polish press created such a fiasco... [one Polish tabloid notably published photos of Beenhakker holding the severed heads of Michael Ballack and Joachim Löw]. My main job was to protect the players from this atmosphere that had nothing to do with football but with the history of the two countries. We were capable of matching Germany from a technical point of view, but because certain players thought they were on some mission — due to the influence of the media or maybe people in their entourages — we couldn't win. They put themselves in a situation where the match was too big for them because they wanted to gain revenge for historical events. Poland has a painful history; they have been battered from both sides, once by the Germans, once by the Russians. That generates a lot of frustration. The older generations of Poles still can't accept that Germany has rebuilt itself and become such a rich, powerful country with a very good standard of living. They say to themselves, "Hang on, they lost the war." As the match got closer and closer, I noticed more signs that suggested this frustration would spill over in to the game. We had the same problem in Holland in the 1970s. That's the main reason we lost the 1974 World Cup final. At the time, a lot of players had lost family members, an uncle or an aunt, during the Second World War. That was the case, for example, with one of our defenders — Wim Van Hanegem. When you play with emotion you can't play well.

🌀 *You recently worked in Hungary. Like Poland, it seems the ghosts of the great past teams are preventing the Hungarians from reinventing their football?*

The principal problem there is nostalgia. I don't know... I get the impression they are unable to shake off their memories. It is as though they are stuck at a certain point in history. When I was in Poland, the people at the FA and the older generations always talked to me about how great they were in 1974 and 1982. Ok, but bloody hell, we're in 2012! It's the same in Hungary. Of course they had some great teams, in the fifties and sixties, but what have they done since? Nothing. Football's constantly evolving. You can't afford continually to refer to a glorious past. If you do that you're dead. Every year, if you're a trainer, you have to make an evaluation of the state of football, the way it's being played, in order to translate the general trends according to your means. In Hungary, there is no philosophy, no awareness of the present moment. They work the same way as 10 or 20 years ago. They have been left behind.

🌀 *Were you able to have an influence as sporting director of a club like Újpest?*

It wasn't easy. There is a form of intellectual inertia. Every change causes some soul-searching that they don't appreciate because it makes them uncomfortable. It destabilises and exposes them. You always have to be convincing — I couldn't just say 'we did it like this in Holland' because that wouldn't work. Back home, training, youth development, is a constant process, day after day. We detect the talents, we put them in the right conditions and we possess the expertise. That's what enables a small country likes ours to produce the likes of Van Persie, Sneijder or Van der Vaart. In Hungary you can watch an Under-15 match and spot some very good players, but then what happens? It's tricky because the structures aren't good, starting with the pitches. At Újpest, they have a training pitch that you wouldn't even dare walk your dog on because he might get injured. I had the same problems in Poland. They told me, "We have a population of 40 million and we produce as many talented players as France or Portugal." And I replied, "Ok, but what do you do with these talents?"

⊕ *Why do you think Dutch coaches like Rinus Michels, yourself, Guus Hiddink or Louis van Gaal are able to adapt to different surroundings?*

Firstly, we have been well trained. I think we are talented enough to be able to learn foreign languages. As we are a little country, we learn German, English, Spanish and French from a young age at school. But I think the main reason lies in the awareness we have of others. We try to understand the person opposite us and how he functions. I'd say that's our principal quality: our capacity to take an interest in others. We are like robots with lots of antennae that allow us to absorb a lot of information. This ability to adapt is a gift from God. When I arrived in Saudi Arabia, Turkey, Switzerland, Trinidad or Poland, I never felt threatened; I could work as though I was at home. And I always gave the same talk at the start: "You have your lives, with your own social, cultural and religious habits. That's your business, don't change anything, keep that to yourself. But for the rest, for the football, we are going to try to do something together."

⊕ *If you were still coaching a club, would you rather be in the dugout at Manchester City or at Ajax?*

City. I know Ajax already. I spent eight years there.

⊕ *Ok. What about a different club renowned for youth development where you could bring through a generation of 20-year-olds...*

Of course I'd go for the club that focuses on youth development. It's so enjoyable to see young players progress. That's sort of what I did in Hungary. There was a coach, but I always hung around at training. When I can help a young player fulfil his potential, when he manages to carry the advice I've given him at training in to a match, I go home a happy man. It makes my day. I love it! On the other hand, if at the start of the season a kid is making 50 mistakes per game, and he's still making 50 at the end, the conclusion is he has no talent. Talent is the ability to learn quickly.

⊕ *You were responsible for bringing Zlatan Ibrahimović to Ajax...*

Yes. We paid Malmö €9m to buy him. That was a record for Ajax. I spent hours trying to convince our finance director. And yet I'd never actually seen Ibrahimović play in a match. Only at training. I'd received a phone call from a contact of mine who said, "Hurry up, come us see this youngster at Malmö." The team was on a winter training camp in Spain, near Alicante. I watched him and thought, "Jesus Christ, I've got to have him!" So we splashed the money after an almighty battle with Malmö. The first week was a disaster. Then after three weeks, the 50,000 supporters at the Arena started whistling him. The coach, the rest of staff, the directors... everyone started avoiding eye contact with me. In the end, there were only two people left who believed in Ibrahimović: Zlatan and me. Then he exploded in to life. But my word it was tough. Everyone wanted to kill me.

◆ Did he already have a big ego?

Yes, and that's why I adored him. I loved him, I still love him — I love his personality. I always told my bosses, "Give me 11 arseholes like him and we'll be champions." Great players are always strong characters. Do you think it's easy to manage Hugo Sánchez or a guy like Bernd Schuster? Of course they're arseholes! But they'll never let you down on the pitch. They're capable of changing the course of a game. From the start, Zlatan was a silly sod. In the dressing room, on the pitch, at training, I used to think, "Fucking hell, who is this guy?" That's why I loved him, because of his nature.

◆ Weren't Arsenal and Wenger also keen to sign him before Ajax came in?

I don't know about Wenger, but Capello, oh yes, he was more than interested. He was coaching Roma at the time. Three or four days after I had signed Zlatan, we bumped in to each other at a game. He came over to me. "Hey you, son of a bitch!" he said. "What's wrong Fabio?" He screamed, "I almost got the green light from my president for Zlatan." I replied, "Hard luck, you poor bastard. These things happen."

◆ At Real Madrid, how did you deal with the characters in the famous Quinta del Buitre [Butragueño, Míchel, Manolo Sanchís, Martín Vázquez and Miguel Pardeza)?

It was very tricky. Too complicated really. My problem wasn't explaining to Butragueño, Míchel, Gordillo or Camacho how to play football. The problem with these clubs is finding a way to get so many great players playing together. The other big issue is the intense pressure they're put under by the media and the fans. You have to succeed in creating a healthy working environment every day, ensuring the players are totally focused and keeping their feet on the ground, match after match. That's the real headache. There are so many egos at these clubs... In my entire career, I never worked as hard as I did during those years at Real. It was 24/7.

◆ Who was the most important player in your system?

I don't like to say things like that. I don't like saying this player was the most important, blah blah blah... If Míchel and Gordillo were so influential in midfield it's because we had guys like Butragueño or Hugo Sánchez up front to finish off their work. I had two very intelligent forwards who knew how to defend and which positions to take up. Gordillo as well was a joy to watch because he had Camacho behind him. Michel was free in his head because he could count on the defensive work of Gallego. The hardest job is to mould a team. Let me tell you something: no player in the world is capable of playing at the same level for 60 matches a season. I remember when Emilio [Butragueño] had a bad day he could count on Hugo [Sánchez]. He could say, "I'm not feeling at my best today, you're going to have to get your head down." And Hugo would do the job, with Emilio playing off him. It worked the other way around as well. That's the key to a team's success: coordination and solidarity. By the end we were almost unbeatable.

⊕ *Was that Real Madrid side even more talented than the Dutch team you took to the 1990 World Cup?*

The Dutch group I had wasn't a team. I never had a real team during the 1990 World Cup. The talent was unquestionably there, but Ruud [Gullit] was coming back from a long injury, Rijkaard wasn't at his best, Van Basten was struggling mentally. The team gathered a few weeks before the tournament. I only had six weeks to prepare everything and it wasn't me who planned the team's preparation program. We found ourselves in places where it was impossible to train properly.

⊕ *Where were you?*

In Yugoslavia. The conditions were dreadful.

⊕ *Because the country was heading towards war?*

Yes, but not only that. The infrastructure wasn't good enough. I accept my part in the failure but half the team were against me. A few weeks before the World Cup, the coach [Nol de Ruiter] was sacked. The press then put pressure on Rinus Michels, the technical director, to appoint Cruyff. But as Michels didn't get along with Cruyff he couldn't appoint him. So I was chosen and found myself in charge of a group of players, half of whom had requested the return of Cruyff. I tried everything to get it to work, but when you aren't speaking to your players it becomes impossible. In Marco Van Basten, I had the greatest

phenomenon of the nineties. I had Gullit, Rijkaard, Koeman… The Netherlands will never have a better generation. But it didn't work. Not only that, it was a disaster. Once a player thinks he's bigger than the team you've lost. That remains the most frustrating experience of my career. I didn't sleep for the entirety of that three-week competition.

⊕ *Why, through the decades, have so many Dutch players and coaches gone to Spain?*

It's not a coincidence. The connection started with Rinus Michels, then carried on with Cruyff, and Guardiola was the heir. In a way the Spanish have even overtaken us because they incorporate an obligation for results as well. Like the Italians, they are prepared to win a game playing horribly when it isn't possible to play nice football. If they have to get 11 men behind the ball and then hoof it in to the stands, they can do it. That's the way it was when I was at Real Madrid — a kind of compromise between Latin pragmatism and the Dutch school. You know, us Dutch, we're a strange race. Before the 1994 World Cup, a TV presenter summed it up nicely. He said, "At the start of the competition you have 23 teams who are there to win. And one team who is there to show off how much talent they have: the Netherlands."

⊕ *How has the actual game changed since you started coaching?*

Firstly, everything is so much quicker. Not in the sense of running or moving quicker, no. Quicker in the head. There's no longer space, which means there's less time to think, analyse and control the ball. You have to find a solution before the ball arrives at your feet. Secondly, we no longer defend to protect the goalkeeper, we defend high to try to win back the ball as quickly as possible. That's the wonderful thing about Barcelona. It's impossible to play like that for 90 minutes. Even horses can't keep that tempo up. Yet Barça manage to do it because all the energy of every single player — from the defenders to the forwards — is channeled towards regaining control of the ball as quickly as possible. Then once the team has possession, they take their time, they all have a feel of the ball, they pass it about some more. As they prepare their next move, they are recovering from the efforts of the pressing they've just done.

Do you really think this is something new?

No, but Barcelona sometimes carry it out to perfection. Because after doing all that, you have to take a decision, a collective decision, and I don't know how to explain this but I get the feeling their players think the same thing at the same time. There's always a moment, I don't know where it comes from, when you feel like there's a signal and then bang! They all attack together at an unbelievable pace. Bing, bang, boom! The speed is infernal.

Do you not think we misinterpret Barcelona and Guardiola? People seem to think they incarnate football, yet in reality they only represent one way of playing football...

It's quite simply today's football. That team has such a high level of notoriety, so much visibility, and so much quality, they influence the entire planet and have

become an example for everyone. I don't know what the future will hold but today everyone tries to have possession and to control the game. That's sort of the way we think in the Netherlands: if you have the ball for 70 minutes you have 70 minutes to try to create chances and only 20 minutes to defend. So if the best way of defending is to have possession, then try to keep the fucking ball! You don't want a sterile form of possession or to pass without going forward. That's irritating. You need to think of how you are going to bring the ball forward. Even the Germans, who for a long time looked to win the ball deep and then use the space to counterattack in to, are thinking along these lines. When you watch a player like Rooney, you see how he fights like a madman to defend and to try to win the ball as high up the pitch as possible. A few years ago, if a coach asked his star forward to defend, he'd have said, "Go fuck yourself, that's not my job." Nowadays everyone is involved in closing down. There's no longer room for lazy players. If a player doesn't help out defensively, the opposition has so much quality they'll always find a teammate in space.

We don't know much about your time in Mexico in the nineties and early part of the 21st century.

It was fantastic. When people ask, I always say that from a professional point of view, Real Madrid is the best thing that happened to me, but from the point of view of lifestyle, contact with the people and the country itself, Mexico was paradise. Mexican players are unbelievable, as keen as mustard. My favourite player there was Cuauhtemoc Blanco. He was brilliant but a bit crazy. A guy who liked to live outside the law. Sometimes you had to fight with him, sometimes you had to hug him. I loved that.

◆ *In 2003, you said, "I have learned that when you win you have to show dignity. That's the lesson I learned at Real Madrid: never be arrogant, never underestimate an opponent." Would you agree that José Mourinho doesn't see things like that?*

No. You have to understand it's like a game for José. Personally what I like, besides his class as a coach, is his personality. I adore him, I'm José's number one socio, I love his explosive side... I find I can relate to him: he always defends his players, always takes their side, although that doesn't mean he's like that in the dressing-room or he isn't tough with them. Everywhere Mourinho goes his players are crazy for him. It was the same back in my day. When I was at Real and Johan [Cruyff] was at Barcelona, we respected each other, but we slagged each other off in the press. Just for the fun of it. Ⓑ

The English Spaniard

Roberto Martínez discusses his conception of football and the difficulties of adapting to the dark nights of Lancashire

By Philippe Auclair

"It was a huge shock — more off the field than on it. The lifestyle... You come from Spain, where you're training in the morning, go home, eat, sleep, then maybe go for a walk, to the shops... But when we got up and went out, everything was shut. It was dark at 5pm. Nobody in the streets. We didn't know what to do. But we found a Spanish restaurant, which is unfortunately closed now, where we'd go for lunch and dinner. You couldn't buy an espresso in Wigan in 1995. There was no olive oil, no jamon in the supermarkets. It was so different."

(As different as the sight of three Spanish players, Roberto Martínez and Isidro Díaz of CF Balaguer, plus Jesús Seba of Zaragoza and Villareal, lining up for Wigan Athletic in front of 3,000 spectators at Springfield Park in the old Third Division. 'Jesus is a Wiganer,' proclaimed one banner. The exotic recruits were made to pose wearing incongruous sombreros. Sombrero is a Spanish word, right? The new owner Dave Whelan's so-called 'Three Amigos' were a stunt, some said, whose novelty value would soon wear off. But it didn't. A homesick Seba beat a retreat to Zaragoza within less than a year but Diaz stayed long enough to see his club promoted to the Second Division after winning their league title outright in 1997. As for Roberto Martínez, the club's top scorer — from midfield — in his first season, he went native. After six successful years at Wigan, he moved to Motherwell, where he met and married a Scottish woman. He was identified as managerial material by a far-sighted Swansea City after which, in 2009, Dave Whelan convinced the Spaniard to rejoin him at a club that had changed beyond anyone but its chairman's expectations, with a new 25,000 all-seater stadium now visited every other weekend by Premier League teams. Little Wigan has changed a lot in the last 17 years, when it wasn't just the shortage of decent ham and proper coffee that made it a very different place indeed.)

"... and the way the coaches and the players behaved was nothing like what we were used to in Spain. That culture — work hard, party hard — was so different from what we knew. In Spain, a footballer had to make so many compromises, give up so much of his youth to become an athlete. That was the real shock. You thought to yourself: that isn't right. Then, what we have in Spain isn't right either. Perhaps what is right is what is in the middle. It gives you an option to choose and I found it really useful to be able to choose from my Spanish background and what I discovered here — I found my own happy medium. The other Spanish boys, they found it a bit harder, they couldn't adapt to the British style as well as I did and they suffered a bit on the pitch. As for me, I wasn't good in the tackle, I wasn't good in the air, I was a technical player. So I found a strange way to be successful in the lower league, in the middle of a very direct football. The whole thing was fascinating for me because I love the tactical side of the game, that's my strength, and that came from the contrast of styles in Spain and in the UK and how, as a technical player, I needed to find a way to survive in a league where the football wasn't based on the possession game."

So Roberto Martínez, the manager, was shaped by Roberto Martínez, the player?

"Yes. Finding the way to survive in the lower leagues as a player gave me a manager's mind, if you will."

But you also had to survive as a manager in the lower leagues...

"I was in a strange situation — at Chester City, at that time [Martínez stayed at Chester for one season only, in 2006-07]. We were travelling to Swindon, on a Friday. Swansea City [where he'd played the three seasons before that] paid compensation, so... Swansea were League One, Chester League Two. And Swansea paid compensation for a player, to make him a manager. That was a bit surreal. One day, I was wearing the tracksuit of a Chester player, the next, I was watching my future team play against Yeovil, as a manager..."

Did you have your coaching badges at the time?

No. I'd always wanted to find out about my method before doing the badges. I always felt that the badges were very good when you had a clear picture in your mind of how you wanted to do things. Then the badges give you organisation, a bit of a structure. But I never felt that the badges were... original enough for an individual to find his own method. I followed many teams, many managers, the way they worked and I came up with my own method which I used when I did the pro licence to expand my thinking, to add a bit more science to what I did.

Do you spend a lot of time on coaching seminars or sharing ideas with colleagues from England or from abroad?

"I don't do it too much. I did my pro licence through the Welsh FA and I really enjoyed the opportunity to share my views on trends in the game with others, but, if I'm honest, you don't get much time if you're a manager in the Premier League. In a club like ours, it's a 24 hours a day job. Even if my position is not a job. It is a passion, a way of life."

You're one of these managers who relaxes by watching more football, aren't you?

"Yes! I don't know if it's the right way or not... but I love to see how other managers find solutions to specific problems. For example, say a manager is confronted by a tactical problem to which I'd think there are three different solutions, I ask myself, 'why did he choose that one?' and... in a way, it relaxes me, it brings me a sort of calmness."

Does that mean that, when you're preparing for a game against a specific opponent, you're also analysing the thought process of their manager?

"Sometimes, I might... But every game you prepare depends on the opposition. If you watch the way a manager reacts with that opposition, it won't necessarily help you to understand the way he'll react against you. So, you can get the wrong information."

⊕ *How much do you rely on technology to prepare for your games?*

"It is a mixture. There are many decisions that you must come to through your feelings. However, you never get enough good information. It has to be well-used, as you can get bombarded with information. I have a backroom staff to help me with that, which is not exceptionally large, but very strong. Richard Evans, the head of sports science, is very important for me; we've been working together for five years now. Then I've got my assistant Graeme Jones, my goalkeeping coach Inaki Bergara and Graham Barrow who used to be the manager at Wigan when I arrived."

⊕ *...and was sacked by Dave Whelan two games later...*

"Yes!" [Laughs]

⊕ *Did you know you'd become a manager when you arrived in Wigan as a player and had to think your way into English lower league football to survive?*

"It's funny, I've never looked back. I suppose it was a natural process. Perhaps I always wanted to be a manager because my dad was a manager. As a boy, you're in awe of your dad. It was just a local club,

CF Balaguer, but everything he did was very professional. So, yes, I always wanted to be a manager but, on the other hand, I wanted to play for as long as I could. There's nothing better than playing. So when I got the offer [to become Swansea manager], I was only 33. I could have played at that level for, probably, another two years. It was a difficult, difficult decision, as I believe it's impossible to be a player-manager, even if there have been many in the British game. I knew I had to give up playing. So, yes, when I was playing, I was always thinking — but not because I wanted to be a manager, because I needed to in order to survive. What I didn't realise is how much it would help me later from a tactical point of view. I'm very demanding with my players now when it comes to thinking on the pitch. I don't like players to do 'jobs', go through the motions. I want them to make decisions, I want them to use their brains, as I did, as I had to play."

⊕ *You're very flexible as a manager, quite daring at times when it comes to in-match tactical decisions. For example, quite a few people were surprised when you switched to a back three, a very flexible back three — in the game at Chelsea last season, for example, you kept altering the shape of your team...*

"That's correct."

⊕ *...how then do you get the players to express themselves, and make their own decisions, as you say, when, at the same time, you must make sure they are in tune with your own vision of what's happening and should happen on the pitch?*

"That's...coaching! [Laughs]. I've always thought that coaching can become a negative tool. Talent wins you games, raw talent. That's my belief. Coaching comes in when the individuals play as a team and when they express themselves and, at the same time, take responsibility for their roles. That's where coaching is so valuable. But I'm wary of over-coaching — that can take the raw talent of players away from them. Everyone becomes average and I want my players to be outstanding in the areas where they're good. They take responsibility, we take risks. If every individual takes his responsibilities, it becomes a team effort. And that's where coaching comes in. Every individual needs different things. As a manager, you need to find whatever the player needs to understand what the team wants from him — without the player losing what makes him what he is. Some players need to watch video clips or review tapes of their own performances, some players need to find out in training, some players need to create partnerships with other players, others need to have it very simple and don't want to think. The background is important, the age of the player, his experience, the events he's been through... as a manager, I'm happy to work with anything that'll help the player. Sometimes, at training, I work with small groups, sometimes with individuals..."

Isn't there a danger of being swamped by details when you have as flexible an approach as this?

"That's why you can't micro-manage. What you can manage are concepts. You can never, never ever make a decision for a player but you can give him the concept of what the team needs — then allow him to express himself, to make the decisions himself, knowing what his team-mates expect from him as soon as we lose the ball and have to switch to defensive duties."

And do you have your own clear concept yourself of where you'd want Wigan to be, in terms of the way you play?

"Absolutely."

And how closely do you stick to that vision?

"You have to adapt. Our major aim is to stay in this league which isn't guaranteed. Small margins will affect that so you have to compromise at times. But not as far as my footballing philosophy is concerned. I'll never compromise on that, never. The fans know it. We want to be a team that takes control of the ball, a team that imposes itself in possession, that is going to be brave, will defend from the front, and will take risks. But that's a philosophy, not a tactical system. In tactical terms, we must be flexible. And we must have players who are committed to suffering for the team. I wanted to carry on the recruitment policy started by Paul Jewell and Steve Bruce, which was very good in attracting players from Central and South America: these players leave everything to come to England, to make their families proud at home. So, yes, in modern football, tactical organisation is a must, but as a means to an end. Remember that tactical organisation is a way of allowing your talent to be effective, to win a game. There's a danger of trying to be too clever. The perfect tactical system doesn't exist: it's the players who make the system look perfect. I don't want to rely on a system to win a game; I want to rely on a player to win a game. I want him, them to express himself, themselves. I love open-play goals; in fact, if I could, I'd get Fifa to give half a goal for a set-piece and a full goal for open play. The system is there to enable the player to be as good as he can be. There is no absolute truth in terms of systems. 4-6-0 works because it is Spain, who are the best at possession football; and when you're so good at possession football, you need players around the ball; it wouldn't work as well — for them — with a traditional target man in the box. An ability to be flexible is more important than sticking to a system."

Is that flexibility one of the first assets you look at when you're bringing in a new player?

"For a player, the ability to play in different positions and understand what it means is far more important than being good in one system. That's not a talent; it's something that has to be learnt, between the ages of 14 and 19, something that, sometimes, we haven't done well enough here in the UK. We've been too concerned about winning, winning, winning, when we should be more concerned about tactical awareness. If you're a winger, you should know how to play in a 4-3-3, a 4-4-2, a 4-2-3-1 and all their variations. I feel very strongly about that. Success, in the development of a player, is not how many titles he's won at each level but how he's learnt how to play in different systems. That flexibility will allow him to be successful at senior level. For me, the idea of good enough, old enough is not quite right. There are stages a player must go through, to learn. We gave Joe Allen his league debut when he was 16

at Swansea [a 6-3 defeat to Blackpool on the last day of the 2006-07 season], and he was fantastic in that game. But he had to grow, to learn; so he spent some time at Wrexham, and when he came back, he could model himself on a superb midfielder, the Dutchman Ferrie Bodde. He didn't become a £15m player simply because of his raw talent. Of course, the importance of tactical awareness varies according to the player's position. Midfielders need to be able to read the game; in other areas, let's say a wide player who's good in one-v-one situations, that's not so crucial. Every single position has its own demands."

It's well documented that you have turned down offers from a number of 'bigger' clubs — Liverpool, most recently. Is it because you see yourself as someone who needs continuity, and not just in technical or tactical terms?

"I do feel very strongly about thinking in the longer term. I don't get satisfaction from just seeing the first team winning. I also get it from being in a club that is financially stable and which is developing in every area, making sure the youngsters are getting a certain type of coaching that'll enable them to become professionals, hopefully in our first team. That's vital. As a manager, I feel that I have to take decisions the impact of which will only be seen four, five, six years down the line — as with Joe Allen. Maybe I won't be here then, but that's the only way I can do my job. But that's not why I'm still at Wigan. I'm here because my chairman [Dave Whelan] is unique. He is a very persuasive man. The power of Wigan Athletic is that it is a club which is built on a person's dream. That's why it is so special."

✦ *Are people in Spain starting to realise what you've achieved in English football?*

"No, not really, and this doesn't bother me. Football is about players; we managers are here to help them. Back in Spain, people have heard about Wigan, because it's the only Premier League club managed by a Spaniard... but they don't really know my story. I left when I was very young, only 21. I'd prefer them to know about my players rather than myself."

✦ *But should you go back to Spain, wouldn't you be able to bring something different to its league, as you're a man who belongs not to one, but two football cultures?*

"Whatever happens in football has happened before. Look at Terry Venables and what he did at Barcelona. He succeeded there by bringing a very British kind of intensity to the Spanish game. As for me, I am Spanish. Look at my background, and look at the way I want the game to be played. But I'm well aware of what is needed to survive in the British game. It is a fascinating argument — different footballs, different cultures, and the way they can communicate with each other, not just in one direction. I suppose that it's the kind of dialogue I have with myself." Ⓑ

96

The Vanishing

"Their actual name was Gidanansky,
which they couldn't spell."

The Strange Disappearance of Leslie Goldberg

How the right-back who became Les Gaunt encapsulated the experience of many 1930s Jewish footballers

By Anthony Clavane

In the late seventies, the *Jewish Chronicle* rang Bob Paisley to enquire whether his new signing, Avi Cohen, was orthodox. "Orthodox what?" the Liverpool boss replied. "Orthodox midfielder? Orthodox defender?" If Avi was an orthodox Jew, the journalist explained, he couldn't play on a Saturday. "But I've got half a dozen like that already," quipped Paisley.

The Israeli defender was so unorthodox he actually turned out for Liverpool on Yom Kippur — to the horror of his country's media. Some Jewish writers even invoked the concept of divine retribution to explain the goal he gifted Southampton on the Day of Atonement with a badly misjudged backpass. I have always felt bad about watching football on that day. In fact, despite not being religious, I still suffer slight pangs of guilt watching football on a Saturday. As my old headmaster once explained to me, Saturday is the Day of Rest, not the Day of the Match.

But maybe that's part of the attraction. Like eating bacon, or sleeping with a Gentile, it's a deliciously illicit activity. And, like driving to the synagogue on Shabbat, we all do it — but don't like to talk about it. "It is virtually *impossible in Britain*," David Baddiel once wrote, "to be *Jewish* and *male* and *not* interested in football."

There have always been religious and cultural pressures on Jews not to play football. But Jews have been kicking balls around ever since Norwood Jews Orphanage thrashed Endearment 11-1 in January 1901, one of the first matches played in the Sunday Football League — a competition set up by the Jewish Athletic Association to increase interest in the game. In the first half of the twentieth century, when the community was predominantly a working-class one, several pioneers emerged. Like the black pioneers of the 1970s and 1980s they were held up as an example of integration. To the Jewish community they were a symbol of belonging — but, 80 years or more later, they have become forgotten figures.

Take my favourite ever Jewish player, Leslie Goldberg, who played for Leeds and Reading. I never saw him play, but my dad did — and I have seen a 1938 British Pathé newsreel clip featuring his exploits. In the clip, a plummy voice announcer says, "And we introduce, on the left, Leslie Goldberg, right-back. A footballer, first of all, must be fit, and PT and shadow boxing both help to that end." Goldberg's widow Peggy, who is not Jewish, met him when he was a PT instructor stationed in Kent during the war. "He did not conform to this ridiculous image of the Jewish weakling," she said. "When we first met, he believed that the more Jews exercised, the more they would be accepted. But later on he didn't think in those terms any more. He didn't really think about being Jewish even. When he came from Russia, his grandfather couldn't speak English. The chaps at customs couldn't speak Yiddish. So they gave them the name Goldberg. It sounded Jewish. It was easy, they could spell it. Their actual name was Gidanansky, which they couldn't spell."

Sixty years later, in *The Definitive Reading FC*, the authors David Downs and Leigh Edwards inserted a note on players' name changes. There are two. "Goodman changed his name to Getgood in the 1920-21 season," they inform us, and "Goldberg changed his name to Gaunt in the 1948 season." The note provoked the following exchange in a Reading fans' forum:

"I'm intrigued as to why Gaunt changed his name – Goldberg is a name which might of [sic] aroused anti-Semitic feeling, that's the only thing which springs to mind..."

"No, nothing to do with the move (from Leeds). I remember him here as Goldberg before the name change."

"I have just had the honour of speaking with club historian David Downs. So overawed was I at speaking with the great man that I forgot to ask about Les Goldberg/Gaunt's mysterious name change."

There was no great mystery. It was, indeed, as one of the fans surmised, a reaction against anti-Semitism. Unlike their US counterparts, many first and second-generation Jewish immigrants anglicised their names upon arrival in Great Britain. What's in a name anyway? "If a Cohen wanted to change his name to Cornwallis," wrote Howard Jacobson in *The Mighty Waltzer*, "that was his affair. It was no mystery to any of us how come Hyman Kravtchik could go to bed one night as himself and the next morning, wake up as Henry Kay De Ville Chadwick. Enough with the ringlets and fringes. Enough with the medieval magic."

Name-changing was especially prevalent among those who sought advancement outside the clothing industry. For Jews who entered the exciting worlds of sport and entertainment in the twenties and thirties, it was virtually compulsory. British boxing world champions like "Kid" Lewis, born Gershon Mendeloff, and "Kid" Berg — previously Judah Bergman — adopted English names. The most surprising example of all, perhaps, is the film star Leslie Howard, who specialised in portraying stiff-upper-lip English aristocrats; the son of Jewish-Hungarian émigrés, he had previously been known as Lesley Steiner.

But what made Leslie Goldberg wake up one morning as Les Gaunt? For Goldberg's generation, football had been one of the ways of escaping the old ghetto, a slum just outside the city centre and becoming part of Leeds. Seeing one of their own rise to the top had given "great *nachas*" (joy) to the city's Russian-Jewish immigrants, most of whom were employed as tailors. Like the London and Manchester rag trades, they had lived and worked in a squalid New World *shtetl*, suffering the appalling conditions and poor pay of the notorious sweatshops. Sport had always offered immigrants and racial minorities not just a way out but, more importantly, a way of gaining acceptance. In his performances for Leeds and, at various levels, England, Goldberg had become the repository of his rapidly-integrating community's dream of belonging. Leslie was born in 1918, a year after a notorious mini-pogrom in Leeds; a 3000-strong mob rampaged through the Jewish ghetto, smashing windows, looting shops and beating up anyone who got in their way. The mob had been fired up by a newspaper article accusing sharp-suited "Hebrews" of parading in the town centre while brave young Loiners laid down their lives in France. The ghetto-dwellers, in fact, were a patriotic lot, a higher percentage of Jews than Gentiles enlisting. And nothing gave them more pride than Goldberg's brilliant career. In becoming the first Jew to play for England Schoolboys, he joined a growing canon of Famous Jewish Sports Legends: Ted 'Kid' Lewis, Harold Abrahams, the amateur golfer Lionel Leonard Cohen, the England rugby union international John Raphael and Nathan Rothschild, who played county cricket for Northamptonshire.

The son of an immigrant boot riveter, Goldberg went to Lovell Road School and joined the Leeds Jewish Institute. The declared aim of both institutions was to disprove the charges of disloyalty, cowardice and unmanliness that were the stock-in-trade of anti-Semites. Jewish youths were inducted into the world of sport and taught to admire the host country's imperial grandeur. Max Freeman, who went to school with Goldberg, recalls it promoting "PT", as the Pathé newsreel announcer had called it, as a pathway to integration. At Lovell Road, as at the Brady Boys Club, the Free School in London and the Jews' School in Manchester, physical recreation of all kinds became an integral part of the pupils' daily life. Goldberg's much-loved sports master Nat Collins, who became his mentor, urged pupils to shed their parents' Old World habits and attitudes — but also taught them to stand up for themselves and fight back if they were attacked.

Collins's influence on Goldberg was described by another school friend, Izzy Pear, as "quite astonishing really... he coached him from the start, taught him everything he knew. He was a nice fella, a good teacher, stern and strict. Mr Collins was a good lad, no question about it. He was Jewish and he wanted the school, which was 95% Jewish, to make a good impression on the outside world. So he entered us for the Leeds Schools' Cup — and we made it all the way to the final." Goldberg made his first appearance for Leeds, who were then in the top flight, in 1937, replacing the England full-back Bert Sproston. He was strongly tipped to replace Sproston at international level; he'd already represented the Three Lions as a schoolboy, making his debut at Wembley in 1932 against Wales. A reporter at that match described him as possessing a "very brainy game, depending upon clever anticipation, sure tackling and strong volleying". As a columnist in a Jewish newspaper wrote, "It is the sincerest hope of Leeds fans, and I have no doubt Jewish football followers throughout the country share this wish, that Leslie Goldberg will one day play for Leeds United and England and if this does happen may he serve as magnificently as a man as he did as a schoolboy international."

The Second World War changed everything. The Football League was suspended with Goldberg having made 21 league appearances. During the conflict he guested for Arsenal and saw service in India before being stationed at Hythe, where he met Peggy. When the league began again after the war, he played a few games for Leeds but, with Jim Milburn and Eddie Bannister now the favoured full-back pairing, he was transferred to Reading in 1947. He changed his name to Gaunt a year later. Such an act of reinvention, as George Orwell had wryly observed in his 1945 essay, "Anti-Semitism in Britain", was easier than undertaking speech therapy or removing an unwanted mark on your skin. "It is generally admitted that anti-Semitism is on the increase," wrote Orwell, "that it has been greatly exacerbated by the war, and that humane and enlightened people are not immune to it. It does not take violent forms (English people are almost invariably gentle and law-abiding), but it is ill-natured enough, and in favourable circumstances it could have political results." At public school, Orwell remembered, a Jew could "live down his Jewishness if he was exceptionally charming or athletic but it was an initial disability comparable to a stammer or a birthmark. Wealthy Jews tended to disguise themselves under aristocratic English or Scottish names and to the average person it seemed quite natural that they should do this, just as it seems natural for a criminal to change his identity if possible."

When Goldberg played for Leeds, he had been insulated by a tight-knit community; located in one of the biggest cities outside London, it numbered around 30,000 in the 1930s. At Reading, a town populated by only a handful of his co-religionists, he and Peggy felt painfully exposed. He had tried his best, all his life, to fit in. Not to be different. Peggy revealed that he had once turned away a group of rabbis from the Elland Road training ground — they had been asking for a contribution to their charity — because he didn't want his teammates to see him as "not one of us". In Leeds, he had been feted as the latest in a line of local-Jews-made-good: first Michael Marks (of Marks & Spencer), then Montague Burton (the tailor) and now Our Les. He had been the first to play for England schoolboys, to captain Yorkshire Schools, to play for Leeds United, to appear on a cigarette card and feature in a British Pathé newsreel. Leeds United were keen to attract the-then predominantly rugby-supporting Jewish community to their stadium. In 1932, a *Yorkshire Evening News* reporter wrote, "The United would dearly like to have in their first team a member of Leslie's faith who was an outstanding performer. Such a player, opine the Peacocks, would increase the gates at Elland Road by several thousands every game." His old headmaster at Lovell Road agreed. "A couple of thousand extra supporters will go down to see Leslie play," predicted Collins. "He is extremely popular." But when he and Peggy moved to Reading they began, for the first time in their marriage, to experience anti-Semitism. "The manager of one shop used to shout loudly every time I came in, 'Good morning Mrs Goldberg,'" said Peggy. "Every time I came in — and everyone turned around to see who this foreigner was. He never said anybody else's name. And there were other, worse, incidents. And in games Les started being verbally abused."

In 1950, after 71 league appearances for Reading, Goldberg's career came to a premature end when he broke his leg in a match against Norwich. "They went for him deliberately," said Peggy, "or so I was told. It was a bad break. His friend, up in the stand, heard the bone break. There was anti-Semitism involved." In his column in the *Jewish Gazette*, my great-uncle, Louis Saipe, remembered how Leslie had been hailed as a shining example of modern Judaism. As a schoolboy he had been a sporting all-rounder, excelling at swimming, cricket and athletics. Being a good sport, my uncle warned, was admirable — as long as you didn't, in the process, shed your identity. When I read this column in research for my book, *Does Your Rabbi Know You're Here?*, I began to understand why Goldberg was no longer talked about when I was a child. The community had either forgotten him or else deliberately chosen to ignore his career.

Goldberg's brothers had been close and had lovingly documented his rise in a scrapbook of cuttings. The scrapbook doesn't include any references to the one goal he scored in seven FA Cup ties for Reading, nor his management of the non-league team Newbury Town. He went on to scout for Reading and Oxford United and then returned to the Berkshire club in 1969 as an administrative and technical assistant to the manager, Jack Mansell. As Peggy says, "He moved away from Jewishness when we moved away from Leeds. He'd been in the army for six years. So he lived among non-Jewish people. That was his world. The football world was the same.

He never wanted to go back. He was a good scout. He discovered Steven Death, who holds the appearance record for Reading. And he looked after the third team and was scouting as well. He could sort out a good player immediately. The thing is, he'd lived in the 'English' world more than his other brothers. When we moved to Reading there were no Jews. Well, a few young Jewish men chased him up — but they, like him, married out and drifted from the faith."

When his scouting days were over, Goldberg worked his way up through the ranks of Crimpy Crisps, becoming their London and south-east area manager. Then he moved to the Fuller-Kunzle company, which made cakes, and ran a restaurant in a casino for a while, mixing with an upper-middle class social set. "They didn't know about his footballing past," said Peggy. "One of them turned out to be a crook, but we had some marvellous times with them. We went to very posh dinner dances with them. We weren't following any religion then. We didn't really fit in."

Goldberg is one of the many who disappeared. Other pioneers like Louis Bookman, Harry Morris and Bert Goodman did something similar. There was anti-Semitism, especially during the 1930s, but it was more an attempt to shed their ethnicity and fit in: in the period leading up to the Second World War, Jewish footballers were outsiders trying not to draw attention to their outsiderness, Europeans adopting the outward trappings of Englishness.

Anthony Clavane's book Does Your Rabbi Know You're Here? *was published in October by Quercus.*

Ten Past Ten and Ten Pastis

Gunnar Andersson's journey from Marseille legend to homeless alcoholic

By Gunnar Persson

Paris may historically have disdained the sport but football has always been the passion of the Marsellaises. And some of their heroes have become myths larger than life or just remained enigmatic. Myths, yes, but still unexplained and not fully understood. Gunnar Andersson's story has been told many times but he probably remains the greatest enigma of all. His life deserves to be explained, detailing his early years in Sweden as well as his later years in France. In between comes his football career, those eight seasons for Olympique Marseille in the 1950s that made some supporters believe that the club motto Droit Au But (Straight to the Goal) was invented for him. He scored 169 league goals for the club, a figure that leaves him still OM's leading all-time goalscorer, ahead of the Croat Josip Skoblar with 151 and Jean-Pierre Papin on 134.

Andersson was born in 1928 in Arvika, a small town on the railway line between Stockholm and Oslo. The family relocated in the area a few times, first to Säffle and then to Åmål. On his first day at school in Åmål the teacher noted several Gunnars in the class, so he called Andersson "Säffle-Gunnar". The nickname stuck.

While at school he proved to be a more than useful football player. It was probably because of him that IFK Åmål, one of the local clubs, decided to start their first team for boys. Youth teams, for players in their late teens, were common in Sweden at the time. The final places in those teams were sometimes taken by players as young as twelve or thirteen, resulting in incongruous team photos with a mixture of young men and boys. IFK Åmål decided it was time to give those of sixteen and younger their own team, and in doing so they would secure this young gem of a player.

The IFK Åmål Under-16 team went undefeated in the district league during 1943-44 and were rewarded with a summer tour to faraway places like Örebro, Motala and Stockholm. They won all three games, scoring a total of 17 goals. The last game, in Stockholm against Reymersholms IK, was won 7–0, with you-know-who getting all seven goals. That feat earned him his first mention in a national newspaper. In total he scored 14 during the tour.

That was his farewell to his pals in the boys team. Promoted to the youths, he became their star as well. You must bear in mind that this was, and still is, a remote part of the country. Sport was not very developed in the county of Dalsland and most of the teams in the local youth league were also-rans. At one point the IFK Åmål youths could only gather nine players for an away game. Gunnar agreed to play in goal for the first half and kept a clean sheet. After the interval he reverted to his usual striking position, got three goals and helped his team win the game 3–1.

But even if you play your game in the wilds, ability like his was too good to go unnoticed. And when he was promoted to the first team, which played in a regional section of the third division, he just went on. Information from the local newspapers is sketchy but from his debut late in 1944 to the 1947-48 season he averaged about a goal a game.

The big-timers IFK Gothenburg talked him into a transfer during the winter of 1948. They even had him down for a trial appearance in a friendly game. This was in the amateur days of Swedish football; contracts were non-existent and all you had to do was to sign a player was to persuade him to be non-active for 90 days. After that 'quarantine' he was free to choose a new club. The snag was that the winter months, December to March, only counted for 15 days. So any player who decided to change clubs was bound to sit out almost half a league season. The incentive, if the transfer included a move to a new town, was usually to be set up with a job and an apartment. This was against the rules, which stipulated that the player should apply for a job first, then move and only at that moment tell a club he wanted to join them, but of course it never worked that way. Besides, money routinely changed hands under the table, or via supporters who had no formal connection to the new club.

IFK Gothenburg hoped to play their new striker towards the end of May 1948.

But IFK Åmål hadn't done too well in the autumn. Relegation was looming, so they asked Andersson to break his quarantine and play in the second game of the spring season. Gothenburg agreed. But then, two weeks later, Andersson played for Åmål again and this time the IFK Gothenburg secretary got the news through a journalist. Gothenburg really needed a fresh young striker. But this breach of agreement — and obvious proof of weakness on the part of the player, who let himself be talked into playing by his old mates — was too much. They didn't trust him and simply let him go.

But they were not allowed to forget him. Reports of Andersson's superlative form kept arriving through 1948-49. He scored 34 times in 18 league games as IFK Åmål won their regional group. Since Gothenburg had last spoken to him he had become a father. It seemed he was developing from a goal-scoring boy wonder into a grown man. Gothenburg, still in need of a striker, made another approach.

This time he was ready to move. In fact, he was so eager that he went AWOL from his military service at the Coast Artillery at Vaxholm, outside Stockholm. He left a message with his regiment — "My wife is ill" — and never bothered to return. In his first serious game for Gothenburg, a friendly against their neighbours Örgryte – which was also the farewell game for their established international star Gunnar Gren, who had been signed by AC Milan – he stole the show and scored both goals as IFK won 2–1.

Gunnar, his wife Harriet and their daughter Beryl moved into a flat in Gothenburg. Back home he had worked for Swedish Rail and the board members did their best to find him a similar job. But however hard they tried, nothing worked. He turned up, worked for a day or two, and then never bothered to go back (or was told to stay away). That worried the team manager Josef Holsner and his aides. All of the other players combined day jobs with training in the evenings and playing games at weekends. Not Gunnar.

Andersson was in quarantine and could not to play official games until April 1950. What to do? The Gothenburg board simply put Andersson on the same bonuses as his playing teammates. After all he and his family had to eat. So, why not? They also tried to lessen their embarrassment by agreeing to the Danish club KB Copenhagen's request that the idle striker should join them on a trip to Spain in late November.

KB had been invited, together with the Brazilian side Palmeiras, to play in a mini-tournament celebrating the fiftieth anniversary of FC Barcelona. The Danes lost 1-0 to the hosts but defeated the Brazilians by the odd goal in seven, with Andersson getting the first. His performance was noted by one of the honorary guests among the crowd of 52,000 at Les Corts, a banker named Louis-Bernard Dancausse who was chairman of Olympique Marseille.

In the spring of 1950 Gunnar Andersson was looking forward to his league debut. Gothenburg needed him desperately, as they had fallen apart without the genius of Gren and looked an almost certain bet for relegation. Andersson's seventeen goals in eight friendlies excited the fans and his debut, at home to Jönköping in mid-April, drew the

biggest gate of the season, almost 22,000. But Gothenburg lost 3-1 and they also lost the next game, away to Degerfors, by the same score.

Two games, no goals and then all hell broke loose. The football federation had got wind of the bonuses paid to Andersson during his quarantine and hit mercilessly. The blow was severe — a one year ban for breach of the amateur rules. The chairman and the rest of the board were also suspended. While they were barred from running the club, the team finally collapsed and were relegated as the 11th of 12 teams. And then the Coast Artillery caught up with their missing gunner. Gunnar Andersson had to appear in court. He was sentenced to two months in jail, to be served only if he declined to do the pending part of his military service. He wasn't able to play football anyway, so he went back to his regiment.

Meanwhile the Sweden national team went to Brazil for the World Cup. Their third-place finish paved the way for another exodus of players. Two years earlier the Olympic gold had resulted in seven players leaving the country. In no time another thirteen were on their way. The stopper Gunnar Johansson, from GAIS of Gothenburg, and Andersson's team mate Dan Ekner, a skilful inside-forward, were quickly signed by Olympique Marseille. But OM were also hunting for a striker. At first Tryggve Granqvist, a sailor who had succeeded the suspended Andersson at IFK, was the target. Negotiations came to nothing, though, and without knowing it the club avoided signing a player who managed just 25 Swedish league games before turning to a life of petty crime.

Both Gunnar Andersson and the board members had appealed against their severe punishments. The highest sports authority in Sweden agreed to investigate. But these were times when the authorities felt threatened by the foreign agents snatching their best players, so nothing much happened for a long time. They didn't give their verdict until November: "A year is clearly too much here. Four months would have been more reasonable!" So, in November Andersson learned that he had been (theoretically at least) free to play since late August.

As soon as the verdict became public, Dancuasse, remembering what he had seen a year earlier, made his move. On November 25, the French paper *Sport-Express* carried the headline, "Saffle (l'Ouragan) arrives Dec 2." His nickname had been translated, or rather transformed, to "Tornado". Nothing less would do for the readers, and this was only the first of many exaggerations that surrounded his name from then on. (The name Säffle actually translates from Iron Age Swedish to mean 'bay with birds').

Andersson caught the first train to Marseille but was pulled off in Avignon by two reporters who wanted an exclusive. In Marseille he was made welcome by his two fellow countrymen and made his debut on December 9, against the touring Swedish side Helsingborgs IF. The new boy got two goals as OM won 4-2. A Swedish reporter who travelled with Helsingborg analysed Andersson's game: "I have not seen this player before, but it is evident that he is very quick on the turn and shoots rather well with both feet, though mostly with his left." He also stated,

matter-of-factly, that, "I saw fourteen Swedes, three Arabs, a Pole and four Frenchmen (of which three had Italian parents) play a game on French soil."

Gunnar Andersson had arrived. He told people an apartment was waiting for him and that Harriet and Beryl were expected to arrive after the holidays. Today his daughter Beryl says, "I was of course too young to know or understand anything at the time. But my mother has told me that she made all the arrangements and got a passport. Still, we never left Sweden. Maybe she thought moving from Åmål to Gothenburg was far enough. She was close to her family and south of France would have been too far away."

Andersson had left Gothenburg in a haze with only football on his mind. He never saw his signing bonus of SEK 60,000. His agent insisted it wasn't his fault. The only arrangement made was with the Swedish Army The club guaranteed time off in the autumn of 1951, so he would be able to finish his military service once and for all. Andersson didn't start too convincingly in the league, but still finished as OM's top scorer with twelve goals. He was a man around whom stories flocked: in that first season he, together with Ekner, helped a young Dane escape from the Foreign Legion, which had recruiting offices in Marseille.

It was the start of the next season, 1951-52, that gave Gunnar Andersson a place in the hearts of the Marsellaises. He scored in the first game, away to Rennes, got another in the second and continued to hit the target for nine consecutive games, totalling thirteen goals. Still, the team struggled. It was typical that his first hat-trick came in a

10-3 defeat to Saint Étienne. The club was left scrapping against relegation. Andersson did what he did best, scoring 31 of their 54 goals. They finished 16th, which meant *barrages* (a play-off) against Valenciennes, who had finished third in the second division. Andersson had flu, but still played in the first game, the away leg, which was lost 3-1. A week later, though, he was back to his best, scoring two as OM won the home leg 4-0.

OM had the sharpest striker in the league. Andersson was top scorer, six goals ahead of the Dutchman Bertus de Harder of Bordeaux and Marcel Rouvière of Nîmes, but their defence was poor. They changed their goalkeeper every year while the veteran Roger Scotti was shifted back and forth from wing-half to inside-left, either helping the defence or supporting the attack, always needed in both spots.

The team lacked some basic elements, just like the stories — the mythical ones — about Andersson. A local favourite tells how Andersson and a team mate had a bet. Could he drink pastis before a game and still be sharp enough to score? Andersson had 10 shots, scored a hat-trick during the first quarter, and then... well, passed out, probably.

I once met Jean Robin, an early teammate, and asked about Andersson's drinking habits. It is no secret that drink eventually got the better of him. But Robin still surprised me by offering a story without much truth in it. "When he had arrived," he said, "and he sat down for his first team dinner, he asked for milk. But grown men don't drink milk down here. He was offered wine instead. And he liked it."

If true, this would have meant that the club, or his teammates, unwittingly led him on to the path of alcoholism. I retold the story to a veteran sports writer in Gothenburg, who calmly replied, "I think he knew his way to the bottle even before he got to France."

What is not in doubt is that Andersson enjoyed Marseille immensely. This large port, then as now the gateway to France from Africa, was like no other city. Its connections to North Africa were very close. OM's successes in the 1930s and 40s had been truly cosmopolitan. After professionalism was legalised in 1932 and the French league established, there was an influx of foreigners — Germans, English amateurs, Jews from the old Austro-Hungarian empire, a Swiss, a Pole, a Greek, an exiled Catalan (who had escaped Franco) and a stray Brazilian goalkeeper. The club frantically built and rebuilt a team that won the league in 1937 and reached five cup finals between 1934 and 1943, winning three of them.

The team also had its share of *pieds-noirs*, descendants of the tens of thousands of French who had colonised North Africa during the 19th century. The foremost member of that generation, which had a major impact on French sport in the 1930s, was the middleweight boxer Marcel Cerdan, *le bombardier marocain*, who was born in Sidi-Bel-Abbès, Algeria, in 1916. He was world champion from 1948 to his death in a plane crash in June 1949. Although married with three children, he had a much publicised affair with the singer Édith Piaf and he was the inspiration behind her song *"Hymne á l'amour"*. Players like Joseph Gonzalès (born in Beni Sal, 1907), Georges Janin (Aïn M'lila,

1912), Mario Zatelli (Sétif, 1912), Manu Aznar (Sidi-Bel-Abbès, 1915) and Jean Bastien (Oran, 1915) formed an ever-present nucleus at OM and were more or less seen as locals.

Marseille was a place in which you could turn up from nowhere and invent or, indeed, reinvent yourself. The Algerian would-be revolutionary leader Ahmed Ben Bella was posted in Marseille after enlisting in the French Army. He also played football and was part of the OM squad during 1939-40. Marseille was a world apart from the rest of France. Crime, gangs, guns and the emerging Corsican mafia influenced the everyday lives of ordinary people. Marseille also served as a hotbed for comedians and entertainers. There was a particular stage, called l'Alcazar, where Maurice Chevalier had his first solo engagement, that was noted as a testing ground for new shows.

It didn't take Gunnar Andersson long to become part of all this. He soon met Laurence, who would become his second wife. In 1952-53, while scoring ferociously for OM, he dealt with his divorce from Harriet, applied for a French passport and looked forward to the spring, when he would marry Laurence, a Parisienne. Gunnar had a penchant for older women. He had met Harriet when he was 15 and she was 18. Now, approaching 25, he was marrying a woman who had two daughters, the older in her teens. Soon enough, with sons born in 1954 and 1955, they were a family of six.

Andersson was advised to open a bar to make the most of his name. But Chez Gunnar wasn't treated as a business

venture. It was more like an extension of his living room, where he was happy to treat anybody with a friendly face to a drink. Besides, Gunnar and a bar? He was a rabbit in charge of the lettuce patch.

But he was the North Star, visible all over town, popular as no one else and in 1952-53 once again top scorer in the French league. His teammates had improved, so his 35 goals (out of 62) were enough to clinch sixth place in the table. It was also a new record — one that would stand for 13 years.

Stardom, wife, kids, booze and lots of money (not necessarily in that order) created a lifestyle in which it was not uncommon for Andersson and Laurence to charter a private plane and fly from Marseille to Paris after his early training session. She would do some shopping and he would hang out with Egon Johnsson, a fellow Swede, known as 'Atom Egon', noted for his ferocious shot and his goalscoring record for Stade Français.

Late in 1953 OM made a major acquisition, bringing the much-loved veteran Larbi Ben Barek back to town. He had started out with US Marocaine of Casablanca, leaving for France in the summer of 1938 and playing one season with OM before the war. While crossing the Mediterranean his passport was somehow altered, with "born 1914" changed into 1917. The famed coach Helenio Herrera did the same in the 1930s, losing six years with a stroke of the pen as 1910 suddenly became 1916. After the war the reputation of Ben Barek had grown steadily while he played under the tutelage of Herrera at Stade Français and Atlético Madrid. He was a goal-scoring inside forward who early on attracted the nickname "the Black Pearl". Now, at 39, he had a wealth of experience. Marseille spent £12,500 to create what they thought was a world-beating strike duo. But it was not to be. The old man was too old, the young prodigy too independent. They never connected. Ben Barek invariably kept the ball for too long and Andersson's strike rate sank to human levels: 19 in 1953-54 and 21 in 1954-55.

Their one achievement together was reaching the cup final in 1954. Andersson played his part, scoring five times in the five games leading to the final. He also scored early in the second half of the final against Olympique Nice, at the Stade Colombes in Paris. But OM were already two goals down and they couldn't get back into the game. They never fired in the league, either, ending 14th and 10th in those two seasons, with Scotti buzzing all over the place as usual and Gunnar Johansson holding the reins as stopper.

With Ben Barek on his way back to Morocco, Andersson felt the air clearing. He resumed scoring (20 in 1955-56 and 23 in 1956-57) as the team rose in the league, finishing fifth and then sixth. Andersson also won a call-up for the national team. Not Sweden, which still had a ban on professionals, but France — his citizenship paid off. His original intention had been to earn a place in the World Cup squad for 1954. He failed in that effort but he was picked to play for France B v Italy B, a game staged at the Stade Vélodrome in Marseille in February 1956. The French won the game 2–1, with the winner scored by Rachid Mekloufi of AS St Étienne.

The two strikers faced each other a year later, when OM lined up against ASSE in front of 36,000 at the Stade Vélodrome. Andersson wasn't going to be overshadowed again. He gave his team an early lead and had completed his hat-trick before half-time. Mekloufi struck back; he scored in the 53rd minute, banged in a second five minutes later and completed his own hat-trick soon after.

With half an hour to go, the score was 3-3. Mekloufi had created havoc in the OM defence, leaving them in danger of losing the game. What to do? Score another goal, of course. Andersson hit his fourth in the 61st minute. The game was still far from over. But OM had the guts to stand firm and hold out. Perhaps this was the game preceded by those 10 shots of pastis?

OM ended the season in style, winning the Coupe Charles Drago by beating Lens 3–1 in the final in Paris. This was a comparatively short-lived competition (1953–65), aimed at the professional clubs who had suffered early elimination from the Coupe de France. Andersson did not score in that final, but it was the only trophy the team won during his eight years with the club.

These tales from 1957 mark the apex of Andersson's days with OM. The tide would turn quickly. The team had grown old together and by 1957-58 it was breaking up. It was the last year for both Andersson and Johansson. Gunnar's winner against Alès in the 23rd round of the league proved to be his eighth for the season and last for the club. He would play only four more games before departing for second-division Montpellier in the summer of 1958.

The move was a disaster. Montpellier went nowhere and he soon lost his place in the starting line-up. Halfway through the season he was sold again, to Girondins de Bordeaux, another second division outfit. There Andersson found some form, scoring 14 goals in 10 games as Bordeaux secured the fourth and last promotion spot. The same season OM were relegated for the first time since the start of French professional football in 1932-33.

Andersson had ousted Bernard Baudet as striker at Bordeaux and the team found a reinforcement in the outside-left Laurent Robuschi, signed from Monaco. But the years had taken their toll and Andersson was now a former star. He played just 14 games that season, scoring 10 goals. Robuschi was the team's top scorer with 20. But the defence was worse than anything Andersson had experienced with OM. They were constantly bombarded, conceding 102 goals in 38 games. Bordeaux finished bottom.

Disappointed supporters began to use the old nickname 'Ten past ten' more and more often —a name derived from his Chaplinesque way of walking, feet angled out like the hands of a clock showing 10:10. Andersson's physique had never impressed anybody. His game, and subsequent success, was based on his speed and positional sense. He was quick off the mark and also packed a powerful shot. But this was all inside the penalty area. When his legs gave way he wasn't impressive at all.

That became increasingly evident during his last professional season, with Aix in 1960-61. He was lured there by his old team mate Gunnar Johansson, who was player-coach. The aim was to help them improve on their twentieth-placed finish (out of twenty) the previous season. They did that, but only because the division was cut to 19 teams. Andersson managed 10 goals in 28 games and left at the end of the season.

Andersson's star was clearly in descent. What would he do? The bar was long gone, so were his legs. But he still had a family to support and all he could hope for was a position in football. He got just that. It was a job where he was needed, one nobody else dared to take — as player-coach of CAL Oran in Algeria.

Civil war had raged in parts of the vast country since 1954. One faction, the Muslim FLN, wanted to break free from France. Meanwhile, the French descendants gathered under the flag of the OAS. They were outnumbered 10 to one and fought desperately to retain ties with the mother country, aware that a free Algeria would mean the end for the French-Christian minority.

In 1958 three leading players in the French league, all three full France internationals — Abdelaziz Ben Tifour and Mustapha Zitouni of AS Monaco and Rachid Mekloufi — were banned from French football for playing for the FLN team, an unofficial Algeria national side. It was in this climate that Andersson arrived in the summer of 1961 to work for Club Association Liberté d'Oran. The club was amateur and played in a league administered from Paris by the French federation. The competition had started in 1959 and was boycotted by Muslim clubs from the outset.

It was quite clear that his job would last only as long as Algeria remained under

French rule. The FLN and the French government reached agreement on a ceasefirein Évian in March 1962. Within a month about 900,000 of the one million French had fled Algeria, most of them across the Mediterranean. The French government hadn't anticipated the full impact of their agreement with FLN and was shocked by the influx. The refugees may have looked French, but they were mostly strangers to French society and it was then that the term *pieds-noirs* became common.

Andersson returned to Marseille and in the midst of this vast upheaval still made the news. *Marseille Magazine*, an oversized lifestyle journal published locally every two weeks, carried in its June 15 issue a large photo-essay on the refugees arriving from Africa. But it also had a piece under the headline "*Un Certain Andersson*". The story, adorned with two large pictures — taken from a distance, making them look candid — of Gunnar shuffling boxes in a portside warehouse, told of how he now had to work to earn his money. "We meet him at a café, exhausted from a full day of manual labour, up and about since 6.30am," the story read. While he was shifting his boxes the FLN hit hard at the French remaining in Oran, perpetrating a massacre on July 5. The number of deaths is still debated, somewhere between 95 and 3,500, depending on who you ask. As the FLN attacked, the 18,000 French troops still in Oran obeyed orders not to act. The Algerian police also stood back. It was French Gendarmes who eventually put an end to the killing after a full day of violence. At around the same time Ahmed Ben Bella, the former OM reserve team player, was released after spending six years in

a French prison. He returned to Algeria to challenge the leaders of FLN and eventually became the first president of an independent Algeria.

Regular work meant exhaustion for Gunnar. But he still found time to play football, for the amateurs AS Gignac in nearby Gignac-la-Nerthe. This only lasted a season (1962-63) and during the summer and early autumn of 1963 he was distressed by uncertainty. In the end he was invited by an uncle to return to his home town of Arvika to discuss his future. His uncle offered him a deal by which Gunnar would be the player-coach of IFK Arvika in the Swedish 3rd division and also run a plumbing business in his own name. They reached agreement late in 1963. Andersson's new life was to begin that winter, getting his business started and preparing the team for the new season.

But it wasn't going to be easy. Once again he got trapped in Sweden's sporting bureaucracy. He was a French citizen and so needed permissions and clearances to be eligible. The Swedish federation wrote to AS Gignac. Or so they thought. There are four towns or villages with this name in France, two of them large enough to support a sports club. The federation picked the wrong one and got no reaction at all. As April and the start of the league got nearer there was still no word from the federation.

IFK Arvika still felt they could officially present Gunnar Andersson as their coach (at least) and staged a press conference. Gunnar had been in Sweden for a few months, without his family (Laurence never even considered a move to Sweden) and clearly suffered from his new bachelor status. One story says that he turned up badly hungover at the press conference. A young reporter couldn't believe his eyes and started to take notes frantically but was taken aside by the club chairman. The reporter was told that "measures would be taken" if he wrote about what he had actually seen (and smelled).

Arvika played their first game on 19 April 1964. Gunnar was finally cleared to play a month later, making him eligible for the seventh round of league games. But he still didn't make the team, reported as being "ill". He had a warm-up game with the reserves the weekend after and finally made his debut on June 5 away at Hillringsberg. Arvika lost 2-1 and the reports were devastating: "Säffle-Gunnar made his long-awaited appearance at inside-left, but had no stamina and seemed completely lost. He wasn't fit and his moves were rigid in a way that caught the eye."

He was left out of the side for a friendly against a touring Brazilian side, Piracicaba, but played two games in the County Cup during the summer, scoring two goals, and got his next serious outing with the first team on August 9 away to Vansbro. Arvika lost again, 1-0, and it proved to be Andersson's last game for the club. In early October he was interviewed in his parents' home. "I'm going back to France now, to my wife and family," he said. He was bored out of his mind: "Everybody here goes to bed at 10 o'clock. My brother only goes on about his boat and his summer house. What kind of a life is that?"

Gunnar went to Paris, to work at the bar owned by his brother-in-law. Perhaps

that was the life he wanted but that life also drew him to disaster. On Christmas Eve 1965, after little more than a year in Paris, he turned up at the doorstep of a Swedish journalist. Gunnar wanted money so he could fly back to Marseille. The journalist refused. Instead Andersson reverted to a life in the Paris Métro, as a full-time *clochard*, a bum sleeping in his clothes with nowhere to go.

He developed ulcers and was seriously ill when Marcel Leclerc, the newly elected chairman of OM, was told of his struggles. Leclerc, a publicist who ran several sports magazines, had an eye for PR. He immediately located Gunnar and took him to the Bichet hospital in Paris. After several operations and a few months of much-needed rest and recuperation, Andersson was fit to be exhibited by Leclerc. He took him to Marseille and invited to him to take the ceremonial kick-off as OM played the Swedish side IFK Norrköping in a friendly in late November.

That was the beginning of another phase of his life. He was installed as caretaker at the private swimming club Chevalier-Roze-Sports at Boulevard Michelet, close to the Stade Vélodrome. He was still newsworthy material. The features portray a sad man, grey beyond his 39 years, with another broken marriage behind him and a medical history that now included a blood clot in his right leg.

Roger Magnusson, the Swedish right-winger, arrived in Marseille in the summer of 1968. He was 23, at the start of a great career in the city. He knew about Andersson's misfortunes but he was still taken aback. "He used to turn up at our training sessions, chatting with the players," he said. "He usually wanted a loan, not much, just to take him through another day. But the thing was that he never dared to ask me for any money. He probably felt ashamed of it, in front of a countryman."

Gunnar had calmed down but at the same time he lost the thing that gave his life meaning: football. He was supposed to take courses to get a coaching certificate, but he never completed his badge. He trudged on, often seen in the company of portside lowlifes.

Having lost all sense of direction in life, he died in the evening of 1 October 1969 on his way to the only place in town he could still call home — the Stade Vélodrome. Andersson had been to the offices of a newspaper to get a ticket for the game against Dukla Prague in the Cup-Winners' Cup when his heart stopped. He fell to the pavement at the crossing of Rue Breteuil and Rue Sainte and died on the spot. He was buried three days later at the Saint Pierre cemetery, a tragic reminder that those who have a talent for football don't necessarily have a talent for life. **Ⓑ**

End of the Road

Gretna's rise was a romantic fairy-tale; their collapse provides grimly real lessons for all of Scottish football

By Richard Winton

Graeme Muir leans back on a rickety plastic chair in the centre of a grubby portakabin and surveys his surroundings. "Little Gretna, eh," he says, shaking his head in bemusement. "You know, this shouldn't work..."

It's April 2007 and little does he realise just how prescient his words are, not just in relation to his own club but also — as the 2012 close season proved — for every other side in Scotland. As he speaks, the chief executive glances out of the grimy window towards the ramshackle stand and sloping pitch, upon which his side have just spurned the opportunity to earn promotion to what was then the Bank of Scotland Premier League. A listless performance against their closest challengers St Johnstone, for whom Jason Scotland scored twice in a perfunctory 2-0 victory, has cut Gretna's lead at the summit of the first division to five points with three games remaining.

Ultimately, it took until the final few moments of the last of those three matches for the Raydale Park club to secure a third consecutive title in one of the most fraught conclusions to a campaign imaginable. When the whistle blew on St Johnstone's 4-3 victory over Hamilton Academical, they were notionally champions, with Gretna

being held 2-2 by Ross County in a game delayed by five minutes while a tortured soul was talked down from the parapet of the nearby Kessock Bridge. But a stoppage-time James Grady goal, some 10 minutes after the conclusion of the game at New Douglas Park, ensured the helicopter carrying the trophy changed direction.

"I've another operation on my stomach this week and I'm not supposed to be taking long car journeys," said Brooks Mileson of the 500-mile round trip to Dingwall, the stricken owner and benefactor having eventually been located behind the main stand sucking furiously on a roll-up despite his health being so poor that he was barely able to walk.

Within 18 months, he would be dead, the boy who broke his back in a quarry accident at the age of 11 growing up to be the man who suffered from chronic fatigue syndrome and, fatally, a brain infection. Upon his hospitalisation in February 2008, his financial support for Gretna was withdrawn by his family, bankrupting the club. By the time of his death that November — the 60-year-old was found unconscious in a pond after suffering a heart attack at his Carlisle home — Gretna were no more, their liquidation and the end of a glorious six years encompassing a Scottish Cup final and Uefa Cup qualification having been confirmed two months earlier.

To those who had long harboured disdain for the manner in which Gretna advanced through the leagues, such an outcome was vindication. Yet even for Muir, the most devout disciple of Mileson, there was an inevitability about the demise.

Speaking to him that sunny April afternoon less than two years earlier, there were hints that not all was well. "What do you want to know?" was his regular, exasperated response to requests for an interview; cryptic references to the fairy tale having ended became more frequent; while the mysterious absence of manager Rowan Alexander with a "stress-related illness" and the consequent arrival of Mick Wadsworth was never satisfactorily explained.

Still, once he did finally agree to sit down and talk, Muir was an engaging, almost evangelical, communicator. Sentences tumbled forth with more clauses than a Scottish Football Association rule book, the lilting brogue of this unlikely missionary evincing an endeavour for answers, posing rhetorical questions that seem to hang in the air like speech bubbles waiting to be pricked by explanation.

At times, it was difficult to keep track as the 40 year old's whirring mind hurled the discussion off on a tangent. Yet, at the same time, Muir was able to view issues with the untainted mind of a child, stripping away baggage and deconstructing arguments so as to make even the most divisive appear easily salved. Perhaps it was a consequence

of his relative inexperience in the incestuous world of Scottish football administration, but his tenure at Gretna mirrored the incredible rise of the club.

A player who burned brightly but briefly at Queen of the South, Muir was running a project to bring his church closer to the community when he received the phone call that changed his life. Mileson recognised a kindred spirit and wanted their Christian beliefs to work together in aligning the club with its own parish. Soon enough, though, Muir's enthusiasm ensured personal promotion.

Yet as the fairy-tale accession neared its denouement, Gretna metamorphosed from everyone's favourite wee club into a soulless entity lacking support who bought their way to success. The introduction of Wadsworth as director of football and a clinical overhaul of both the playing staff and youth structure, which involved picking up talents released by bigger clubs and, they hoped, selling them on to make Gretna self-sufficient, sparked suggestions of malcontent; the favoured theory being that Mileson's well of benevolence had run dry, with the restructuring an attempt to slash overheads. Failing to win promotion, critics said, would actually suit a club that had come too far, too fast.

"I hear it every day," said Muir that afternoon, smiling mischievously. "But if we've no money, if we're cost-cutting, if it's all dried up, why haven't we cut the community programme, which gives free football to schools every day? Why is Danny Lennon [now manager of St Mirren] taking kids in our youth set-up through scholarships at Cumbria College? In economic terms, the fairy tale's gone and there's been restructuring, so there's been contrary stories to the wee happy story. But if that hadn't happened, we could have been in danger of a boom-and-bust scenario.

"People say Gretna are successful because of Brooks Mileson's money — rubbish. It's helped — we are glad of his input — but let's look at it this year. We've taken a substantial amount off the payroll and we're now doing spreadsheets and budgets, five-year plans, when before we didn't even have basic administration and it was a case of throwing money at things. Everybody thought this Gretna story would not last but I'm not sure of that now. In fact, I'm convinced that's not the case. If things go as we expect, we'll need to rely less on Brooks. If our figures are right there is a case that if we were seventh or eighth in the SPL, we could break even groundsharing at Motherwell."

Within nine months his claims would have been proved hopelessly naive, but Muir's defence of the decision to use Fir Park as a temporary home during the planned renovation of Raydale — one he now concedes was ludicrous — was undermined even then by his own candour. "I've listened to this, Gretna playing Inverness at Motherwell on a foul February night, and how the crowd would be an embarrassment," he said, leaving his words to hang before delivering the punchline. "I'd ask, why are we playing in February then? Why do we sell short-sleeved replica shirts at £47 and then play in the winter? Okay, I'll be the first to admit that on New Year's Day you can't beat being at the football, but I've got to put my hand up and say, 'Come on, the game's bigger than this and we've got to look at it.'"

The plea was made five-a-half years ago yet Muir still finds himself making it, albeit more quietly and from the periphery. Now disenfranchised and disengaged and focusing his attention on community work with his church while helping run his local youth club, Greystone Rovers, he can reflect on the solitary season he spent among the guardians of top-flight football and wonder why nothing has really changed.

"I met some really genuine guys trying to do their best for their clubs but I'm not so sure the SPL board was the most visionary committee I've ever sat on," he admits. "I think it was tired and didn't take into account what people, fans and communities really wanted. There wasn't a lot of enterprise or forward-thinking; it was people battling with their budgets and just trying to pay the next bill. They gave the impression to me they were firefighting and just treading water."

As Rangers' scarcely believable third-division campaign continues to cause consternation, Muir recalls his prophetic words when Gretna became the last Scottish club to be wound up. "I didn't think we would be the last and people laughed and sniggered when I said that it just might be some of the bigger boys that go first," he says, his tone more sad than smug. "I didn't expect it to be Rangers, mind you, but the whole thing just didn't add up for me and it still doesn't."

The picture he paints is evocative of LS Lowry's celebrated 1949 work *The Football Match*, a scene that, somehow, remains redolent of 21st-century Scotland. Hundreds of working men are depicted gathered around a pitch against a backdrop of factories and billowing chimneys. It is, we suppose, a Saturday afternoon in post-war Manchester; the men warming themselves with hot drinks and meat pies after a morning of graft, aligning themselves to one team or another and giving vent to their emotions free from the constraints of the workplace.

It is a snapshot of another world, one a lifetime away, but one Scottish football is still clinging to. "When we were groundsharing at Motherwell, I still got a feeling they expected Ravenscraig to empty at midday on a Saturday and all the workers would fill their ground," says Muir, evoking another Lowry masterpiece, *Going To The Match*. "Even now, clubs are waiting for miners and steelworkers and shipbuilders to come out and fill their grounds because the game was built upon industrialised Britain. But the world has changed. The days of miners finishing a shift and going to football are over. They'd come along and you'd give them a pie and Bovril because that was the working man's sustenance. That's gone but Scottish football is still delivering pie and Bovril."

Football has, insists Muir, become dislocated from the communities it used to represent. Clubs that were once focal points for whole towns have allowed the erosion of that identity and, with it, lost the support of those who ensured its viability before the pernicious influx of broadcast revenue. "If you put a hospital into a town, it delivers healthcare," he says. "If you put a football club in, it should deliver football. Why should people come in here on a Saturday and support us if we don't support them Monday to Friday?"

Football is now part of the service sector but has not grasped that fact and supporters have, consequently, been lost to the game. Muir, himself, can count on the fingers of one hand how many SPL matches he has watched since leaving his post at Raydale four years ago and he knows he is not alone in walking away from the game. Indeed, even as Gretna were preparing for their Premier League campaign, he and Davie Irons — Alexander's assistant and the man at the helm when the promised land was reached — would fret over the future of a club without an established fan base.

Amid it all, did he enjoy that season? "Yes and no," Muir says, after a pause long enough to accommodate another chapter of Rangers revelations. "I enjoyed the second division more because it was fun then. The minute we threatened to get into the SPL, the constraints, demands and legislation meant it all stopped being enjoyable because the steamroller of the first team meant I had to stop the community work I had been doing and become chief executive. Once you have to stop selling ice cream in case fans throw it at each other, and have to arrange to get police horses in for a Sunday TV game against Hearts where 500 fans come through, it gets daft. I admire Ross County and the way they have gone about it; the lesson there is they did it at a slower place and built gradually."

Gretna simply outgrew their slight frame. It is remarkable to think how little time has passed since Mileson's largesse took them to within a missed penalty kick of winning the Scottish Cup, then into the Uefa Cup and the SPL. Yet somehow the Galloway club have been airbrushed from the annals of the Scottish game, the only trace of a once proud club the existence of semi-pro side "Gretna 2008" in the East of Scotland League.

Many blame the philanthropist Mileson for chasing an unrealistic dream by committing more money than he could afford but Muir insists his admiration for a man who, lest we forget, set up supporters' trusts at various clubs, is undiminished. "Brooks, I suppose, will be remembered for how Gretna collapsed but he blew all his money on taking a small village through the divisions, to a Scottish Cup final and into Europe. People forget the massive amount he tried to do for the good of the community and that's the sad thing about it. How is David Murray going to be remembered at Rangers? And Craig Whyte? You just wonder...

"Liquidation is a surreal process, whether it's Rangers, Gretna or Woolworths. The administrators come in and your feet are taken away from you. It's never nice but it's the same for anybody; people said, 'Come on, you can't lose Woolworths from your high street,' but we did. Look at the banks, too, so why should football be immune? For years you were able to get pick'n'mix up the high street but not anymore and that might happen with football if we don't act now.

"We're almost going to the cinders but I'm hoping that amid all this the green shoots of recovery can come through and, in 10 years' time, we will maybe see clubs become more focused on the people who support them and we'll have a more productive national sport with more integrity about it."

Safe as Houses

Espen Baardsen was a Norway international but at 25 he gave up football to work in finance.

By Paolo Bandini

Every now and then, Espen Baardsen gets a reminder of his former life. "One of the guys in the office will come in and say they were channel-surfing and saw **Premiership Years***," he says. "It's a TV show where they have the save of the season, the goal of the season, all sorts of stuff for a particular year. And I guess I had the save of the season [for Tottenham] against Bolton in 1998."*

It was indeed a remarkable stop, Baardsen uncoiling the full length of his 6'5" frame to tip away Jimmy Phillips's right-footed strike as it arced towards the corner of the net. For Bolton it was also a pivotal moment, the save condemning them to a 1-0 defeat in the closing weeks of a season that would finish with them being relegated on goal-difference.

For Baardsen and Tottenham, however, it was a false dawn. The player, then just 20 years old, would go on to enjoy a fantastic year — representing Norway and being named as goalkeeper of the tournament at the European Under-21 Championships, then making his senior international debut in September. Yet despite such achievements he could never hold down the first-team job at Spurs and was sold to Watford in the summer of 2000.

Three years later, Baardsen retired. Aged just 25, he had suffered no critical injury, nor had he been discarded by the game. His form and career trajectory had undeniably taken a dip and he found himself temporarily without a club following a short-term contract at Everton, yet he still had his suitors. The thought of carrying on, though, simply did not appeal. Baardsen had, in the classic sporting parlance, 'fallen out of love with the game'.

If that can be a difficult concept to grasp for the many supporters who have lost countless hours daydreaming of how it might be to play for a living the sport they love, then Baardsen had identified a path that he believed he would find altogether more fulfilling. Rather than football, he wanted to work in finance.

Time has borne out that judgement. When I meet him at the west London offices of Eclectica, the asset management fund where he is now a partner, Baardsen is not only happy but in remarkably good shape. Despite having retired from football nearly a decade ago, he — seven years younger than Tottenham's present goalkeeper, Brad Friedel — claims to be in better physical condition now than at the end of his playing career.

Simply put, giving up football was the best decision Espen Baardsen ever made.

⊕ *I suppose the obvious place to start is 2003. You're 25 years old and you've just decided to walk away from professional football. What happened next?*

What happened next is that I went off travelling. I spent three months driving around the United States — despite having grown up in the country that was the most I'd ever seen of it. I set off from San Francisco, bought a car and travelled through Nevada and further east, through Yellowstone, Utah, the corn belt there, into Chicago. Saw a bit of the Midwest, then looped up into Canada, back down the whole East coast, stopping in Boston, New York, Washington, the South, around Florida. Then across the south of Alabama and into Texas, then back through Arizona. It was a long trip but it was very fun.

⊕ *Was there a particular highlight for you?*

There are certain towns or cities that I thought were really interesting to see and as a tourist looking for a different destination I'd recommend going to Savannah, Georgia. The place where I really didn't find anything interesting would probably be Texas.

⊕ *And did you just get sick of travelling at a certain point?*

Well I kept going for pretty much 12 months. After the three months in the US it was two months in South America before going on to New Zealand, which was a lot of fun, then Australia and south-east Asia. I remember driving north in the Atacama desert in Chile — I hired a car and I ran out of petrol, which

was a real concern, so I had to just walk into this village of about 20 people and ask around. There was one guy with a jerry can who I could negotiate with to get enough to get to the station. That was a bit scary. And the desolation there … when you go for hours driving and you don't see any other car or any other person, then you look outside and you see no life, it's like being on the moon. There's literally no life, if you're away from the coast there's no birds either.

⊕ *Rather different to the kind of travelling you would have been used to in your football career...*

Football travelling is seeing the stadium, seeing the hotel, looking out from the side of the bus and that's it. It's not the same thing.

⊕ *Did you take in any games during that post-retirement voyage?*

Not really. I have to say that since I retired from football I've been pretty bad at actually watching football. I like to go and see live matches occasionally but... maybe I see a couple of Tottenham matches a year and that's it. I did watch the Chelsea v Bayern Munich [Champions League] final. But apart from that I don't watch much.

⊕ *Are you just not interested?*

Finding the time is a big thing. I enjoy watching a big match but I'm not a dedicated follower of any team. I would say I support Tottenham, but I'm not an avid fan.

⊕ *You grew up in the States at a time when not many people were watching* soccer at all over there. Did you follow the professional game as a kid?

I would certainly try. Nowadays in the States there are so many television channels and I believe there's a soccer-only dedicated channel. But back when I was a kid my Friday nights were so exciting that at 10 o' clock at night there was a once-a-week programme called *English Football League Highlights* and I was definitely a dedicated watcher of that from the age of about 12 onwards.

◈ *I guess in light of how things have moved on since, it's interesting to know that at a certain point you clearly were passionate about football...*

Oh, I was engrossed in it. I would have known all the players, watched loads of videos. From the age of 13-14, I really dedicated my whole teenage years to football. I would go to school, but everything else was football.

◈ *Who were your idols?*

Erik Thorstvedt was a hero of mine, someone I looked up to as a teenager. It was also fun watching other big Scandinavian keepers like Peter Schmeichel.

◈ *Were your parents fans of the sport?*

My mum was very into it. She did a lot to make my football career happen, in terms of finding me the right coaching and helping me have the connections that I needed to find the best teams to play with, as well as driving me everywhere. She was definitely very inspirational in making that happen.

◈ *Was it you pulling or her pushing?*

Oh, both. No, no, no. It was me pushing and her excited that I wanted to be part of it.

◈ *You mention Thorstvedt. The story goes that you were on holiday in Norway and he saw you playing ...*

That's right. In fact that was something that my mum helped organise. It was a football summer camp where he was going to come out and coach the goalkeepers for a couple of days. It was not too far from the area of Norway where my mother grew up.

◈ *That must have been pretty special, getting to work with one of your idols.*

Oh, yeah. There was this great coincidence that my mum went to high school with Egil Olsen — 'Drillo' — who is the current manager of the Norway team [and was interviewed in *The Blizzard* Issue Three]. I don't think they were close friends but they knew each other as you do with classmates. She had tried to make contact with him, and he had told her to go to this football school. So that was where I met Erik and he along with another chap, my previous coach who made me a goalkeeper, the two of them were able to help arrange for me to come over the summer after that camp to train with the youth team boys at Tottenham.

◈ *At what point did you start to think "I'd like to do this for a career"?*

I was about 15 years old and after having made that contact with Erik, the Norwegian team had a trip down to the United States to play against USA and Mexico. My mum and I flew out to watch the match — Norway against United States — in Arizona. I believe Norway actually lost 1-0 [actually, Baardsen had just turned 16 and Norway lost 2-1]. And then they flew to San Diego to play against Mexico. So I flew with them and Drillo, the Norway manager at that time as well, said, "Well, we could use another goalkeeper for training." It was incredible. Because I think I was 15 or just about to turn 16 and I was suddenly joining training with the Norwegian full international team. And I did quite well — they would do shooting training and I was up and down the whole time trying to make a save. I think I made a good impression. That was when I think I realised I could make it and also that I really wanted to — that this was really what I wanted to do.

And yet you stayed in school till 18 — even though Tottenham would have taken you sooner.

Being a high school drop-out by American standards isn't quite an achievement, so I needed... well, I certainly wanted to finish and get a high school diploma. They wanted me to come a year before, they were willing to give me a junior professional-type contract but I told them I wanted to come but a year after if they would give me a provisional agreement. And they did that.

With the benefit of hindsight, it's tempting to wonder whether you wanted to hang around because you were interested in things outside of football too, or maybe you were hedging your bets?

I guess, relative to what I currently do, it wouldn't make any difference really. I didn't need a high school diploma to get into the Open University, so that part doesn't really matter. But you kinda had to do it, it would have been something to drop out of high school.

When did you start taking an interest in finance?

I think the interest in finance began a little bit in high school but it certainly wasn't any focus of mine. I would say the point where I got quite interested in it was at 19. It stemmed partly from just having an initial small amount of money to save from football. Not that I was earning very much at 19 but at least having something... wanting to set aside stuff and wondering how to look after it. And then recognising that the financial world is fairly dodgy in terms of the way it operates, the fees it takes, and the poor quality of returns that professional managers have largely given. You look today and there are things that are just disgusting out there. In a world where you have incredibly low, 0%, interest rates globally, and you're talking about someone's pension pot over a 30-year period, 30 or 40% of it gets consumed in fees. That's 30% of the total capital. That's just an enormous amount — virtually unfathomable — and that still exists.

So you thought it best to look after your own money instead ...

Exactly — if you look after your own money the fees are virtually zero. That was one element to it, but I was also just more curious at 19 and I was concerned because you can't play football forever and you don't even know how football is going to go.

Would it be fair to say footballers also have a lot of free time to do things like that?

Sure. There's definitely a lot of free time but it's a strange kind of free time. I have much more flexibility in terms of what I want to do now. If I want to book a summer holiday or time over Christmas I can. My work does follow me now, in the sense that if you're running positions in trades it's very hard mentally to switch off but it's very easy to be physically detached. You don't have to physically be anywhere. Football is the exact opposite. You only have to be mentally attached for certain periods — in training and then in meetings... ish! And obviously games. The rest of the time you could be mentally unattached but physically you were predetermined to be in a certain area at a certain time with a schedule that was totally fixed and not necessarily to your liking. And totally unpredictable, too. You'd anticipate that you'd get the Sunday after a match off, but the manager could change his mind on a whim and say, "You're all coming in tomorrow." So in terms of planning anything socially it was difficult. I found that part to be horrible. You couldn't say to a friend, "Oh do you want to grab dinner on Wednesday?" because you didn't know what was going to go on on Wednesday.

If you'd allow me to indulge in a moment of pop-psychology, self-determination theory holds that all people need three things to feel nourished: a sense of relatedness, competency and autonomy. I guess that last one feels salient because you had

a career where you were told where to be and what to do — and then the minute it finished, you went off on an adventure where you could completely set your agenda...

I think that's a very good point. I think of those three autonomy is the one I value most of all. For me that's really the goal of money — it's not so much to spend it as to have the flexibility where you won't be forced into doing things which you might not want to do. Which is difficult, because a lot of jobs make you do those things. But I think that one of the main drivers from the age of 19 for me was that I wanted that degree of independence that would be afforded by having some money. That would mean having flexibility to pursue the interests that you want to pursue, regardless of how well compensated they are.

Plenty of people who work in your new field, finance, would say they have chosen it for similar reasons — to make some money now so that they can retire at a certain age and then have financial freedom.

I can understand where those people are coming from. But at the same time it leaves a bad taste if you're only doing it for that reason. I hugely enjoy the intellectual satisfaction of trying to piece together what is going on in this macro-economic political environment and how that relates to financial instruments and financial assets. And the interaction of those different forces. I find it hugely interesting and complex — it's like a maze or a puzzle that I'm trying to put together. Getting that part right is exciting in and of itself — even if there was no financial reward attached, it would still be exciting. I wouldn't enjoy winning the lottery — not that I would ever play because I think it's a scam — but it would be unappealing because at the end of the day you would know that it was just an extraordinary, improbable amount of luck that made it happen. Whereas succeeding in business or through investments is exciting because you've pieced together the way you think the world works and you've then had that idea, put it into practice and things came about in the way you anticipated. That process is an enjoyable one.

⟳ *Graeme Le Saux has spoken before about taking a lot of flak from teammates and opponents in football simply for being the sort of person who has an intellectual curiosity and because he read the* Guardian. *Did you ever have that sort of trouble?*

Well, I never read the *Guardian*! I was reading the *Financial Times* and yes, my colleagues would take the piss. But after they've done that about 10 or 20 times it probably gets a bit boring so they give up on that after a while. The ones who found it the most threatening were the managers. Gianluca Vialli and Ray Wilkins didn't like it, whereas a couple of the Tottenham managers I had didn't care. They found it curious but they didn't care. I think the first two found it threatening in some ways. I would have some bizarre book like... *The Handbook of Fixed Income Securities* by Frank Fabozzi on the bus and they would make it clear that they didn't like it at all.

⟳ *Do you think there is an extent to which certain managers don't want you to be getting smarter, because they don't want you to think for yourself?*

Oh, I think there's definitely some element of that, yes. Oh yes. The element of control is what you're talking about and there's a bit of implicit control in kind of dumbing players down to a certain level.

⟳ *As soon as players get too intelligent, they might actually start challenging the coaches...*

Right — football and girls is all players should think about.

⟳ *What was the lowest moment for you in the game?*

To be blatantly honest, the lowest point was staying in a hotel in central Liverpool for the two months I was at Everton. Completely nothing to do with Everton... Everton clearly was and is a well-managed club, especially when you consider that they don't have the same monetary resources some others have. So credit to them and credit to the manager David Moyes, who was the one who brought me in. I have a lot of respect for the club and the manager. But for someone who has lived in London now for 17 years and feels like a Londoner, it's a different country. To go from living in central London to living in central Liverpool... And it happened at a time in my life where I was almost egging myself on to fail. I was so fed up with football at that stage that I was sabotaging myself. I was overweight and not in good shape and I spent all my time reading finance books and trading stuff on my own. I must have been 24 and I just was not enjoying it, I wanted to get away. I was spending all afternoon eating bad food and drinking beer, which was a subconscious way of making sure I was going to fail. And making sure I was going to fail meant I could move on.

⊕ *How did you get to that point?*

Well, it came just after another low point which was the last period I had at Watford. I had been bought from Tottenham while Graham Taylor was the Watford manager and I was getting paid the exact same amount as I did at Spurs — I left for no improvement, because I wanted to get first-team matches. But the simple fact was that for Watford it was still a relatively high salary. Then, after a year, Gianluca Vialli came in to replace Taylor and he lost the plot thinking he was at Chelsea and that Roman Abramovich was the backer. The directors clearly lost the plot as well and he went on some massive spending spree, spending tonnes of money, bringing guys like Ramon Vega up to the same salary apparently as David Beckham. So that's when everything got totally out of perspective. And then the inevitable happened which is that the club blew up financially. Then they're having to get rid of people as quickly as possible to slash the wage bill. The problem was for me that we'd dropped a division, I'd not really been on good terms with Vialli and if I was a stock or a share my price would have fallen significantly. But I was still on the same contract, I still had two-and-a-half years left on the contract, and I was never going to get near those terms anywhere else. So that created a very difficult situation because I would have been happy to move to another club but I wasn't going to do it and take a 70% wage cut, not knowing what the future holds. As we've discussed, I wanted the autonomy and the independence that

those, my best contract years, were going to afford me. So that created a horrible environment because then the club was trying to make things as miserable as possible for you, almost purposefully because they wanted you to say, "OK, I give up, I'll walk away, forget the remaining two-and-a-half years on my contract, you don't have to pay me for that." So that created a six months, well, almost a year period where it was just miserable.

⊕ *You're talking about quite a long lead-in time there. So really you were thinking about life without football by even the age of 23?*

Yeah, I think when I left Tottenham I was already thinking I would like to have a Plan B that's not just a distant Plan B but a close Plan B. Then as Watford went on and I found myself liking it less and less, then Plan B came closer and closer to Plan A.

⊕ *Do you think that your form dipping was an element — that added pressure of having the supporters getting on your back for the first time?*

To be totally honest, being in a football environment... I guess I have a certain geekiness to me. Let's just say I was dying for a vent — a place to have intellectual thoughts and ideas and discussions, and there was no source of release. It's like steam building up. I just wanted somewhere to vent the steam, these ideas and thoughts I had in my mind and there was nowhere to do it. Instead you were in an environment where that just wasn't available. The whole football community is somewhat that way. I don't mean to say it in a negative way,

I just mean to say that I didn't fit in with that mould. And that made it hard for me. Wanting to put myself in a different environment where I could vent all these thoughts and where I could get intellectual ideas thrown back at me, I think that just started to develop more and more in my early 20s. And that kind of led to Plan B becoming more like Plan A in terms of my future career.

🔅 *Did you find other footballers along the way who felt like you about that?*

Yeah, I think there are some smart guys out there.

🔅 *Do they feel they have to hide it?*

Maybe things are changing. I was reading the *Financial Times* writer Simon Kuper just the other day about the poshing up of English football, I think it was a great article — it actually mentioned Erik Thorsvedt in it. But I think when I was playing it was less that way.

🔅 *What was the straw that broke the camel's back? When did you know you were going to do it?*

There was no single point. I knew while I was at Everton that last game I had [Baardsen conceded four in a 4-3 defeat to his former club, Tottenham] was sort of a make-or-break for my career — that if I didn't play well and get a bit of momentum, my career was only going to head further south into an area where it would be very, very difficult to get out. After Everton, it was pretty much all over in my mind. Then my agents at the time got me to go up in March up to Sheffield United to see… I can't even remember the guy's name…

🔅 *Neil Warnock.*

Yeah, Neil Warnock. He had a bit of a reputation as a loud mouth. I went up to see him and I certainly wasn't in good form in training but after the training I went to see him and got offered about £25,000 per year. It was actually quite funny — I think it was £2,000 a month he was going to give me, gross, as a wage, but then he had this interesting theory that, "Oh yeah, but you would get £1,000 per game appearance bonus — which includes if you're on the bench." Then he takes a pause, then he says, "But I don't put a goalkeeper on the bench." At the time it was almost like I wasn't sure if he was joking. But actually the money didn't really make any difference. If I'd really wanted to do it I would have. I walked back to the hotel in Sheffield — and this is after being in a hotel for two months in Liverpool — and I just burst into tears basically. At that moment I just got in our car, drove back to London, and that was it. I called the agent and said, "Forget it, don't call me back." So that day there was no going back.

🔅 *A few weeks later you were in America.*

Yeah, a couple of months of planning, then I was off.

🔅 *Was there any moment where you woke up in the next months, or years, where you woke up and thought, "Shit, what have I done"?*

No. Absolutely not. I felt like I had bottomed. I had hit the bottom and I was only going up. Since then I've only felt like that.

⊕ *If you had your time again, would you do it the same or differently?*

I appreciate so much both the memories and the advantages in life that football gave me. So I would never take those back. And it will be a super-fun story to tell my kids and grandkids about the experience. I finished when I was 25, and I now have eight years working in finance under my belt. You can't start on this career I'm in now at 35. It was either do or die, you either make the decision at 24 or 25, or you continue what you were doing. Really if I was going to do what I do now, there was no choice in the matter. So I have no regrets. I'm very happy, and I feel very fortunate.

⊕ *Since you mention kids and grandkids... would you have them being footballers?*

[Laughs] Probably not! But I certainly wouldn't stop them if that's what they wanted to do.

Ⓑ

WHOEVER YOU FOLLOW...
DO IT WITH STYLE.

AS PART OF GOALSOUL'S CONTINUED EVOLUTION AND AS A COMPLEMENT TO OUR RENOWONED GRAPHC T-SHIRT COLLECTION, WE ARE DELIGHTED TO INTRODUCE THESE STUNNING, STYLISH HIGH NECK ZIP-UP HOODED SWEATSHIRTS. AVAILABLE NOW IN CLASSIC BLACK, NAVY AND CHARCOAL.

SPIRIT, STYLE AND QUALITY
IN THE BIRTHPLACE OF THE BEAUTIFUL GAME.

GOALSOUL (SHEFFIELD'S INDEPENDENT BRAND OF CHOICE FOR THE DISCERNING FOOTBALL FAN) AND **SHEFFIELD FC** (OFFICIALLY THE WORLD'S OLDEST FOOTBALL CLUB) HAVE COLLABORATED TO BRING YOU **CLUB1857**... A CELEBRATION OF THE BEAUTFIUL GAME, AND THE ONLY STORE IN THE UK CATERING FOR THE THINKING, STYLE-CONSCIOUS FAN. POP IN TO SEE US ON **SHARROW VALE ROAD** **(S11 8ZF)** NEXT TIME YOU'RE IN SHEFFIELD.

KEEPING THE GAME BEAUTIFUL
WWW.GOALSOUL.NET

128

Polemics

"a body of titanic ineptitude."

Breaking the Mould

Last year Johnny Saelua became the first transgender person to play in World Cup qualifying

By Zac Lee Rigg

After try-outs in 2010, the coach of the men's football team from the University of Hawaii at Hilo tapped Johnny Saelua on the shoulder. Perhaps it would be better if Saelua didn't come back. Talent had nothing to do with it; others in the locker room would be uncomfortable.

Johnny Saelua prefers to be called Jaiyah. She also prefers to go by feminine pronouns. Saelua is a *fa'afafine*, a 'third gender' specific to and highly valued in Samoan culture — born male but embodying both gender traits. A year after rejection in Hawaii, she was sleeping on the concrete floor of a locker room with a cluster of sweaty, snoring men, preparing to represent American Samoa in World Cup qualifiers, as perhaps the first trans person in international football.

The Polynesian island, a US territory, has a population of less than 70,000. According to the CIA website, they lead the world in obesity levels, at 74.6%. Although American Samoa has produced a significant number of NFL players, including Junior Seau and Troy Polamalu, their football team has been awful. Rugby, wrestling and martial arts are more popular.

Since joining Fifa in 1994, they hadn't won a competitive game, tallying 30 straight defeats. American Samoa ranked last in the Fifa rankings, tied for 204th by the time Saelua and the team began preparations for 2014 World Cup qualifying.

Two things changed before 22 November 2011 when they played a qualifier against Tonga. First, the former MLS and US Under-20 head coach Thomas Rongen joined through a deal with US Soccer, and he set about transforming the team's psyche with yoga and meditation, aside from implementing a sterner tactical shape. Second, the day before the game, Rongen promoted Saelua to a starting spot.

"It was very clear to me early on that Johnny — she prefers to be called Jaiyah — was one of our better and tougher defenders," Rongen said. "She was very good in one-v-one duels, our strongest and fittest player. To me it was a no-brainer that when you're trying to get your best XI on the field that she was one of those players. I didn't know till afterward when she gave an interview that she'd never been a starter."

Rongen was also starting Nicky Salapu, the goalkeeper who had conceded 31 goals to Australia in April 2001, the biggest loss in international football history. Salapu still bore the psychological scars, as well as a self-confessed alcohol problem. Rongen, who calls himself a "soccer witch doctor," performed an exorcism of sorts at the final whistle of a 2-1 win over Tonga in the first match of qualifying. He held his goalkeeper as both of them cried.

Salapu was the elder statesman at 31. Shalom Luani, a 17-year-old high schooler, scored the winning goal, which was set up by Saelua. Saelua was named man of the match for her performance, which also included a late goal-line clearance to preserve the win. "I knew that the keeper moved up and I felt like someone needed to cover the goal post, and that's what I did," she said. "I felt like I needed to be there and I was at the right spot at the right time." It wasn't the only time Saelua was there for her teammates.

"When you travel, there a lot of things that males don't like to do, like pick up after themselves," Rongen said. "You know how we are, we leave some tracks on the floor. Every morning I woke up after I'd rested, it was not always the cleanest." But when he'd come back, the dressing-room of the stadium — where the team slept ("We had to bring our own blankets and pillows and stuff," Saelua said) — was spotless. Inevitably, Rongen's questions would uncover that Saelua had tidied up. "She was just used to doing female and male chores, and had no quarrels with doing that," Rongen said. "She became the glue in a lot of areas, especially off the field, and that was pretty awesome to see."

The team hung together in a 1-1 draw with the Cook Islands in the second match but a last-minute goal conceded to Samoa ended their Oceania qualifying campaign.

That was a year ago. American Samoa are up to 182nd in the Fifa rankings. Rongen took a job overseeing the academy system for Toronto FC and does some analysing and commentating work on TV. Saelua is a Performance Arts major at the University of Hawaii and never went back to the football team after that first day of try-outs. She doesn't foresee a future in the sport. "Right now it's just dance for me," she said.

Saelua's role in giving some dignity back to one of the worst teams in the world made waves across the globe. "Korean TV came to my house to do an interview. It was kind of weird," Saelua said. "I would have people from New York call in and say they wanted to come to my house and do a photo shoot and interviews and stuff. All the attention was very overwhelming."

There was less of a ripple in the trans community. Plenty don't care about the "macho" elements of sport, according to Juliet Jacques, a writer who frequently tackles trans and football topics. "Those who do like football realised that the anomaly of a 'transgender' woman playing for a men's team owed much to American Samoa's lowly international position, the small resources and pool of talent available to them etc," Jacques said, "and that Saelua's debut was a good thing to see but unlikely to change the deeply ingrained sexism, split between male and female and lack of space for anyone between male and female in western professional football."

Jacques bristled at lumping Saelua in with the trans experience in the Americas or Europe. "Saelua is part of the *fa'afafine* community in American Samoa, with a very different history and culture to 'transgender' people in the West," Jacques explained, "so there's some anxiety about calling Saelua 'transgender' because that means imposing a Western concept onto her."

Saelua, now 24, says she experiences prejudice and a lack of acceptance in Hawaii. Transphobia might go some way in preventing others from pursuing sport. Tricky logistics don't help. Jacques pointed out someone would have to transition early, likely as a teenager, to have any shot at a professional career. International Olympic Committee rules dating back to 2004 demand transsexual people be on hormones for two years and have cost-prohibitive sex reassignment surgery (SRS) before they can compete as their chosen gender.

There are a smattering of examples of trans individuals in sport, most of whom transition after competing. Football's most famous was Martine Delaney, a 47-year-old who played in the Tasmanian Women's League. Neither Rongen nor Jacques expect many more to follow Saelua. "I think American Samoa is probably more the exception than the rule," Rongen said. "You won't see this in Italy or Spain in the next few months."

But global impact wasn't the goal. Football was always the end, not the means. "The only reason why I play is because I love the sport, not because I want to get famous or popular being a transgender," she said. "It's just sad to me that people have to stick within their comfortable zones. I don't understand it too much."

In Arsène We Trust

However frustrating this season, the numbers suggest Arsenal would be worse off without Arsène Wenger

By Zach Slaton

A Premier League manager's existence is highly transitory. Supporters expect immediate success and if it doesn't arrive, call for the manager's sacking, while managers who succeed seem always to be looking for a better deal at another club. Thus, the average tenure of a Premier League manager is less than two years. Smart clubs know that over the long term a manager and his system matter when it comes to extracting the best value from the money spent on players. When they get a good one, they do everything possible to hold on to him.

It is therefore no coincidence then that the three managers who have spent more than seven years at a single club over the Premier League's twenty years happen to work for some of the most consistent clubs: Everton, Manchester United and Arsenal. David Moyes's Everton sides should be finishing in the bottom half of the table, yet his teams have over-performed on average nearly 3.5 table positions and 5.1 points per season against his club's wage and transfer bills[1]. At the opposite end of the spectrum is Sir Alex Ferguson, without

whom Manchester United wouldn't have won nearly as many as the twelve Premier League titles they now have in their trophy cabinet. In between these two ends of the achievement spectrum sits Arsène Wenger, who is now in his 17th year at the helm of Arsenal.

To watch Wenger on the sidelines of most matches is to see a man frustrated by the unfulfilled promise of a team in which he has ultimate faith: the over-the-top gesticulating while wearing an oversized down coat; the haranguing of the officials for perceived fouls by the opposition or missed calls that would have favoured his team; the sullen, inconsolable figure slumped in the manager's chair when his team is behind; and the coup de grâce — the water bottle, which he nurses all match, flying in the air after another late goal conceded by his team.

Wenger, like Ferguson and Moyes, is an anachronism in today's money-filled internationally competitive game in which managers and players alike are always looking for a better deal at another club. Wenger has the trust of his players because the club has

---

[1] *All figures are quoted from models built upon the Transfer Price Index (www.transferpriceindex.com), which combines Companies House-reported salaries with publicly reported transfer fees to build a Premier League-inflation based constant cost model of teams' player valuations.*

trusted the manager to build all facets of its existence as he wishes. Allowing him to build that bond with players has been critical to the club's success at each stage of Wenger's career and in turn has allowed him to succeed as a contrarian within the different phases of the Premier League's history. No matter the manager's level of success — the trophy-laden early years, the trophyless youth project era and during what might now be called the post-youth phase — Arsenal's management, its players, and its supporters have built the club around a supreme faith in their manager.

While Wenger may have arrived to newspaper headlines of "Arsène Who?", the leadership at Arsenal knew that they had hired the one man capable of shaking things up at one of the most British clubs in the Premier League. Arsenal required a change in strategy both on and off the pitch to beat the dominant sides at the time and they foresaw the changes that the game's globalisation would bring to the professional leagues in England. They needed an outsider to institute new ideas and Wenger was their man.

Wenger began changing the club by enacting a well-documented training, tactical and dietary revolution. Out went the Mars bars in the dressing-room and the drinking after the match. In came protein-and-carbohydrate paired menus and an intense focus on recovery time. Out went direct, conservative football and in came fluid passing. Even with all the changes, Wenger's efforts would have been irrelevant if he hadn't been able to change the types of players he had available to him and build upon the solid foundation left by previous

managers. It was the outlay in terms of player purchases and resultant salaries in which Arsenal's management demonstrated their full trust in Wenger and his philosophies.

In its fifth year when Wenger arrived at Arsenal in September 1996, the Premier League was already undergoing some modest change in the nationalities of the players who made up its clubs. Over 85% of first-team player registrations were from the UK in the league's first season. That number had been reduced to 77% the season before Wenger's arrival. Who better than the man from Alsace to accelerate the transition to a worldlier Arsenal? In only two seasons at the helm Wenger would take a team that was 84% British the year before his arrival and transform it into one that was one third British and half continental European, with the remaining 16% coming from outside of Europe. He used his knowledge of France's golden generation and advanced global recruiting networks to add Nicolas Anelka, Luís Boa Morte, Gilles Grimandi, Marc Overmars, Emmanuel Petit and Patrick Vieira to his squad. These players were added to a stable of British players such as Tony Adams, Lee Dixon, Ray Parlour, David Seaman, Nigel Winterburn and Ian Wright. The combination of an established British core with new European flair would take Arsenal to the top of the Premier League table by the end of Wenger's second year.

That was far from inevitable. Such a drastic change in diet, training and tactics could have gone disastrously wrong even with the best manager leading the way. The key was in getting the whole organisation, down to the individual players, to trust the use of the new disciplines. "At first," Ian Ridley wrote in the *Independent* at the close of the 1997-98 season as Wenger secured his first Premier League title, "the English players were sceptical when Wenger assembled them for stretching exercises on the morning of a match but the proof of the bread-and-butter pudding has been in the eating. They feel physically fitter and can see their careers — and earning capacity — being extended and respond accordingly."

As the players bought into the system, they also bought into each other. Feeling more comfortable with their new Dutch and French teammates and recalling the tough days at the close of the George Graham era, the English defenders who had earned a new lease on their playing life started the conversation that changed the fate of Arsenal's season. "A team meeting was called [by the players]," Ridley wrote. "Home truths were exchanged; home thoughts on those from abroad expressed... It was never a question of them-and-us, domestic v overseas, conflict in the dressing room; more a meeting of footballing cultures and how best to integrate the two. The French and Dutch were coming to understand the physical demands of the Premiership... while the English were beginning to appreciate the flair that the overseas players could bring to the party, the flair they had pined for as complement under Graham."

Wenger's goal of getting the players to open up, to communicate with each other and not always require him to solve the club's challenges had been realised. He had created a self-sustaining system that permeated the entire club. His master plan had worked.

In executing such a plan Wenger delivered two advantages to Arsenal. The first was the knowledge and use of undervalued talent from continental Europe within the Premier League, which was virtually unique to Arsenal at the time. The only other team in the top half of the table with as much non-UK talent was Chelsea, who not coincidentally were led by the Italian Gianluca Vialli [2]. Like Wenger, Vialli would manage a team of great European and British players and beat the economic models of the time by delivering 11 points per season more than his player expenditures would suggest he should have achieved [3]. Where Vialli and Wenger differed was in the aggressiveness with which Wenger was willing to pay for such overseas

---

[2] *There were only three managers from outside Britain and Ireland in the Premier League that year —
Wenger, Vialli and Tottenham Hotspur's Christian Gross. Most of the league's management structure
still comes from Britain and Ireland but there were seven managers from elsewhere at the start of the
2012-13 season.*

[3] *This would rank him sixth all time in over-performance on the TPI's mEXIR model that takes into
account the cost of two squads and the venue to generate an expected points total for each match.
In Vialli's 94 matches managing Chelsea he would average 0.30 more points per match than his
player valuations suggest he should have earned. Alas, such success was met with dismissal when the
unrealistic expectations of players and management were not met.*

talent, and this is where he delivered his second deadly advantage for Arsenal.

Simon Kuper's book *Why England Lose* (known in the USA as *Soccernomics*) and the Transfer Price Index (TPI) exposed what English football clubs had known for years: there's no substitute for spending big on good players (at least in terms of wages), and those players are increasingly coming from other places than the clubs' own youth academies. Arsenal had the seventh highest wage bill prior to Wenger's arrival and the fourth highest squad valuation in terms of cumulative transfer fees. Within one year he had moved them into the third position for wages and second for squad valuation in terms of transfers. The dizzying investment continued throughout the trophied years and by the early 2000s, Wenger's teams were constantly battling Manchester United for top spot in terms of wages and transfer valuation. Ferguson's United were the only ones who could match Arsenal's combination of financial might and management genius until Roman Abramovich's financial resources arrived at Chelsea in the summer of 2003. One fallacy is thus exposed: Arsenal haven't always been a financially conservative club. Wenger ended up

spending nearly £145 million on player transfer fees alone between the 1996-97 and the 2003-04 seasons (£327M 2011-12 CTPP [4]) , with a net spend of around £60 million (£130M 2011-12 CTPP) due an offsetting £85M (£197M 2011-12 CTPP) in player sales. The player wage bill nearly quadrupled from £13.3M (£61M in today's wages) in 1996-97 to £61.3M (£113M today) in 2003-04. The net effect of the spending, when inflation within Premier League wage and transfer valuations is taken into account, is that Arsenal moved from 1.39 times the median total team valuation (TTV [5]) in 1996-97 to 2.23 times by 2003-04.

Arsenal's board had put their complete trust in Wenger to spend such sums of money in an effort to transform their style of play and return them to the top of English football. They got everything they wanted from their manager and then some. With a less than 10% chance of winning the league the year that Wenger took over, the new manager's investments and tactics moved the club to be odds-on-favourites for the title with a 30% chance of winning the 2001-02 and 2002-03 trophies. Wenger delivered on such favourable odds, winning three Premier League titles and three of his four FA Cups

[4] *CTPP = current transfer purchase price, which is the price of each transfer fee inflated year-by-year by the percentage increase or decrease in the average transfer price paid from one season to the next. This is done so that all transfer fees can be expressed on a constant pound basis. CTPP valuations can then be summated into squad values and allow for comparisons across different Premier League seasons as an estimate of how much it would cost to construct such a team of players in today's Premier League economic environment.*

[5] *Total team valuation is a TPI metric that combines wages and transfer valuations (both inflation adjusted) to estimate the cost to construct a specific season's team from scratch. It is then inflated and deflated like CTTP via the current total team value (CTTV) metric.*

Arsenal's Team Valuation (1992/93 through 2010/11)

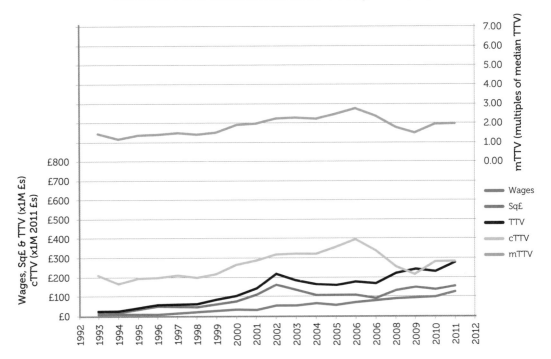

Current Total Team Valuation and mTTV (Big Six – 1992/93 to 2010/11)

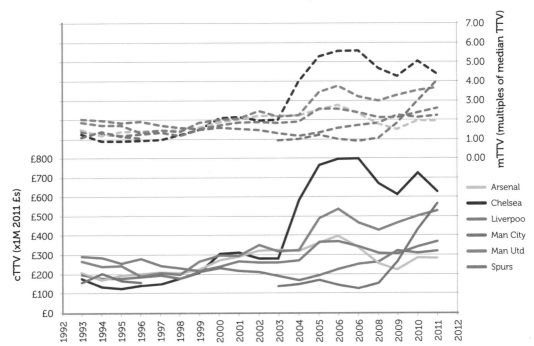

between 1997-98 and 2003-04. The culmination of Wenger's efforts would come at the dawn of the Abramovich era with the Invincibles' 2003-04 season. On a player valuation basis the club's title chances had dropped to 10% that season given Chelsea's heavy investment, and their odds of completing the season undefeated were less than 0.01%. Nonetheless, Wenger and his side expertly navigated the season's 38 matches, winning 26 and drawing 12 to finish top of the table with 93 points [6]. At the time it seemed the sky was the limit, but this would end up being Wenger's finest achievement at the club.

Two substantial changes that would diminish Arsenal's ability to win additional trophies came at the end of that season. The club had decided that if it were to make its annual challenge for the title permanent, it must generate the match-day and commercial revenue of their chief rivals, Manchester United. Arsenal had certainly grown into a worldwide presence with their attractive football and multiple trophies, but they needed a bigger home to house the club's growing ambitions. What wasn't initially clear was how extravagant the stadium might be and thus how much it would cost to build. Xavier Rivoire's *Arsène Wenger: The Biography* contains an account of the debate about the stadium from the perspective of Alex Flynn, a British specialist in the business of football. "I don't think Arsène wanted all the money from this partnership with Emirates [Airlines] to go to this new home," he

said. "I think he wanted a functional rather than a luxurious home... Wenger and [vice-chairman David] Dein certainly wanted the stadium to be built, but... they didn't want it to be at the expense of transfer monies."

The Emirates would indeed be built as a lavish home for Arsenal, with nearly 60% more seats than Highbury and a great increase in the number of luxurious executive suites that would raise match-day revenue to more than £90 million per year. The stadium and redevelopment of Highbury would come at a cost of nearly £380 million, with £260 million paid for by various term bonds. "The stadium initially cost us a lot," Wenger said in Rivoire's biography. "Now, though, the financial situation will improve given the size of the arena we have moved to and the off-field benefits it will bring. It is true that it has been a painful few years, though. We have steadily had to cut the wage bill and invest less in transfers."

The wage and transfer bills were also cut due to the second major change — the rise of Chelsea via Abramovich's resources. While Abramovich had invested heavily before the Invincibles' 2003-04 season, he and the club went into overdrive the following off-season. The purchase of Didier Drogba for £24 million (2011-12 CTPP of £48 million) was part of a nearly £100 million (CTTP of £200 million), nine-player buying spree that would raise Chelsea's TTV to £333 million (or equivalent to £757

---

[6] *That season also stands as the best performance against the points expected due to team valuation. The Invincibles earned 0.96 points per match (PPM) more than expected or 36.5 points more than expected over the season (PP38).*

million in current wages and transfer fees). The 2003-04 Chelsea squad had blown away the previous record for TTV on a constant valuation basis by more than 63%, and the club then surpassed their own record by another 33% in 2004-05. In two seasons they had more than doubled the previous TTV record valuation and showed no signs of slowing down under Abramovich and José Mourinho. Not even Manchester United could keep up; Arsenal had even less of a chance.

The lack of money due to the stadium project and the lack of inexpensive quality players due to the spending by Chelsea and other clubs meant the Arsenal board had to ask Wenger to do more with less, hoping that his managerial genius could carry the club. Wenger needed not only to mine the furthest reaches of the globe for talent but to find it less polished and much younger than before if Arsenal were to be able to afford it.

Slowly the club lowered its wage bill, selling players like Patrick Vieira and Thierry Henry for profits while bringing in younger, less expensive players like Mathieu Flamini, Cesc Fàbregas, Gaël Clichy, Robin van Persie, Emmanuel Adebayor and Theo Walcott. The change in player strategy would move Arsenal from a buying club into one that sold talent. They would spend £220 million (CTTP £272 million) buying players between 2004-05 and 2012-2013 while the departing players would generate £254 million (CTTP £316 million). Comfortably situated in the top two positions for TTV in the early 2000's, Arsenal found themselves sliding to fourth position by 2007 and

sixth by 2009. What had been a Big Four — Arsenal, Chelsea, Liverpool, and Manchester United — had become the Big Six with the rise in spending at Manchester City and Tottenham Hotspur as the Premier League completed its second decade of competition.

The purchase of such young, untested talent meant Wenger had to have faith in the rapid development of the new players. In turn, they trusted him to give them opportunities they might not get elsewhere. "It was him who placed his trust in me, and Arsenal the club which gave me the confidence I needed," said Fabregas in Rivoire's biography. "Other teams talked about taking me on, but none of them did. Now it is my turn — I want to give something back... I want to help construct the future team."

It wasn't just the older players who moved out to make way for younger, less developed talent. In 2007, Dein resigned as vice-chairman over differences in how he saw future direction. He'd been at the club since 1983 and was instrumental in changing every facet of it via the recruitment of Wenger and faithfully backing each of his initiatives. If the club and its management were content not to spend the money that Manchester United and Chelsea were then spending, there was no future for a man like Dein at the club. Wenger was now the sole man guiding Arsenal's fortunes.

Dein's concern about Arsenal slipping off their pedestal due to a lack of spending was prescient, if not obvious. The Gunners haven't won a trophy since their 2005 FA Cup triumph. There have been a number of up-and-down campaigns in the Premier League.

Percent Chance of Winning Title
(Big Six plus Blackburn and Newcastle vs m£XIR Model)

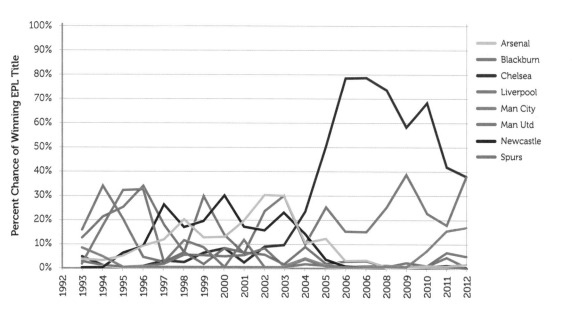

Percent Chance of Champions League Qualification
(Big Six plus Blackburn and Newcastle vs m£XIR Model)

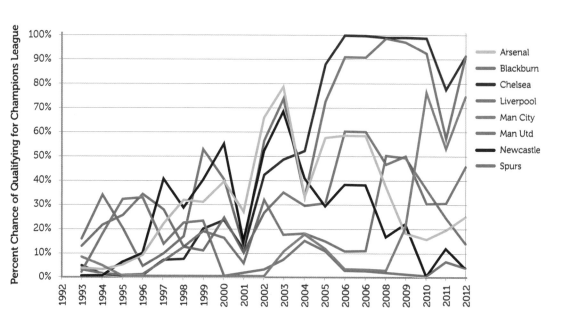

Arsenal's championship odds from 2005-06 through to last season were no higher than 3% given their player expenditures, while their odds of making it into the Champions League have hovered between 20% and 25% over the last four seasons. Premier League title aspirations had been replaced by ones centred on Champions League qualification and the desperately needed revenue it brought to the club.

Dein's frustration would soon show up in the players on whom the youth project was based. Clichy, Fàbregas, and Van Persie were all recruited when Arsenal were still winning trophies and they were to be the centrepiece of a more youthful Arsenal that was to continue such successes on a less expensive basis. Season after season they would come up short, only to be promised that a few more signings would be made each summer to push them over the line the next season. Instead of seeing more proven players added to their ranks they saw teammates like Flamini and Adebayor leave for what were perceived to be more ambitious clubs. By the summer of 2011, the core of youth players had reached their breaking point. Clichy left for Manchester City with the younger Samir Nasri, while Fàbregas left for his boyhood club Barcelona — the club whose youth-centred development and tiki-taka style seemed a more effective model of wat Wenger was trying to do. Fàabregas, long the Arsenal talisman, had lost his faith in the club's strategy, but not his former manager. "It wasn't really the losing, it was the routine," Fabregas explained. "Year after year, it was always the same story. Fighting until the end only to see we didn't have the energy,

in the semi-finals, the finals, to arrive in the final sprint... Wenger is a special person to me. He'll always be a second father to me... I'll never be able to find the words to express my thanks for what he did for me. I think he has been given a bad image here, and that shouldn't be the case. If I'm here, a big part of that is thanks to him."

With the departure of Fàbregas, Clichy and Nasri, there was a sense of finality about the youth project. Arsenal would trudge through the 2011-12 campaign, barely qualifying for a fifteenth consecutive Champions League after their worst start to a season in nearly a century. All of the struggles during the season made last summer's departure of Van Persie all the more inevitable, with the transfer of Alex Song further confirming that Wenger's experiment to win championships on the cheap was dead.

The failure to win trophies has led for many to call Wenger's attempt to buck the money-driven nature of the Premier League a failure, but is it really, given the club's expectations and resultant expenditures? "At a certain level," the Arsenal chairman Peter Hill-Wood said earlier this season, "we can't compete. I don't think [the majority shareholder] Stan Kroenke is going to put in the sort of dollars that Abramovich or Sheikh Mansour are putting into Chelsea or Manchester City... That's not the way he thinks clubs should be run. Luckily, Arsène understands that. He got an economics degree from Strasbourg University so he's certainly no fool... We're ambitious enough but we're not going to end in the same plight as Rangers [who were bankrupted]... That is a fact of life. So my advice is, don't get miserable about it."

While some may debate whether or not the club has spent every available pound on players, what's not debatable are the results Wenger has been able to deliver on such a limited budget. He ranks first overall against player expenditures for all managers with more than one season of experience in the Abramovich era, earning nearly half a point more per match than expected resulting in an average overperformance of 18 points per season. His teams had a less than 1% chance of making more than six straight Champions League group stages during that same time period, yet this autumn they showed up for their ninth straight group stage since Abramovich's arrival in English football. In the long term, clubs who spent as much relative to the rest of the league as Arsenal have in the last four seasons averaged a table position of 7th, while the Gunners never finished lower than fourth. Wenger has done the virtually impossible: he's continually earned a top-four position while five of Arsenal's rivals outspend them every year and their relative player expenditure advantage over the rest of the league has

	Era	Pre-Abramovich	Post-Abramovich
Record	Number of Seasons	7	9
	Seasons	1996-97 – 2002-03	2003-04 – 2011-12
	W/D/L	150/65/43	176/85/60
	% Points	66.50%	63.60%
Honours	League Title	1998, 2002, 2004	-
	FA Cup	1998, 1999, 2003	2005
	League Cup	-	-
	Champions League Quals.	6	9
Team Valuation	Average Total Team Valuation	£121.6m	£201.5m
	Average Current TTV	£260.2m	£305.9m
	Average TTV Rank	3	4
	Average Multiple of Median TTV	1.82	2.15
	Points per Match vs Player Value	0.34	0.48
	PP38 vs Player Value	14.6	18.1

Wage data from the Companies House via Stefan Szymanski.
Transfer data © Paul Tomkins and Graeme Riley via www.transferpriceindex.com.
Analysis © Zach Slaton via www.abeautifulnumbersgame.com.

shrunk — which is exactly what the board has expected of him.

At some point Wenger may decide to leave the club he seems to love enough to guide it through a trophyless transition while getting far less gratitude than he deserves from the club's supporters. Perhaps it will only be then that those on the outside will fully appreciate what he's done for the club, perhaps watching his successor struggle to maintain the former manager's record even if other clubs' spending is reined in via Financial Fair Play. They'll be able to look at the physical monuments to the financial prudence his man-management allowed and his club management drove — the Emirates Stadium and London Colney training ground — and see the trust the club put into him. They'll continue to read about the love ex-players have for the man, the club and his training systems. Some day they may even gain some insight into Wenger's most difficult hours via his long promised post-retirement memoir. The Invincibles, the Emirates, the players, the culture — all bear the mark of a professorial Frenchman who has always insisted on doing things differently and in doing so has earned the love and trust of the club, the players and the supporters along the way. The supporters' banners couldn't be more accurate when they say "In Arsène We Trust".

The author would like to express his gratitude to Paul Tomkins and Graeme Riley for the use of Transfer Price Index data, and to Professor Stefan Szymanski who provided the critical salary data used by the Index's models.

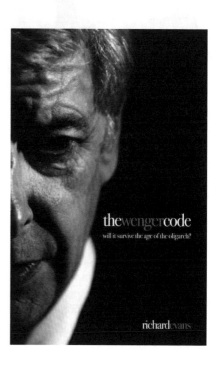

Dictionary of Received Ideas

A guide to what pundits really mean when they use certain terms

By Brian Phillips

From *The Dictionary of Received Ideas, Football Pundits' Edition*

Football is a complex and demanding science, which is why only the most intelligent, articulate and highly trained individuals — the true cream of the crop — are capable of talking about it for money on television. Fortunately, after years of study, mostly conducted from a crouching position behind the rearmost seat of Mark Lawrenson's Nissan Qashqai, we have cracked this difficult code and written the definitive manual in 'how to think like a pundit'. For the first time ever, we can now honestly say that anyone, no matter how thick, can talk about football just as insightfully as the people on TV. Simply order the Dictionary of Received Ideas, Football Pundits' Edition today, and before you know it you'll have the full breadth of knowledge — and possibly the hairline — of Alan Shearer. Godspeed.

ARSENAL Admirable but misguided. Think they can pass the ball into the net. Bemoan their naivety: "You can be as attacking as you like, but it's all for nothing if you don't win." Remind your listeners that the perfect goal is the one that goes in.

ASIA A source of "untapped markets".

BACK To praise lukewarmly in a press conference. Writers: Should only be used in headlines; otherwise reformulate as "a ringing statement of support".

BARCELONA The team of the decade. Mention tiki-taka.

BIG MAN Call him "old-fashioned", or else point out that he has good feet.

BRAZIL Home of samba, Pelé, carnival, 'The Girl from Ipanema,' and kidnapping, not necessarily in that order.

BRAZILIAN FOOTBALL Never bring up without saying "the beautiful game". Elaborate: "dancing and prancing up the pitch to the beat of their own inimitable drummer". Alternately: point out that they know the value of set pieces.

BUMS Always squeaky at the end of a close match/season.

BUS Inferior teams park them; no team yet fielded has ever attempted to drive one.

CATENACCIO Apply to any 1-0 game.

CRISTIANO RONALDO On his personality, be diplomatic: "He tends to divide opinion." Otherwise, alternate between "imperious" and "in his pomp".

DIVING Joke that it was caused by the wind. Of English players: "Did he dive, or did he just lose his balance?"

ENGLAND Expects.

FIERY Admiring way of saying "alcoholic".

FIGHT Blame the referee: "He's lost control of the match." In a derby, treat as evidence that the two teams dislike each other. Downplay: "We're having a bit of handbags just now." In America, call them "extracurricular activities."

FOOTBALL It's a game of two halves. The English invented it. When something happens: "It's a funny old game." Declare it "the winner" after any high-scoring match.

FOREIGNERS Outnumber Englishmen in the Premier League. Technically proficient but don't much like it up 'em, so to speak. Divers (be careful how you phrase this). Have an inexplicable tendency to get homesick.

FORM It's temporary; class is permanent.

FORMATIONS Overrated: the game is about the players.

FOULS (HARD) "There's no excuse for that kind of thing." Alternately: "It's a man's game." "He just let him know he was there."

GARETH BALE The fans will crucify you if you slip up and call him English, since they can't remember either.
GERMANY They always win in the end. Excellent at penalties. You should allude to the war where possible.

GOAL It only takes one to change the game. You're most vulnerable after you've scored one. If ugly: "They'll take it." "They all count."

GOAL OF THE SEASON Any goal you've just witnessed is surely a contender.

GOALSCORER If it's his birthday, point out that he's given himself a present.

HANDSHAKES Refusing one is a declaration of war. Point out that "the media will have a field day with this."

HELENIO HERRERA You don't need to know who he is.

HITLER It's a myth that he was a Schalke fan. If you have to bring him up, identify him: "the German chancellor during World War II."

HOOLIGANS Sophisticated: They're usually middle-class professionals. Ultra-sophisticated: Blame Margaret Thatcher. Everyone else: Publicly deplore them, then turn to YouTube in secret.

IBRAHIMOVIĆ Sneer at his inconsistency: "Give me 10 Frank Lampards any day." He never comes through in England.

INJURY Probably just needs to be walked off. While reviewing the slow-motion replays: "Doesn't look like too much there." After the stretcher comes out, point out that it could be career-threatening.

IRISH A mysterious and seldom-heard-from people whose only known qualities are luck and smiling eyes.

ITALY Home of organised defending,

pasta, corruption, Roberto Baggio and nudity, not necessarily in that order.

JOHN TERRY (Updated, 2012 edition) Refer to his "strong personality" and "bravery".

LA MASIA The incubator of Spain's golden age. Point out that it means "the farmhouse".

LEADS 2-0 is the most dangerous.

LEFT FOOT The only human extremity capable of becoming "cultured".

LITERALLY Figuratively.

LIVERPOOL The greatest team in the history of English football. Should be out of the title race by October.

MLS They call it "soccer" in America. Will never succeed until it cultivates homegrown stars. Offer measured praise: it's as good as the Championship. You don't need to watch any matches.

MANCHESTER CITY If they score a beautiful goal: "All the money in the world can't buy a goal like that." You may find it easier to pretend they were founded in 2008.

MANCHESTER UNITED You can never count them out. Always have a trick or two up their sleeve. It's their belief that makes them invincible. Everything begins with the manager.

MARADONA Better than Pelé. See PELÉ.
MATT LE TISSIER Never mention him. Why? Who knows?

MESSI May be the greatest of all time; it's too soon to say. Could burnish his

credentials by winning the World Cup. Would struggle against lesser English opposition on inclement weeknights. See STOKE.

METATARSAL A part of the body that was discovered shortly before the 2006 World Cup. A mark of weakness: "They didn't have those when I was playing."

MINDGAMES Alex Ferguson is their acknowledged master. Talk about them as though it's obvious why they would work, even though it isn't.

MISSED SHOTS Worthy of contempt: "He really needs to be testing the keeper from that distance." Or else praise: "If anything, he almost struck it too well."

MOURINHO Filter all commentary through the word "special". After an important final: "It's the special-est of victories for the Special One." After a tough loss: "José Mourinho won't be feeling too special after that." If saying this once feels like overkill, say it twice.

NEYMAR The new Neymar.

OFFSIDE LAW (Obsolete) Women never understand it. When confused, state angrily that the attacking player should be given the benefit of the doubt.

PENALTY DECISION Declare that you've seen them given for less. Or else say, "for me, that's not a penalty," as though you were judging wine.

PENALTY SHOOTOUT A lottery. Note that you can't practise for them. England will lose through one in the quarterfinals.

PELÉ Better than Maradona. See MARADONA.

PRAWN SANDWICH BRIGADE Ruining football. No idea how to support a team. Careful; they're also your listeners.

QUALITY Measured in bags. Often a little bit lacking in the final third. You can have all the quality in the world, but you still have to get it done when it counts.

REAL MADRID Their two unforgivable crimes are fascism and galácticos.

RINUS MICHELS Said "football is war."

SACKINGS The list of managers most likely to be sacked: point out that this is not a list you want to appear at the top of.

SCOTLAND Apart from the horrific sectarian violence, home of the nicest fans in the world.

SIR ALEX FERGUSON "The fiery Scot." Also: wily, experienced, magisterial, single-minded, resolute, etc. Mention his hair dryer: the players are afraid of it. After a win, point out that he nearly retired in 2002.

SPAIN Some people find them boring. Explain that Messi is Argentinian.

STOKE Wet Wednesday nights there are a test of manhood. A zone where technique does not operate.

SWASHBUCKLING Any fullback beyond the centre circle.

TACTICS See FORMATIONS

TENSION An invisible substance that conducts electricity and can also be cut with a knife.

TOTAL FOOTBALL Bring up when any Dutch side scores three goals. Always a "breathtaking display".

TRANSFER BUDGET Stored in war-chests the location of which is known only to the club board. Their spiraling growth is ruining modern football. Question why Wenger won't spend his.

TRANSFER RUMOURS A nuisance: "if you believe the talk out of Portugal." Spread them at all costs.

UNITED STATES Praise the strides football has made there since Beckham went over.

UNSETTLED Conscious of needing money.

VOTE OF CONFIDENCE Always "dreaded". When given to a manager, usually precedes his sudden recommitment to the idea of spending time with his family.

WAGs During international matches, bemoan "distractions". Best not to get too specific.

ZONAL MARKING Excessively complicated. "At its heart this game is simple." Ruining football.

Follow the Money

How Nicaragua's national stadium highlights the problems with Fifa's Goal project

By Elliott Turner

A national football stadium is more than concrete and grass, it's a home and a source of pride. In 2004, Fifa agreed to help the Nicaraguan Soccer Federation (Fenifut) build a noble home: a 20,000-seater stadium. After a lot of delays, the stadium opened in 2011 to the delight of local fans. But the buzz soon faded. Fans glanced at the 2,000-seater ground and asked, "We waited seven years for this? How did this happen?" The answers cast an ominous shadow over Fenifut and Fifa's flagship Goal program.

Fifa as an organisation probably lacks your respect. After recent scandals it commissioned a report into its corporate governance. Mark Pieth, a professor of law at the University of Basel, published a 39-page report in September 2011. His section on the Goal program was damning.

The report's "development section" noted that Fifa sent a "substantial volume of funds" to associations through the Goal program. In fact, 26% of Fifa's total expenditure went to assist associations. How that money changes hands, though, raises questions. The statutes show that Goal is run by at least six people, all of whom are appointed by the president himself rather than a committee. No term limits. No elections. Power is

concentrated and indefinite. Why is that a problem? The Pieth report understates the obvious: "Associations may be influenced in the use of their statutory rights within Fifa." Basically, Goal dollars can buy support for other things and the unelected appointees on the Goal committee will probably cater to the President's whims.

The case of Nicaragua's stadium is telling. On 10 November 2004, the Fifa president Sepp Blatter appeared in Managua, Nicaragua, to lay the first stone of the new stadium's construction. However, according to Fifa's website, Goal did not approve the Nicaragua stadium project until 17 February 2005. Fifa boasts that Goal did "intensive research" before saying yes. The available time line indicates otherwise.

Another problem with Goal is the chasm between Goal's reports and the reality on the ground. Fifa claims that on 4 December 2007, Goal approved a second project to increase the Nicaraguan stadium's capacity from 2,000 to 6,540 seats — even though the stadium was still to open. In the first report, Fifa's website proudly shows walls of concrete and a recently razed hillside; in the second it displays a blank white page where pictures should be. On 14 April 2011, Sepp Blatter visited Nicaragua to attend the stadium's ribbon cutting ceremony. The first official game was played on 6 October 2011. Three years after US$400,000 was sent to triple the capacity, the 4,000 additional seats had not materialised.

These inconsistencies point to two possible conclusions: the Goal bureau just does as the president bids, as the Pieth report implies; or the Goal bureau cares little for admitting sidesteps, problems, or delays: transparency and accountability are not priorities. Neither are symptoms of healthy corporate governance.

Of course, excuses for the delay in building the Nicaraguan stadium abound. First, construction always progresses slowly. London's Wembley stadium took seven years to complete. Before every World Cup, Fifa barks at the host country to speed up the building of infrastructure. Second, the global economy nosedived in September 2008. However, decades earlier and with no support from Fifa, Nicaragua's richer neighbour, Costa Rica, built the much larger Estadio Ricardo Saprissa in six years. Despite the global woes, Nicaragua's economy has grown at a steady 5% per year. Neither explanation feels satisfactory.

A look at the original stadium estimates and expenditures raises even more questions. In 2004, Julio Rocha, the president of Fenifut predicted that the stadium would cost $20 million, seat 20,000, and be built in five years. Seven years later, the secretary of Fenifut, Florencio Leyva, claimed that to complete the stadium would cost at least $20 million more. The problem, according to him, was that the government and local municipality had

not paid enough of the promised funds. In 2011, the Central American Football Association (UNCAF) website totalled the investments. The local university, UNAN, had donated $5 million in land and $15,000 in costs. Club Nexaca of Mexico donated stadium plans reportedly worth $750,000. The City of Managua had put in $40,000 worth of labour. Fenifut had spent about $25,000. The Nicaraguan government had contributed about $670,000 to the installation of the playing surface and seating. Fifa had donated a total of $800,000. The total was well short of the $20 million allegedly needed.

Even those numbers are disputed. In July 2011, *La Prensa*, a well-respected Nicaraguan daily, attempted to obtain documentation of where and how all the money was spent. Despite the best efforts of the journalists Anne Pérez and Oscar González, both the local government and Fenifut rebuffed their inquiries. Fifa's own website for Goal only includes a few paragraphs, the date of a project's approval, the amount sent and a pie chart of how the money should be invested. Unlike many non-profit-making organisations that rely on audited statements to show how much money goes to services as opposed to the organisation itself, Fifa discloses no such reports, nor does Fenifut. Nobody knows exactly where or how the money was spent for Nicaragua's stadium.

In February 2012, *La Prensa* reported that Fenifut had opened a luxurious two-storey building in Managua that cost $300,000. Fifa's website shows no Goal program approval for Nicaraguan expenditure on headquarters but Mauricio Caballeros, the regional director for Goal, turned up at the opening. Fenifut has not said how it obtained financing for the building but their website proudly displays dozens of pictures of their new home. The contrast with the barren concrete that forms the national stadium is clear.

So, what do Nicaraguan fans think? Sadly, Nicaragua as a country does not protect freedom of expression. The Committee to Protect Journalists ranks the country low in terms of the protection of free speech, journalists have fled the country due to death threats and defamation is a criminal offence with a hefty fine and possible jail time. Fenifut, meanwhile, has had the same president since 1990. The independent and excellent Nicaragua football website Futbolica has been critical of Rocha at times. The result? For games at the national stadium, Futbolica reporters have been shut out of the press box and left outside in the pouring rain.

Still, the anonymity of the internet offers an insight into Nicaragauan fans' angst. In the comments of an April 2011 *La Prensa* article, a fan by the name of Billy referred to Fenifut as a "pack of thieves." Another commenter, Leticia, compared Rocha to Walter Porras, the former head of the Tax Authority who was accused of rampant corruption and mysteriously disappeared in April 2011. Another commenter, Javier, called Fenifut a body of "titanic ineptitude". Many commenters point out with a tint of jealousy that Costa Rica built a nice stadium with little fuss. Some express hope that Fifa will hold Fenifut accountable. Others are embarrassed that Fenifut invited Fifa to arrive for the inauguration of an unfinished stadium. All are frustrated. Few are hopeful.

Nicaraguan fans rightly wonder when the national stadium will be completed. Globally, fans ask when Fifa will be run with transparency and integrity? Everybody can agree with the aim of Fifa's Goal program: to help developing federations with worthwhile projects. However, the Nicaraguan national stadium ordeal is a textbook example of poor corporate governance. A stadium opened, but well short of expectations. Nobody knows the truth, but it's hard not to suspect the worst. Ⓑ

The Third Party

A tax avoidance scandal in Argentina could have ramifications across the globe

By Sergio Levinsky

To most in the football world, the news that some Argentinian clubs have been engaged in a form of tax avoidance will be greeted with a shrug, but this is a scandal that potentially involves some of the biggest clubs in Europe, South America, Mexico and Asia.

The Argentinian judge Norberto Oyarbide is studying 444 transfers of Argentinian players — both those who have moved to foreign clubs or those who have returned from abroad in recent years — as part of an investigation into a system of tax evasion known as 'triangulations'.

In a 'triangulation', the player being transferred passes through an intermediary club for whom he never plays. Typically that intermediary will be in a country in which the tax paid on transfers is much lower than in either Argentina or the country of the club the player is leaving or joining.

Ricardo Etchegaray, the head of AFIP, the Argentinian tax authority, has denounced those third-party clubs as "sporting tax havens" and in many cases those clubs have admitted receiving a fee, often as little as US$10,000, to be used to reduce the tax. In Argentina, 24.5% of any transfer is paid out in fees — 15% to the player, 2% for the Argentinian Football Association (AFA), 0.5% to the players

union and 7% to AFIP. In Chile, that percentage goes down to 19. In Uruguay, it is as low as 2%.

There's nothing casual about the way Argentinian clubs have been cooperating with small clubs such as Sudamérica, Fénix, Progreso, Bella Vista, Cerro, Boston, River and Rampla Juniors (Uruguay), Unión San Felipe and Rangers (Chile) and Locarno (Switzerland). Between the end of August and the beginning of September 2012, AFIP suspended 151 of the 210 agents registered with AFA on suspicion of avoiding taxes through the use of intermediary clubs.

The case of the former Everton forward Denis Stracqualursi provides a case study. He joined San Lorenzo from Everton but the records show that he passed through Fénix of Uruguay. Fénix was also the (very) temporary home of the defender Facundo Roncaglia as he made his way from Boca Juniors to Fiorentina, while the midfielder Ignacio Piatti was briefly registered at Sud América of Uruguay as he moved from Lecce to San Lorenzo.

The secretary of Fénix, Alvaro Chijane, makes no secret of the practice, "It's no crime," he said. "We have the federation licences of the players that we register at the club and pay the corresponding taxes. We agree a percentage in negotiations with the executives of the Argentinian clubs and the business is so good that what we earn on one deal can pay our players' salaries for a month." What Chijane does not say is that the taxes paid by Fénix and the Argentinian clubs are not those that would be paid if the player actually joined the club.

Two cases illustrate the point: those of Jonathan Botinelli and Gonzalo Higuaín. Botinelli, the former Sampdoria defender, joined River Plate from San Lorenzo before the start of this season. On the way across Buenos Aires, he was briefly registered at the small Chilean club Unión San Felipe — for whom, of course, he never played. His contract stipulated that if Botinelli played more than five official matches for River — which he has already done — River would pay the Chilean club an additional US$550,000. That aroused AFIP's suspicions.

Their investigations found that the football section of Unión San Felipe is owned by Old Oask Invest which is managed by the Argentinian Raúl Delgado, a former journalist who was secretary of media communications for the government of Carlos Menem between 1995 and 1999. Old Oask Invest is based in the Virgin Islands. Delgado had a similar position in Argentina with Brown of Arrecifes, a club in the National B (the second division) that ended up suffering three straight relegations without winning a single game. In 2003, a Brown player, Walter Chazarreta, said that the club was being "emptied".

Something similar has been going on at Sud América of Uruguay, who are run by the Argentinian Vicente Celio, a former

vice-president of Chacarita Juniors. He arrived at Chacarita with the backing of the AFA president and Fifa vice-president Julio Grondona. In his time at the club, Chacarita sold such players as Facundo Parra (to Larissa of Greece) and Ignacio Piatti (to Saint-Étienne of France) and were relegated from second to third flight.

But the most startling case is that of Higuaín and his move from River Plate to Real Madrid in December 2006. River sold Higuaín to Locarno of Switzerland for US$6million and a percentage of any future transfer fee received. A few days later, Locarno sold Higuaín to Real Madrid for $18 million. Of that $18 million (effectively the 'real' fee, what Real Madrid were prepared to pay), US$2.7m went to Higuain, US$360.000 to AFA, US$ 4.4m to River Plate and US$ 10.5m to Locarno.

Locarno are owned by HAZ Football World Wide Limited, which has its headquarters in Gibraltar and derives its name from the first letter of the surnames of its three owners — (Fernando) Hidalgo, (Gustavo) Arribas and (Pinjas) Zahavi. The first two are Argentinian executives; Zahavi is a well-known Israeli agent.

Many have asked about Grondona's role in the triangulations scandal. The master politician, who has been president of AFA since 1979 while climbing the greasy pole at Fifa, has been publicly indignant about the tax avoidance. "AFA is happy to review everything, but this is a very difficult structure to clear up and it's impossible to do it ourselves," he said. "I've talked with Etchegaray, telling him the names of the people who have dedicated themselves to the buying and selling of players."

He seems not to recall that in 1997, AFA came close to establishing a business to produce television game shows with Alejandro Mascardi, the brother of Gustavo, one of those agents blocked by AFIP.

Grondona has made himself one of the main collaborators of the government of Cristina Fernández de Kirchner, helping in 2009 to break the contract for television rights that AFA had with TRISA to establish the *Fútbol para todos* programme. It ensures all top-flight Argentinian games are shown on public television and represent a de facto state subsidy for football. It is, of course pure coincidence that TRISA is 50% owned by Grupo Clarín, the main media opponents of Kirchner.

AFIP's activity, few doubt, is motivated by the need to increase revenues and to prevent money leaving Argentina for abroad. Etchegaray has said that if debts are paid, the issue will not be taken further. But very few are paying and that could mean consequences not only for Argentinian agents, clubs and players, but also for clubs in the rest of the world. Among the 444 transfers being investigated by Oyarbide are those involving Sergio Agüero, Ever Banega, Martín Palermo and Gabriel Heinze (to Spain), Martín Demichelis and Andrés D'Alessandro (to Germany), Javier Mascherano (to Brazil), Mariano Andújar (Italy), Gonzalo Bergesio (to France), (Spain) and Diego Forlán (to England).

Etchegaray has already contacted the tax agencies of many countries to collate data. What began as an Argentinian scandal threatens to spread across the globe.

154

Fiction

"...some sad song of betrayed
masculine trust and flighty females."

The Limping God, part 2

His football career ended by injury, John Brodie's life is going nowhere until he is sucked into the world of crime.

By David Ashton

Story so far. I, John Brodie, washed-out, weak-ankled, boozed-up, ex-Junior footballer had been hired as guardian angel to a young talent, Billy Gourlay. This enigmatic boy was the great hope for Hastie's Works team in next Saturday's final. He was last seen by me wrapped in the warm embrace of a bookie's wife in a blue Triumph Herald.

To wit, one Mamie Dunlop, wife of Donny, poison dwarf and nasty specimen, my former employer with whom it was safe to say I was not on good terms. My present commander, Frank Carlin — an affable, untrustworthy Irish smoothie — had offered me the angel brief and two fivers. Being a man who drank and read too much I took them like a shot.

It was now Monday morning and we were sitting in the Willow Bar, over mugs of tea that the bartender Jimmy Lapsley had once more rustled up from the goodness of his heart. The smell of stale beer and whisky still hung in the air. It was nippy but Frank was sweating. One thing I must mention is that mendacity was rife in this whole affair. Rife as potted heid.

Frank Carlin didn't do panic as a rule but he was close this moment. He patted a damp brow with a delicate hankie and pursed his dry lips. "I'll tell you the fallings out of it all," he muttered. "It is a well-known fact that I keep pigeons. My father did before and it roots me to the earth."

How pigeons connected Frank to the earth since they spent most of the time dropping bird shit on the populace of Greenock from the dank heavens was beyond me, but I said nothing and sooked at my tea.

"On Sunday night after the holy Sabbath day," Frank continued, "I was scattering seed and scouring out the doo-house when came a knock at the cage-door. It was Billy's father, Tommy. He spoke through the chicken-wire. The boy never came back Saturday night. Nor it would seem Sunday. I rang my mate in Hastie's office and he's not turned up this very morning."

"Office boy. You got him that job," I said.

"Ye remember that much," replied Frank grimly.

"Billy done this before?"

"With a pal maybe but not for so long and always left a note."

He suddenly hit his open palm down on the table and Jimmy, who was polishing a framed photo of Greenock Morton FC's latest bunch of misfits, ducked as if shot at.

"Where the hell is he?"

"Beats me." I sooked on. "How come you're so worried?"

Frank tried to look innocent, aggrieved and compassionate at one and the same time. It gave him the appearance of a man with a bad ulcer. "I'm his uncle."

"Not by blood."

"Friends of the family. Uncle Frank, that's me. Pure concern!"

Jimmy began to whistle a few bars of some latest hit, *The Tennessee Waltz* — some sad song of betrayed masculine trust and flighty females. The bar telephone rang and he answered it as Frank drew further breath.

"What are you going to do about it?"

"Finish my tea."

He stood up and gathered his camel-haired coat around him like a prelate. "I paid you good money. See you earn same. Find the boy. Pure concern!"

With that he swept out to avoid the look of disbelief in my eye. Frank had fingers in many pies; rumoured to be a big gambler, a real lady's man despite a stolid local wife and progeny to boot, plus an import-export business where the cargo might alter shape if bound for Ireland.

I hadn't mentioned Mamie's Saturday night clinch with Billy because I felt my employer was dissembling somewhat — just an instinct but that's all I have left these days.

One thing had surprised me about the weekend though. I hadn't had a drink and I'd spent Sunday walking the hills above Greenock where the old railway lines used to be. Lost in memories. My parents had walked these hills, arm in arm. I have a picture taken with the Kodak box camera. A small photo and out of focus, but they look happy. The sun was shining and I was so proud to be their son as I keeked through the viewfinder. Lost in memories.

I reached down to rub a throbbing ankle: old football injuries never die and it still flared up at unaccustomed usage; Jimmy banged down the phone and ambled over, pop-eyes agleam.

"Guess whit?" he announced. "My mammy jist clocked in." He had bought the old biddy a phone and being the gossip of this pendant world, she used it to lethal effect. "Murder polis," Jimmy carried on. "Mamie Dunlop's in hospital. Car accident. Women drivers, eh?"

The Greenock Royal Infirmary was where my father died, Capstan Extra Strength tracking him down like the Hound of the Baskervilles. I had mixed memories of the place because as I'd trailed miserably to and fro till the old man muttered that for God's sake brighten up it was him dying not me, a pretty dark-haired nurse had taken pity on my plight. Rosalind Connor her name, green eyes, a wicked humour and black stockings to raise Lazarus. The legs inside them, that is. When we finally parted company, she said, "You read too many Russian books, John."

True enough. Dostoyevsky does not lend himself to foreplay and though she might drink me under the table, Rosalind didn't need whisky for a crutch. So she gazed upon me one day as 'twere someone she could not cure, put on her black stockings and moved to another shift.

Now she was a junior matron looking at me again, same eyes, same wicked glint. "Are you in love, John?"

"Not yet," I replied. "But I need to see the woman. Life and death, you know?"

Rosalind laughed and moved a little closer, her starched uniform made a cracking sound like far-off bones. "Ye still on the booze?"

"Down to a steady torrent."

She pulled back slightly, poker-faced, and jerked her head. I followed. That was the deal.

It was a private room, the blinds drawn. Mamie was sat up in the bed as I slid in. A magazine of some sort lay on her lap with a horse on the cover. Not a racehorse though, a show pony leaping over a fence. She turned it over and signalled to the side table where a bottle of Lucozade was waiting. I poured her out a glass and it fizzed with healthy promise.

As she sipped through puffy lips, I tried not to gawk too obviously at both black eyes and the swollen nose — normally she would put the bookie's smoke-

filled den in a flutter of lust but now she looked like a beat-up bulldog.

"Walk into a door?" I asked.

"My hand slipped. Accidents will happen."

The wry smile turned to a grimace of pain at the effort and she looked at me appraisingly through slit hazel eyes. Mamie might have been, I had sometimes wondered, fond of me — women often are at the beginning — and even in this bruised condition she gave off a sexual come-hither quality that could rouse the nearest caveman. I put my club firmly to the side and shot for the truth instead.

"I saw you Saturday night with Billy Gourlay. You seemed... on friendly terms."

Mamie's battered face revealed little. "He's jist a boy."

"Now you're hammered and he hasn't come home."

She shook her head. "He's no' the violent type." Then oddly a tear squeezed out from the swollen eyelids and found its course down her cheek. "Told anybody ye saw us?"

"Not yet."

"How come you were on hand?"

"I was paid to be the boy's guardian angel. Frank Carlin. Two fivers."

A twisted smile was the response, and then she snapped her eyes open best she could. "It was an accident," she muttered. "If ye don't believe me, look at the state o' the vehicle."

I nodded. Silence. Then a sharp rap at the door indicated from Rosalind that a Doctor's visit might be imminent. As I walked away, Mamie closed off the exchange.

"He's jist a boy," she said. But as I closed the door she mumbled something that sounded very like... *dirty wee bastard*... of course it most possibly would be her midget in wedlock, Donny Dunlop, to whom she was referring — but you never can tell.

White's Garage was tucked away in the cul-de-sac of Bruce Street not too far from the Willow Bar in what appeared to be a large corrugated iron shed but inside was tidy as a soldier's grave. That fitted the owner, Geordie White, ex-Boys' Brigade, born to serve.

He had a sharp, sleekit face with pale skin and slatey eyes that never looked direct; George had come in now and then to the bookie's but rarely put on a line and spent most of the time laughing compliantly at Donny's lousy jokes. I figured the damaged car would probably be stationed there and, as the Irish say, not often you're wrong but you're right this time.

Luckily the bold boy and his mechanics were swarming over a white Jaguar when I strolled through the open doors of the archway with Doris Day belting out *Secret Love* on the radio, so I was able to examine the Triumph Herald stuck forlornly in the corner at my leisure. It had a big dent at the front where the radiator was stove in but, strangely enough, no attendant gouges or scrapes.

As I was pondering this on my haunches, footsteps approached and into my line of vision came the immaculately shined toecaps of a pair of heavy working shoes, laces in a double-knot. I straightened up with some difficulty to almost meet Geordie's shifty gaze.

"I'm looking for a second-hand vehicle," I said. "Is this for sale?"

"Very funny," he replied. "It's Mamie's car as well you know. Been in a fracas."

"Women drivers," I remarked sagely. "Still — she paid a price, eh? The car got off light."

George squinted while his Boys' Brigade brain put two and two together . "Ye seen her?"

"Photo in the *Greenock Telegraph*," I lied nonchalantly. "Where did it happen?"

"The Lyle Hill. Took a corner too fast. Straight intae a hedge."

"A hedge gave her two keekers, a fat nose and lips like flying saucers?"

"There was a post behind it."

"Was she alone?"

"Definitely," he said like a dutiful NCO. "Donny was working late." He squinted again to indicate intelligence at work. "Whit're you doing here anyway, Brodie?"

"I told you. Looking for a vehicle to purchase," I responded making quickly for the door with the errant thought that the Lyle Hill was a notorious winching spot strewn over which were more

French letters than Cragburn Dance Hall on a Saturday night.

"The polis are happy enough," George called suddenly as if I had asked him a question.

"The police are always happy, Mister White," I said stepping across the threshold. "It's to do with their innocent nature."

I pressed the button and four pennies rattled down into the coffin of the telephone box at the Orangefield, just opposite the chip shop and past St Patrick's where my mother used to genuflect to Father Scanlon in the good old days. A note to ring Frank had been left at the Willow Bar but I had been in no rush to do so — questions in the mind, slow the feet. Had Mamie taken a header into the steering wheel or met with more human contact? If so — whose fist? There was some dark purpose behind all this or might it be I read too many *Black Mask* magazines?

I had an image of a dark sludgy stretch of water with various large sharp-toothed fish, pike perhaps, lurking in the depths, circling each other but not yet breaking surface. Not yet.

It was a typical Greenock day, rain dripping down the panes of the box and I was reminded of the single tear shed by Mamie Dunlop. Crying for herself, or someone else? A squawking voice sounded in my ear but not a message from the inner depths, just Frank Carlin. I could hear what sounded like a cacophony of children in the background as he bawled out to someone called

Cathy and then a distant door slam signalled silence. Possibly shut the poor little buggers in the coal-bunker.

"Good news and bad," said the bold fellow. "Good. Billy Gourlay's back in the bosom of his family, safe as houses and returned to work this lunchtime."

"Where was he?"

"With a pal, he says and will say no more. He rules the roost in that home."

"Talent often does."

Silence ensued. The phone began complaining and I slammed in another four pennies. Frank coughed as if handing out a cue of sorts.

"And the bad news?" I asked, watching a man come out of the fish shop, deliberately open up his wrapped offering and allow the rain to mix with the vinegar therein. Simple pleasures unite the human race.

Frank coughed again as the man outside tucked into his sodden chips. "The bad news is you're off the case. To be truthful John you're a sad apology for a guardian angel and a waste of money. It was only out of pity for your poor dear departed mother that I doled out the two fivers."

"You keep my mother out of it," I said tightly, an unexpected rage rising in my head like a red mist.

"All right, all right," was the tinny response. "But you're off the case."

"You hear what happened to Mamie Dunlop?"

"I did indeed. But accidents will happen. See you around, John."

The phone disconnected leaving me with my rage and an echo in the mind.

As a factory hooter sounded the men poured out of Hasties like a horde of oily insects; it being a Monday night most were headed home and not for the pubs, though there was a shared feeling of being let off the leash into open, if dank, air. Big Neilly, who was shoving among the mass like a good-natured grizzly, waved over and then growled as one of the apprentices nicked the bunnet from his head and made off like a whippet pursued by the ursine avenger. A roar of laughter rose up and the lined faces of older men softened a touch as they cheered the boy on. I remembered meeting my father when he used to saunter out, a part of yet somehow separate from the heaving mass and a strange lost feeling echoed in my heart, but then I saw Billy's mop of hair in the crowd.

Office suit, neat black shoes, head down dribbling a tennis ball through the forest of legs and skilfully resisting efforts to prise it from him. Though the workmen jostled and poked out their big boots, there was an innate respect — as I said, the boy had class. Someone bumped him from behind and the ball scooted forward to be trapped by my one good foot.

Billy stopped. The men passed on, a few greetings thrown my way by my dad's former workmates. As the flow thinned out, I carefully passed the ball back to him so that he could flip it up to catch in hand and then stow it away in his pocket.

"If I didn't know better, I'd think you were a tanner ba' merchant," I said. "Small fry. Not for the big time. Lose your nerve."

A damp sniff was the response but as he made to move past, I blocked him off like a dogged defender. "Show me your hands," I requested.

He held them out. No bruising, no contusions. Another move. Another block. "I saw you with Mamie Dunlop on Saturday night."

Billy froze. No body swerve. "Dinnae know whit you mean, eh?"

"I thought she was going to swallow you whole, is what I mean. Now she looks like 10 rounds with Sugar Ray. What happened, Billy?"

He bit his lip, shook his head then suddenly bolted past me up Kilblain Street, running as if the devil was on his trail till he reached the top where he turned to bawl through the mirk.

"You're nothing. A big keech. Everybody says. A chanty man. A fucking has-been!!"

Then he vanished, leaving the childlike insults to hover in the mist while above a sea-gull screeched as if to mock my investigative efforts. A fleeting white shape in the grey sky.

The rest of the week passed by in a blur due to the fact that I recommenced my hand to mouth relationship with John Barleycorn. Jimmy Lapsley looked on with mournful eyes as I poured the last of Frank's money down my throat, winced as it hit an empty stomach, but persevered till the feelings of pain were numbed. Still there, but dead to the world.

It wasn't just the case, I had an attendant lifetime to drown. So many voices in my head, swarming like soldier ants, each with its own wounding sting. And the seductive dark taste of the bitter bane drew me in like an addict. Oh, it was a fine caper.

I sat in the corner of the Willow Bar hunched over *Crime and Punishment* thinking how clear the writing seemed when drunk but in the morning, the sense had somehow slipped away.

Things do slip away — life is a greasy business.

This was on Thursday night, late and an immaculately conditioned fingernail flicked at the book cover with a snap. I recognised the digit and did not look up. The snap was repeated and for the sake of Fyodor D, I raised my eyes.

Donny Dunlop towered over me, all five feet but I was seated and getting up might have its difficulties. "Let me buy ye a drink, John," he smiled, little pointy teeth edging through the thin lips. "Ye look thirsty. Like a fuckin' dromedary." Laughter greeted the statement but not from me; he always had three goons at his back like a cut-price Jimmy Cagney.

"M'all right," I muttered from the drunken depths of Saint Petersburg. "M'okay."

"Ye don't look it." Donny raised his voice. "Jimmy! A double for John here. Black Label. Best in the house, don't want to poison the boy."

Jimmy hesitated but then like a good barman, poured out and slid it up the counter where one of the goons picked up, brought it to the table and planked the glass right in front of me.

"Drink up," said Donny. "Ye must be dry as a bone."

The pub had gone quiet, gazes lowered; no-one likes to see a man humiliated unless it's safe to do so — in a movie maybe but not before your very eyes. I hesitated but what would be the harm? The searing contempt in Donny's eyes would fade with the passing years and perhaps he wished to kiss and make up, offer me my job back — in fact it struck me suddenly, why did he want to make this effort in any case? Why? But while this was going on in my mind, on the other hand as it were, my fingers were inching towards the heavy glass.

Donny ran his own fingers through the immaculate coiffure piled up on the side of his head in a startling ginger quiff to add some much needed height, and one of his dry lizard-like eyes drooped in an encouraging wink.

As the whisky was lifted I caught sight of myself in one of the grainy mirrors that framed the bar. A man of indeterminate features, who might once have been a contender, blinked a slack-jawed acknowledgement of approaching self-debasement and then bowed his head towards the glass. But at the last moment his wrist turned and liquor splashed out onto the table spurting all over a small man, perhaps an innocent bystander.

I looked up into Donny's puce face, the quiff electric with rage at the stains below on the blazer and flannels, and smiled vaguely.

"Sorry," I mumbled. "Must be the drink. Accidents will happen, eh?"

One of the goons made a move forward but Donny raised his hand a notch and the man was still. Just as well. He was built like a shipyard crane.

"You'll be sorry for that," Donny hissed quietly. "Very sorry. You can bet on it."

And yet I sensed something behind his eyes, perhaps the reason he had baited me. He was worried. It was as if everybody in this game thought I knew more than I did. I had a twisted realisation that this might even include myself, laughed suddenly, beckoned Donny a little closer so I could smell the polo mints he sucked on a daily basis, and whispered, "It's a dangerous game Donny and I know what's going on – but don't worry – your secret's safe with me. Saturday will come – and all will be revealed, eh?"

Then I laughed again and he left abruptly. No one else had heard the exchange, I could have been pleading forgiveness as far as they knew. The pub went back about its business then Jimmy Lapsley slammed something down on the table. I peered down at what transpired to represent itself as a meat pie. The crust looked invincible.

"Been on the shelf three days," said Jimmy dourly. "Fit for a king."

Her lips were still puffy but the eyes concealed behind large sunglasses —

in Greenock a wasted gesture, hiding behind an umbrella might have better passed without comment. The nose was a little thick but almost back to normal.

Mamie Dunlop. She rapped on the door at eleven Friday morning and I had fallen out of bed, donned the yellow dressing gown and stumbled to the summons, hungover, unshaven, full of misplaced hope that it might be Rosalind Connor, post night-shift and full of beans, it being her delightful habit when we were thrown together.

Instead of Rosalind's sharp odour of hospital carbolic, however, it was the allure of some French midnight fragrance emanating from the bruised but mysterious form presented. The damaged glamour and the peekaboo blonde hair falling over one eye put me in mind of Veronica Lake.

But this was Greenock and it was Mamie. No doubt. A pocket Venus risen from the sick-bed. She looked somewhat disdainfully at the piles of books scattered around like so many prehistoric rock formations, put one hand on her hip and ran a tongue over the aforesaid swollen chops.

Oddly Donny had not mentioned her the previous night and neither had I. Perhaps that was the reason she had made an appearance. Or perhaps I was shooting in the dark.

Anyway, hip outflung, tongue on the move, Mamie was the embodiment of black and blue temptation. "How would ye like tae nail that wee bastard?" she enquired.

I pulled the velvet collar up to disguise an eleven o'clock shadow and asked a question that had been running in my mind. "Did he punch your lights out?"

She smiled brokenly. "He put on the gloves first. Kid gloves. A nice khaki colour."

I nodded. That explained the lack of ancillary abrasion on Donny's hand that I had noted last night as he flicked at *Crime and Punishment.* "Was Billy there?"

Mamie shook her head whether in denial or to indicate the end of this line of enquiry was not clear as she moved in closer and her perfume wreathed around me like a noose. Our bodies were not quite touching but you couldn't have got a roll-up in there especially the upper half where her pointed bra strained like a dog on a leash. She then brushed her leg against the nether reaches of the yellow dressing gown and giggled.

"Is that a torpedo in your pocket or are ye jist glad to see me?"

Burns once remarked that a standing cock has no conscience. But I had seen *Pinocchio* and Jiminy Cricket was my watchword.

"What do you want, Mamie?" I managed from a dry throat.

She laid her mouth against an equally aroused ear and let out a little hot breath before the soft words followed.

At the back o' White's Garage, a wee room. A filing cabinet. Where he hides everything. A' the crooked deals, John. You could nail him.

"Why should I?"

When you father died – know whit he said – Donny?

I shook my head. But I didn't feel good. Poison ivy.

He said. Donny. He said. A waste of space. Like his son. Cancer's too good for him. Scum o' the earth — dirty communist bastard.

Her hazel eyes darkened. "Whit do I want?" she repeated. "The same as you."

Then she turned and left — only the scent remained. Jasmine, vanilla and a faint trail of musk.

I stood there like stone.

Somewhere in the distance, came the sound of an ambulance bell. As it faded, the deep chime of the Orangefield Church clock tower tolled out a doleful Protestant warning against excess emotion.

To be continued...

165

Greatest Games

"All that stands between Ipswich and a place in the
third round of the Uefa Cup is the unspoken threats
of a violent second leg in Rome."

Lazio 4 Ipswich Town 2

Uefa Cup, second round, second leg, Stadio Olimpico, Rome, 7 November 1973

By Dominic Bliss

They say there are two sides to every story, but it isn't often that you can identify precisely the dividing line between those two sides. When discussing the events that followed the Uefa Cup second round second leg between Lazio and Ipswich Town in November 1973, differing accounts come from either side of a locked changing-room door.

On one side, an army of Lazio supporters (including several players) raged, furious about perceived injustices during the tie, and fuming at the referee, the visiting supporters, the ambulance service and even their own stadium. Meanwhile, the victorious Ipswich team had locked themselves into their changing room and refused to come out until all fell silent in the corridor outside. As the Ipswich midfielder Bryan Hamilton put it, "We didn't know what was going on outside, we just knew it was bad."

When they finally did emerge into the tunnel of the Stadio Olimpico, there was a smell of tear gas in the air and the pitch outside was littered with broken glass. After all the anger, resentment and embarrassment of those moments that followed the second leg, it would be some time before people were able to reflect on the fact that these teams had just played out two classic football

matches, ending in a 6-4 aggregate victory for the English club.

Over the course of 180 frenetic minutes, Ipswich had taken on a group of players that specialised in histrionics and put them through the wringer, in both a footballing and an emotional sense. The drama of a crazy second leg in Rome was so intense that, had a world-famous striker sworn into a television camera following the final whistle, it probably wouldn't even have made the highlights.

Combining the pride of strutting divas with a snarling aggression, Tommaso Maestrelli's Lazio had already displayed the shortness of their collective fuse to the English football community when they brawled with Arsenal players in a restaurant following a Fairs Cup tie in 1970. Violence had broken out after some apparently hurtful gags were made by the Gunners players about a post-match gift from their hosts. Presenting leather purses to a group of sideburned, quintessentially seventies, working-class British men was not seen as the most masculine of gestures by the recipients and their amusement caused hurt feelings and then a flurry of angry fists and upturned dinner plates in the centre of the Italian capital.

The Ipswich Town side drawn against Lazio three years down the line were an earnest, restrained bunch, still in the process of being moulded by a hard-working young manager, whose coaching career had not begun well but promised a brighter future. Still just 40 years old, Bobby Robson had transformed his Ipswich side from perennial relegation battlers to Uefa Cup qualifiers over the previous four seasons. In the first round, they beat Real Madrid.

Ipswich Town 4 Lazio 0, Portman Road, Ipswich, 24 October 1973

The angst and frustration that led to the mayhem had its roots in a first-leg performance by Ipswich that would have humbled a less arrogant side than Lazio. As you might expect from a team made up of aggressive showmen, Maestrelli's Lazio were at their best when playing to

a home crowd or when their blood was up. But on that cold, late-October night in Ipswich, the psychological factors that made this intense team such a dangerous opponent were absent and Robson's team took full advantage.

Lazio sat far too deep at Portman Road, allowing Ipswich to mount attacks in front of their massed backline and ceding space in wide areas. These problems were partly a consequence of changes made to what would be deemed their first XI — the line-up that ultimately led them to the Serie A title that season.

Lazio's system under Maestrelli is best described as a 1-3-3-3. Made up of two full-backs, a stopper centre-half (Giancarlo Oddi) and, behind him, a libero (Pino Wilson), the backline was used to lying in wait, organised and well-positioned to nullify opposition

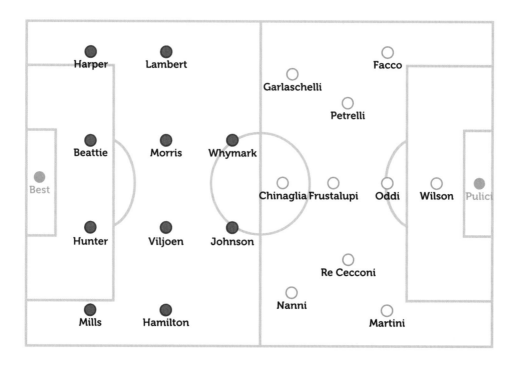

strike forces. In front of them were two battling midfield players — usually Luciano Re Cecconi and Franco Nanni — who often took up old-fashioned wing-half positions, either side of a third central midfield player, Mario Frustalupi. The attacking threat came from a trident made up of two tricky wingers, Vincenzo D'Amico and Renzo Garlaschelli, who were capable of bursting past defences on the touchline or of cutting inside and shooting, and the talismanic Giorgio Chinaglia, who led the line with power, talent and clinical intent.

In East Anglia, for one reason or another, the eleven names that trip off the tongue for Lazio supporters of a certain vintage did not trot out in their usual order and the changes affected the balance of the team. The skilful left-winger, D'Amico, was named only as a substitute as Maestrelli selected Sergio Petrelli, an uncompromising right-back renowned for his robust challenges, to play in the No 11 shirt. Adding to the confusion, despite the number on his shirt, he wasn't asked to play on the left-wing — that task was given to Nanni, who moved out wide from his usual role in central midfield, where Petrelli was included to add some steel. Mario Facco, meanwhile, was the man called in to play in Petrelli's usual right-back slot, as Lazio went into the game looking to keep things tight.

It didn't work. They were too deep and too narrow, leaving exploitable gaps. For much of the game, there were large swathes of open space for Ipswich's wide players to run loose in. Meanwhile, the Ipswich centre-forward Trevor Whymark positioned himself in the centre of the Lazio penalty area, where he could compete for the balls Lazio were effectively inviting Ipswich to cross into the box. It was not in the make-up of Lazio goalkeeper, Felice Pulici, to leave his line and claim these crosses, so the game hung on the battle between Whymark and the Lazio defence as the ball was slung into the penalty area over and over again.

Ipswich's approach play, though, was not simply a case of knocking long balls into the box. They used the left flank to particularly devastating effect that evening, as Colin Harper pushed forward from left-back frequently, making runs on the outside of Mick Lambert on the left of midfield. The movement left Petrelli, floundering in his unfamiliar role on the right of a three-man midfield, unsure which player to close down.

On two occasions in the first half, he chose incorrectly.

With 16 minutes gone, Lambert, under very little pressure in a deep position on the left touchline, was afforded the time and space to push the ball inside onto his right foot and send an in-swinging cross onto Whymark's head. Cutting a dominant figure in the middle of a crowded penalty area, he guided his header over the dive of Pulici and inside the far post to open the scoring.

Harper was the man behind Whymark's next goal, scored three minutes before half-time. The full-back strode forward unchallenged and struck a left-footed cross on the run, once again from a deep position. In truth, he scuffed the cross slightly but it was misjudged by Facco, who threw himself headlong at it, connecting with nothing but clean air. The ball evaded everyone in the crowded penalty area as it bobbled across and awkward autumn pitch before finally reaching the back post, where Whymark reacted quicker than the left-back Luigi Martini and plundered his second goal of the night off his left shin. Pulici was criticised for appearing to dive out of the ball's way as it rolled unconvincingly into the centre of his goal but in retrospect he could be forgiven for leaning to his left in anticipation of a well-struck shot towards the far corner only to be deceived by the mishit. Either way, the tame effort made it 2-0.

Ipswich had discovered Lazio's weakness and they exploited it mercilessly. The confidence of Petrelli and Facco had been destroyed before half-time by the simplest of British tactics — an overlapping full-back and winger combination in a 4-4-2. The psychological advantage was clear as, just two minutes into the second half, Harper and Lambert used the same formula again with the visitors looking a disheartened rabble on their right flank.

Whymark claimed his hat-trick after Harper was allowed to make a driving run inwards from the left touchline, before shrugging off a desperate attempt at a tackle by Petrelli and playing a pass into the penalty area that split two Lazio players. Petrelli's challenge was almost apologetic — the attempt of a man who knew that he should try to do something but didn't know what. The pass wrong-footed Re Cecconi but Lambert, anticipating perfectly, latched onto it, before furrowing his way towards the goal line and squeezing a pass between two flat-footed defenders at the near post. Whymark pounced on the ball inside the six yard box — to a confident

goalkeeper, an unthinkable outcome — and his forceful left-footed shot had too much power for the timid Pulici.

Three times Ipswich had exposed the unfamiliar Lazio right flank and the unnecessarily deep backline. The Italians were architects of their own downfall and it got worse 10 minutes later, when Whymark scored his fourth goal of the night in fortuitous circumstances. Colin Viljoen carried the ball into the Lazio half unchallenged (a recurring theme that night) and, as Frustalupi belatedly closed him down 25 yards from goal, the South African-born midfielder dropped his shoulder and cut inside to strike with his right foot. The shot hit Whymark either on the back or on the left arm, depending on whose account you listen to, before he swivelled and lashed the ball into the bottom far corner of the net.

Immediately, Lazio hands were raised in protest, appealing for the goal to be disallowed for handball and in the scenes that followed, the Swiss referee was surrounded by eight Italian players. 4-0 was an embarrassing result for Lazio and the dismay at conceding some poor goals turned into anger at what they perceived to be a refereeing injustice. It proved the tip of the iceberg.

From Ipswich's perspective, however, the tantrums of their vanquished Roman foes were merely an amusing sideshow after a rout that left not just the East Anglian town but the whole country brimming with confidence and pride. "Whymark's four goals against a panic-stricken Lazio defence sent a thrilling message racing through English football," James Lawton wrote excitedly in the *Daily Express* the following day. "It proclaimed in every phase of this savage beating of a top Italian side that an English team can still take on a massed defence and cut it to pieces."

The result and the performance were further signs that Robson was creating something special at Portman Road, after a fourth place finish in the 1972-73 season. The manager claimed in his autobiography to have constructed three great teams at Ipswich, reaching their peak in 1975, 1978 and 1981. As they put Lazio to the sword in front of their disbelieving supporters on 24 October 1973, he was still in the process of the building the first of those legendary sides.

Under the ownership of the eccentric John Cobbold, the club was renowned for its belief in putting the manager first and that was precisely what the future England and Barcelona boss needed as he looked to make his way in the coaching world. After traumatic experiences with Vancouver Royals and Fulham — both clubs in a state of disarray in the boardroom — Robson could have been forgiven for turning his back on management, but he applied speculatively for the job at Ipswich and was successful. What's more, he was given the time to learn and build at Ipswich and the club ultimately reaped the rewards.

It was not a straightforward rise to prominence for Robson and Ipswich, though. In the four seasons before they claimed fourth spot in 1973, Ipswich had finished 12th, 18th, 19th and 13th, reaching their lowest ebb during the 1970-71 campaign, when Robson came to blows with two of his players after omitting them from the team. After the

manager and his assistant, Cyril Lea, had gone toe-to-toe with the offending players — Tommy Carroll and Bill Baxter — the pair were eventually offloaded and the squad rallied around their beleaguered boss. Crucially, they were joined in that respect by the board.

"Our manager's name is not written in chalk on his door with a wet sponge nailed by the side," Cobbold said when Ipswich found themselves bottom of the table in the same campaign. He was vindicated in the years that followed, as Robson's network of scouts began to come good with some bargain signings — Whymark, Lambert, Mick Mills and Kevin Beattie among them — while the club won the FA Youth Cup in 1973 (they would repeat the feat in 1975). As the new faces settled into Robson's way of doing things, the club's fortunes took off.

Beating Real Madrid and then racing to a 4-0 first leg lead over Lazio must have sent confidence soaring around Ipswich but they had to ensure that their chastened opponents didn't let their appetite for vengeance spur them onto an unlikely comeback in Rome. This Lazio team came with a reputation and, having lost face in England, they were expected respond at the Stadio Olimpico.

Lazio 4 Ipswich Town 2, Stadio Olimpico, Rome, 7 November 1973

"All that stands between Ipswich and a place in the third round of the Uefa Cup is the unspoken threats of a violent second leg in Rome," claimed Jeff Powell in the *Daily Mail* following the 4-0 victory at Portman Road. Hindsight tells us that he understood the situation well but the proposed threat from Lazio should

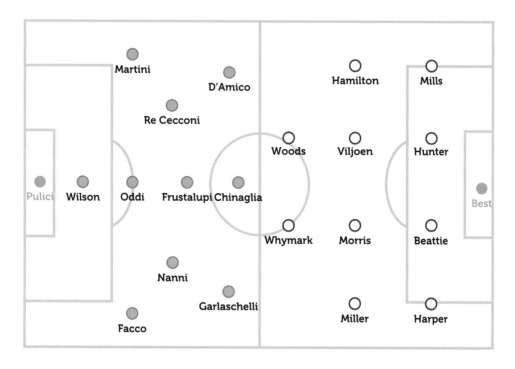

not have been reduced to violence and petulance alone. This was a team, after all, who had lost out on the 1972-73 *scudetto* following defeat on the last day of the season and who would go on to put that disappointment behind them with their first Serie A title success the following April. A 4-0 defeat away from home was bad, but Lazio, and the Italian press, refused to accept that it was terminal, particularly for a team who were so much more dangerous in their own stadium than they were on the road.

Lazio, while by no means poor travellers on the whole, did show a degree of frailty in particularly high-pressure away games during the 1973-74 campaign. They leaked a combined total of 18 goals in away games against their four closest title rivals and their two European opponents. Indeed, they had progressed despite conceding three

times in the away leg of their Uefa Cup first-round tie against Sion, albeit in very different circumstances.

The *Biancocelesti* had arrived in Switzerland with the cushion of a 3-0 lead from the home leg, courtesy of a hat-trick from Chinaglia, who was in almighty form that season. His personal tally of 24 league goals amounted to one more than Lazio conceded in total. Never lacking in bravado, Chinaglia was brimming with confidence but it may be that a certain amount of complacency entered into the team's psyche when they went ahead in the second leg to open up a 4-0 aggregate lead. Whatever the reason, Lazio revealed a porousness to their usually watertight backline that night in Switzerland. Sion recovered to win 3-1 on the night, falling just short of a memorable comeback, although little was made of their mini-recovery.

But Lazio were more or less impenetrable at the Stadio Olimpico, where their formidable record and the aggressive atmosphere could cause opponents to wilt before a ball had been kicked. This intimidation factor was summarised emotionally in 1975 by the proudly Communist Perugia player, Paolo Sollier, after he was subjected to deafening abuse by right-wing Lazio Ultras that reached fever pitch when he was substituted. "Perhaps it is incorrect to talk about 'Lazio's fans'. 'The Lazio fascists' is better," Sollier is quoted as saying in *Calcio*, John Foot's history of Italian football. "They beat people up, attacked buses, slashed tyres. I had been whistled every time I touched the ball... I walked off with *Sollier Boia* ['Sollier Executioner'] being screamed out by those shitty people, their hands in the bastard form of a fascist salute. I went into the tunnel without doing anything... once I was inside I was afraid... shivering... I wanted a rifle to kill the whole *curva*."

Sollier's was an extreme case, given his well-known political beliefs, but his account gives an impression of how the Olimpico could affect Lazio's opponents when the heat was on. With such a potent psychological weapon, even when faced with a 4-0 starting deficit, Lazio's players genuinely believed they could win by the required margin on their own patch. Spurred on by baying *Laziali*, this fiercely proud and tactically astute force lost just one home game all season.

Ipswich's players, meanwhile, had little idea of what lay in store for them. When they landed in Rome, Robson's men were simply looking forward to seeing the sights in the ancient capital before playing out the second leg of a tie they had firmly under control. Hamilton remembers sitting with fellow Northern Ireland international Allan Hunter in Saint Peter's Square, marvelling at the surroundings in Vatican City and planning to return with his wife. However, he also recalls the atmosphere in the build-up to the game turning on an incident at the Ipswich training base: "The whole situation was hyped up out of sight at some stage, somewhere. In my mind, it was from the moment we came off the plane, but there was a turning point at one of our training sessions in Italy when a group of men came with a trophy for Trevor Whymark."

These men were representatives of an AS Roma supporters' club — the *12° Club Giallorosso* — and they had arrived, with a photographer, to stoke the fires of their own rivalry with Lazio (one the *Giallorossi* were undoubtedly losing on the pitch at the time). Their plan worked. Several Italian newspapers carried the same photo above their match preview articles the following day. In it, a rather bewildered looking Whymark could be seen accepting a gold plate from a smiling club president, Pietro Magliocchetti, who was decked out in a patterned suit jacket that wouldn't have looked out of place on a Roger Moore-era Bond villain. A further detail acted as a twist of the knife, though: the plate was inscribed with a personal message incendiary enough to elevate the Ipswich striker to the kind of nemesis status Sollier had endured during his ordeal at the Olimpico.

To Whymark, in recognition of Ipswich-Lazio 4-0
Il Roma Club F.C. "12° Giallorosso", with affection and gratitude

Affection and gratitude. Sparked by those words, the fuse on Lazio's infamous *Curva Nord* was lit.

On the same day that Roma supporters made Whymark a club icon for his disservices to Lazio, Maestrelli was making plans of his own for the Ipswich centre-forward. Alarmed by the ease with which he dismantled his defence in the first leg, the former international striker was ready to tinker with his tactics, a drastic step for a team that was rarely altered and even more rarely reacted well to such changes.

Facco, the experienced right-back, kept his place for the second leg ahead of Petrelli, who was dropped following his humiliation at Portman Road. D'Amico was recalled on the left-wing, with Nanni returning to central midfield, offering more flair going forward but, in a move considered by the Italian press to have been planned for "psychological reasons", Lazio planned to give Whymark closer physical attention to prevent him from running amok once again. In other words, the Ipswich frontman was being earmarked for rough treatment, both in the dressing-room and on the terraces. Briefly it appeared as though these plans were to be scuppered too, as Wilson, the linchpin of the Lazio defence and a strong, steadying force at the back, suffered a knock in a 0-0 draw at home to Fiorentina in the intervening Serie A game. On the morning of the second leg against Ipswich, the captain and libero was considered a doubt by the Italian press, but that evening he trotted out at the head of the team to take his usual place behind the backline.

As Hamilton explains, Lazio made their intentions clear immediately. "At the start of the game, the first ball was played up to Trevor Whymark and he got a smack in the back of the head. That set the standard for the rest of the game."

Moments after clattering their chief tormentor from the first leg, Lazio took the lead. Just 43 seconds into the game, D'Amico, the talented winger returning to his position on the left of a three-man attack, pushed the ball inside and saw it rebound fortuitously off Hunter's knee into the path of the right-winger Garlaschelli, who gratefully drove his shot past Best. With a goal on the board inside the first minute, Ipswich disorientated and the crowd roaring them forwards, Lazio's players felt even more conviction in their pre-match belief that they could recover the deficit.

36 years later, Chinaglia recalled the dead-eyed will to win which permeated through that team in moments of crisis. "I remember one game later that season, against Verona," he told me. "We were losing 2-1 when we went in at half-time and I said to them all, 'What are we doing in here? Let's go outside now!' So we put ourselves on the pitch and just waited for Verona to come back out. We came back and won the game 4-2. We thought it was better than sitting talking to go out there and get on with it straight away because we believed we were better than them. And the fans went crazy — they loved it — so it was good. They were shocked at first, but then they started cheering, going crazy. So the Verona team came out on the field saying, 'What the hell's going on here?' In six minutes we had scored two goals, so that tells you everything — the psychological aspect is important sometimes. After we lost 4-0 at Ipswich, we said to each

other that we could beat them 5 or 6-0 at home."

Taken aback by the ferocity of their wounded hosts, Robson's team struggled to cope. Lazio continued to push forward and, after just nine minutes, Chinaglia nearly scored a second with a well-executed overhead kick that rebounded off the Ipswich crossbar. Much had been made in pre-match media discussions of the upcoming international friendly between England and Italy (a game that saw Fabio Capello score the only goal in a famous first win for Italy at Wembley). With that fixture in mind, the Azzurri manager, Ferruccio Valcareggi, was in the stands at the Olimpico and one of his key men, Chinaglia, played a leading role in a stirring opening 30 minutes from the hosts.

Every so often, a centre-forward of a certain stature and prominence appears to force himself upon the narrative of a game and cast himself as the protagonist. Like any hero, or antihero, he does so with an air of certainty that he will succeed. That night, Chinaglia was like a force of nature. When he played that way, he filled the Lazio players and supporters with confidence.

Three first-half minutes in particular did much to raise pulses in the stadium. After 24 minutes, Hunter made two goal-line clearances in quick succession to deny Chinaglia. After his second shot was blocked by Hunter, it rebounded onto the post and into David Best's arms — it seemed faintly ridiculous that the ball had stayed out of the goal but even more infuriating for Lazio was the feeling that, once again, the referee had overlooked a handball.

Chinaglia believed that sense of injustice was the final straw for an already incensed Lazio. "I took a shot and the guy on the line parried it out with his hand, but the referee didn't give us a penalty," he recalled with a lingering sense of frustration. "That's when it all started."

Despite the disappointment of Lazio's players, they refused to yield and the momentum remained as they scored two minutes later. This time he had reason to be disappointed with himself after Garlaschelli's cross went unclaimed and Chinaglia powered it home in anger. With over an hour left, things looked ominous for Town; Lazio were performing like a team possessed. An Ipswich fanzine described the second goal as having "put the game in the melting pot" but the final meltdown was still to come.

At the end of the first half and the beginning of the second, chances were created at both ends as the game became increasingly open and increasingly tense. That anxiety then exploded into rage on one side, and fear on the other, as the Dutch referee, Leo van der Kroft, once again took centre stage with a brave, but contested, decision. On 73 minutes, Clive Woods — who replaced David Johnson alongside Whymark in attack for the second leg — tripped over the leg of Oddi as he looked to latch onto a free kick. A penalty was awarded.

It was at this point that one or two of the personalities within Robson's squad came to the fore. With the Lazio players and supporters out of control and the atmosphere on a knife-edge, teetering between intimidating and dangerous, the cool head of Colin

Viljoen shone through."[Viljoen] was an outstanding footballer," Robson wrote in his autobiography, "quicksilver over the ground, smart brain, intelligent first touch... but he was not the most popular person... He had that arrogant, self-confident bearing... and it rubbed people up the wrong way in our down-to-earth dressing room."

That night, Ipswich were thankful for Viljoen's "self-confident bearing" as he converted the penalty. Most of the team trotted back to their own half almost surreptitiously, sensing the fragility of the mood inside the Olimpico and hoping not to enflame matters further. But one player failed to read the warning signs, something Hamilton will never forget: "Poor old Trevor Whymark! He made the decision to cheer and go over to Viljoen, and about four or five of their players started chasing him. He ended up behind David Best in our own penalty area!"

According to one report, a scissor kick was among the blows aimed at Whymark as he beat a hasty retreat and nobody was surprised to see Wilson booked four minutes later for flooring Woods with a hefty challenge. What they weren't expecting, however, was the pitch invader who got past a heavy police presence, a metal fence and a moat.

With the interruption over and the game all but won, it might have been time to calm things down. Maestrelli, however, decided to make a substitution that would have the opposite effect. He replaced one of his most technically gifted players, D'Amico, with his trusty enforcer, Petrelli, who must have still been seething from the run-around he had been given in East Anglia.

One of his targets was Johnson, the Ipswich substitute, who had been left out of the starting line-up that night, in part because he had failed to recover fully from the rough treatment he had received in the first leg. According to Hamilton, it was not an easy night for the future Liverpool striker. "David Johnson, for whatever reason, had become a marked guy," he said. "He was on the bench in Rome and, I can't remember who said it, but I heard they were all sitting on the bench — and we were all very decent, sensible players — and someone apparently ran past and spat on him. He was shocked that someone would do that in a football match, a European club football match. It was just an unsavoury night, where we wanted to get the match over with and get home."

Before they could do that, however, they had finally to extinguish the fight from Chinaglia. The forward had already had a second goal disallowed for offside, shortly before Viljoen's penalty, and he refused to give up with the aggregate score at 5-2. With eight minutes remaining, he won and converted a penalty, before completing his hat-trick five minutes later, pulling Lazio to within a goal of Ipswich, although the away goals rule meant that the *Biancocelesti* needed another two goals for victory.

Then, in injury time, probably the worst thing that could have happened, given the fraught situation inside the stadium, happened. Johnson, who later admitted he hadn't dared to stop moving in case the injuries he had incurred two weeks earlier were tested by his markers, scored a screamer. He chested Viljoen's cross down and struck the ball left-footed into the net to settle the tie. Then, all hell broke loose.

"Afterwards the fans went crazy — everybody went crazy," Chinaglia said. "Their players couldn't come out of the dressing-room because 75,000 people were waiting for them, and that's a difficult situation."

In the race to reach the tunnel before the supporters and opposition players could get to them, the Ipswich keeper, Best, was badly hurt by a kick and was eventually carried inside, before the changing room door was locked. It remained bolted for almost two hours.

The Ipswich supporters on the terraces, however, had nowhere to hide. "Fighting on the terraces was rife and supporters from Ipswich were terrified," remembers Barry Collings, an Ipswich fan who had travelled to the game across Europe by car with three friends. But, having met the squad outside their hotel earlier that day, he and his friends were among the lucky ones.

"We were herded out safely by the police because we were in the players' guest area, but in the street we were set upon and jostled. We ran and merged with the host of Lazio supporters, hiding our scarves. We walked for a long time to get out of the vicinity of the stadium and eventually found our way back to the hotel."

Collings had seen the situation in the stands developing from his seat in the *tribuna* and his account helps to explain why the police were unable to stop the pitch invasion at the final whistle. "The playing surface was surrounded by a moat and a high fence, while the police were sitting on benches in 'V' shapes behind the goals, looking out at the crowd. When a goal was scored

during the match, a coloured rocket was fired up in the air for the benefit of the people outside in the city — white or blue depending on the team scoring. However, as the match descended into chaos, the rockets were directed down at the police benches and the police were jumping around in smoke."

There was little sympathy for Lazio's players and supporters, even from their compatriots in the Italian press. In Rome, the newspapers were filled with condemnation and concern for the image of the ancient capital. "Madness at the Stadio Olimpico" read one headline; "The Night of Shame" was another, while a more philosophical sub-heading offered the sentiment, "Better to lose a contest, or not to play at all, just to save the city a defamation for which it is not to blame".

The Turin-based daily, *La Stampa*, went for "Thugs of the Olimpico", reporting that the referee was forced to leave via a hidden exit as the battle raged within. As he did so, an ambulance departing the stadium was targeted by a mob who believed the Dutch official was inside. They succeeded only in damaging an ambulance filled with fellow supporters.

The club would pay dearly for the violence that night. Crowned champions of Italy for the first time in their 74-year history at the end of the campaign, their celebrations were cut short by the knowledge that a Uefa ban, imposed after the Ipswich game, would prevent them from competing in the European Cup the following season.

The squad then began to fall apart, in traumatic style. Chinaglia, whose wife was American, longed to move to the United States, where he was offered the chance to play alongside Pelé and Franz Beckenbauer for the New York Cosmos, and he took the opportunity in the summer of 1976. By then Maestrelli was battling the cancer that would eventually claim his life. Tragedy also claimed midfielder Re Cecconi who was shot dead in a jewellery shop when he shouted "This is a robbery!" as a joke, not realising that the jumpy owner had recently been robbed and wasn't going to ask any questions before shooting. Years later, after Frustalupi had died in a horrific car crash in 1990, it was claimed that the team was cursed.

On the pitch, there was little to cheer about following the 1974 *scudetto* party. Lazio had slipped to 13th by the end of the 1975-76 season, finishing on the same number of points as relegated Ascoli in a 16-team league. With just six wins in 30 games, a team that had won the league two years earlier avoided relegation on goal difference. They wouldn't lift silverware again until 1998.

As for the victorious Ipswich players, they returned to England battered, bruised and exhausted, while the overriding emotion was not of delight at another famous European victory but relief that they had got away from the hatred and intimidation of the Stadio Olimpico that night. The team reached the quarter-final stage of the Uefa Cup that season, but their second round heroics in Rome did not feel too much like a victory in the immediate aftermath.

Robson, addressing the journalists who had gathered to meet his squad at the airport, was unequivocal in his condemnation of what had happened after the final whistle in Rome. Pointing angrily to the walking wounded among the Ipswich party, he said, "Look at my players here! Colin Harper has a serious injury to his leg, David Best has a sore shin and almost every one of them has bruises all over their bodies. It's a miracle we don't have five or six players out.

"Believe me, it was not football; it was war."

179

Seven Bells

"...not before smashing an earthenware coffee set he'd just purchased in the duty-free shop."

Fouls and Fisticuffs

A selection of unsavoury incidents we're supposed to condemn

By Scott Murray

1 Ron Harris and Ian Hutchinson on Eddie Gray (CHELSEA v Leeds United, FA Cup final replay, 1970)

The 1970 FA Cup final at Wembley between Chelsea and Leeds retains a period charm, a beguiling snapshot of more innocent times. Jack Charlton flaps his scrapeover at a cross. The ball trickles over the goal line, getting there slowly, half-turn by half-turn. Eddie McCreadie tries to kick it away, but takes a fresh-air swipe and falls on his arse like a drunk in a Frank Randle film. Big Jack jogs back to the centre circle wearing an uncomplicated expression of benign happiness, floating upfield like a balloon with a pair of dots for eyes and a U drawn on it. Peter Houseman equalises, then accidentally spits all over his shirt. The pitch is a quagmire. Innocent times.

The replay at Old Trafford wasn't quite so pure and wholesome. Had the game been played in 1996, when the referee David Elleray re-evaluated proceedings on video, there would have been 20 bookings and six red cards. It's not even worth contemplating the rap sheet in today's overfussy climate, suffice to say that upon filling out his post-match report, a referee would require several months off to receive lengthy treatment for RSI. Three Chelsea players — David Webb, Ron Harris and Charlie Cooke — did enough in Elleray's eyes to earn three bookings apiece.

Webb spent the opening quarter of an hour booting Eddie Gray and Allan Clarke up the Aris, then just before half time Harris clattered Gray — a delicate, floral genius — with one of the great reducers. Gray had attempted to turn the Chelsea galoot down the left. Chopper was having absolutely none of it. He took Gray's standing leg from under him as he turned, sending the Leeds winger arcing into the air. Clarke went up to remonstrate with Harris, who responded with an expression of stoned amusement. Gray meanwhile was on the turf grasping his left knee, face scrunched up in pain. The trainer Les Cocker came on to bend Gray's jiggered joint up and down, like a good old-fashioned 1970s quack, while Billy Bremner held Gray's hand, wearing a look of concern usually only seen on mothers taking their first-born to the dentist for the very first time.

It has become the signature moment of a brutal game, yet it was not the most outrageous act visited upon poor Gray's person. Two minutes after Chopper's Career Compromiser, Gray was hobbling around on the left wing, waiting for the half-time whistle and some proper rest and recuperation. He didn't really want a hospital pass from Johnny Giles but he got one anyway. Gray went to hoick the ball up the wing, away from personal danger. But it was too late. Ian Hutchison hoved into view, sliding along the grass and whipping the flaccid Gray into the air like a pancake. The recently damaged Gray understandably took exception and meted out retribution by stamping on his assailant's leg. At which point Hutchison sprang up and punched Gray right on the tip of his front tail.

Two red cards right there, not counting Chopper's earlier intervention. Injury having been added to injury, the referee pops a little insult into the mix as well, by doing absolutely nothing. Play went on. The half-time break did little for Gray, who was effectively jiggered for the entire match. The Leeds winger having run riot during the opening game at Wembley, Harris's assault had effectively won Chelsea the cup final, and lost it for Leeds, who had already fallen apart during the league run-in, gifting the title to Everton, and capitulated against Celtic in the European Cup semi-final. A trifecta of torture, and one reflected in the final line of the report by the man from the *Guardian*: "I understand that there is no truth in the report that the Leeds players were presented with statuettes of a blind-folded Justice."

2. Werner Liebrich on Ferenc Puskás (WEST GERMANY v Hungary, World Cup group game, 1954)

The 1954 World Cup is remembered principally for feats of scoring. Tournament records include the highest average number of goals per game (a whopping 5.38), the most goals in a single game (Austria 7-5 Switzerland) and the biggest win ever (Hungary's 9-0 victory over South Korea). All good, clean, wholesome, occasionally-one-sided fun. But the real signature moments of the tournament involved acts of mindless brutality – including one act of wanton hoodlumery which effectively decided where the pot was going.

In the group stages, with West Germany trailing Hungary by five goals, the mists descended on Werner Liebrich. Ferenc Puskás had been walking his team-mate Jupp Posipal around the pitch like a docile dachshund for the best part of an hour, so Liebrich took Posipal's place on the end of the lead, whereupon he began snapping at the Hungarian's heel. "My opponent," Puskas later recalled, "finding his skill of no avail resorted to roughness ... it was inevitable that sooner or later I would be badly injured." Liebrich viciously kicked the Galloping Gut on the back of his boot, putting Hungary's captain out of the next two games, and seriously handicapping him for the Magical Magyars' ill-fated final.

Not that the Hungarians themselves were saints. Their next match is probably the most outrageous in World Cup history, a quarter-final against Brazil that would go down in history as the Battle of Berne. Hungary went two up within seven minutes, Nándor Hidegkuti scoring one, setting up the other, then having his shorts ripped in two by an opponent, no mean feat in an era when footballers' apparel was made from durable, hard-wearing material (unlike today's skimpy confections of cobwebs and candyfloss fused together by the tears of an eight year old in a sweatshop). Hidegkuti's embarrassment was a harbinger of worse to come. József Tóth was forced to depart after finishing last in a midfield brawl. Brazil captain Bauer clanked into József Bozsik, who required lengthy treatment off the field, came back onto it wearing a face and was soon sent packing again after dusting the jowls of Nilton Santos, who retaliated and was also sent off. Djalma Santos went haring after Czibor with the express intention of smacking him in the mouth. Hidegkuti shoved Indio to the floor and went for a jaunty perambulation up and down the prostrate player's thighs. Didi clattered Hidegkuti by way of return. Humberto then walked for launching himself at Koscis.

Puskás later described the match as "a desperate tussle of ruthless brutality". Despite having sat the entire game out injured in the stand, he did his bit for the cause. With Hungary celebrating as they changed after the game, a Brazilian player threw a glass soda siphon into the dressing room, then bust the light bulb. In the darkness, a ten-minute melee ensued, during which Puskás clacked Pinheiro upside the head with a broken bottle, and Toth was knocked spark out. "What the Brazilians hoped to achieve," sighed Puskás, checking the damage to his knuckles, "we will never know."

Hungary went on to play reigning champions Uruguay in the semi. The much-fancied Hungarians, purported to be by some distance the best team in the world, stroked the ball around in a confident manner for fully 15 seconds. Jenő Buzánszky rolled the ball down the inside-right channel for Hidegkuti, who looked to turn cleverly. Víctor Rodríguez Andrade came straight through the back

of him, a no-nonsense early softener which makes Roy Keane's demolition of Marc Overmars in a 2001 World Cup qualifier and Vinnie Jones's reducer on Steve McMahon at the 1988 FA Cup final look like exchanging of handshakes, pennants and air kisses. Fancy football? Not on Víctor's watch, Nándor! And yet the match was subsequently played out in the most sporting of fashions and is commonly regarded as one of the most entertaining and dramatic in World Cup history. "They were really great," said Puskás later. So well done to Mr Rodríguez Andrade for establishing that there'd be no playing of silly buggers early doors.

3 Jair Rosa Pinto on José Salomon (Argentina v BRAZIL, South American Championship, 1946)

Brazil and the beautiful game? *Joga bullshitto!* The stunt Brendan Rodgers is currently pulling on the more impressionable section of Liverpool's support aside, it's the biggest confidence trick in soccer. Look! Here comes the *Seleção* now, all packed into a cab trailing a massive tanker full of snake oil. Of course, let the record state that the Brazilian teams of 1950, 1958, 1970 and 1982 were some of the most aesthetically pleasing in the history of the sport. But the tippy-tappy fun shouldn't obscure their time-honoured embrace of the more thuggish aspects of the game.

The side they took to the 1974 World Cup is perhaps the most depressing. Defending the title they had won with such style four years earlier, but without Pelé, Clodoaldo, Carlos Alberto and Tostão, these toasters were a clodhopping shower. Brazil muscled in six goals during their six games, but three of them came against a travelling circus troupe from Zaire. The only memorable mark they left on the tournament was to be found on Johan Neeskens's leg, which Luís Pereira stopped just short of hacking off with a rusty axe as he lumbered from the centre-circle towards the Dutch star, who was about to break clear down the left, and put an abrupt halt to his gallop.

Brazil's winners from 1994 were decent enough, and nothing more, but could have been something special had Leonardo not decided to crump his elbow into Tab Ramos's cheek and get himself thrown out of the tournament . The 2010 selection would probably have made the final in South Africa had Filipe Melo not morphed into a Tony Pulis wet dream made flesh midway through a game against Holland. And Brazil's first win, back in 1958, is remembered chiefly for the carefree antics of Pelé and Garrincha, yet the victory may never come about had Vavá not cleaned out Robert Jonquet in the semi-final with a malicious trundle through the French captain's standing leg. The score was 1-1 at the time; effectively down to 10 men, France crumbled to a 5-2 defeat.

But at least Brazil were bringing something to the table in 1958. Thirteen years earlier, a 6-2 win over Argentina was overshadowed by the striker Ademir Menezes's leg-breaking assault on José Batagliero. The challenge, egregious in the extreme, allowed resentment to fester, and in a South American Championship decider the following year in Buenos Aires, all hell broke loose when Jair Rosa Pinto showed his studs to José Salomon, resulting in a second broken Argentinian leg. The repercussions were immense, starting with an immediate full and frank exchange of views via the medium of ABH. Salomon's pal Juan Fonda went chest to chest with Jair, whose team-mate Chico soon arrived on the scene. The Brazilian went to grab Fonda, at which point four Argentinians decided it was indeed Chico Time, clocked him to the floor and gave him a good shoeing. Cue crowd invasion.

The game did eventually restart, with Argentina winning 2-0 to take the title, but with Salomon's career effectively over, relations between the South American neighbours soured. Argentina refused to enter the 1950 World Cup as Brazil were staging it and the two countries didn't play each other again for a decade. Beautiful game? They're doing doughnuts in that tanker!

4. Graeme Souness on Iosif Rotariu (RANGERS v Steaua Bucharest, European Cup quarter-final second leg, 1988)

Rangers on the verge of a European Cup semi-final. It seems a long, long time ago now. Mind you, it seemed a long, long time ago back in 1988, too. The club hadn't made the semis of Europe's premier competition since 1960, the year they learned their place in the grand scheme of things: a 10-4 evisceration at the hands of Eintracht Frankfurt, who would in turn get their arses skelped in Glasgow by Real Madrid in *that* final.

But after years in the doldrums, Rangers had started thinking and spending big in the mid-1980s — hell, why not, what could go wrong? — and after winning their first domestic title for nine years in 1987, the investments made by the new manager Graeme Souness started paying off in Europe. Rangers fought their way past a superb Dynamo Kyiv side in the first round — albeit by bringing the sidelines in to negate the left-wing sorties of Oleh Blokhin. "The pitch didn't have to be a fixed width as long as it was above a certain minimum, so I thought: Right, I'll make it the absolute minimum," explained Souness. "On the Tuesday afternoon the Kyiv players trained on the pitch when it was the normal size. On the Wednesday night they came out for the match and must have been shocked to discover that, after 15 paces, they were on the touchline. It wasn't purist stuff but it was within the rules."

If that episode didn't clearly illustrate Souness's raging desire to succeed at all costs in Europe, the quarter-final second leg against Steaua Bucharest at Ibrox — Górnik Zabrze of Poland having been dispatched in round two — would complete the picture. Steaua had won the first leg 2-0 in Bucharest, the home side helping Ally McCoist, who had undergone a knee operation eight days earlier, test his surgeon's skills by repeatedly trying to knacker his tender joint. "They whacked me twice," winced McCoist after the game, "but they picked the wrong leg."

The result left Rangers with a rare old traipse up a hill against a side built around the emerging Gheorghe Hagi. And that journey soon became mountainous when Marius Lăcătuş scored within 150 seconds in Glasgow to leave Rangers needing four goals.

Souness's reaction was legendary and outrageous. In possession of the ball near the centre circle, he looked to advance into Romanian territory. Miscontrolling, he raised his boot and pushed his studs into the upper thigh of Iosif Rotariu, who had otherwise been minding his own business. It was the challenge he had been building up to ever since making his competitive debut for the club at Hibs, which had lasted 37 minutes and ended in a 21-man brawl that saw Souness off and every other participant booked. Some marker.

Admirably, having studded Rotariu, Souness had the chutzpah to bend down and point at an imaginary tender spot on the back of his sock, offering the referee an explanation for the righteous retribution meted out. The ploy worked: he was only booked — and Rangers, still with their full compliment, gave their attempted comeback a good rattle, Richard Gough and McCoist scoring before half time to cut the arrears in half. But Steaua, who had won the trophy two years earlier, and would make another final within 13 months, held out.

Souness's foul would attract understandable opprobrium, but one of the most vociferous critics was his own newly purchased Danish full-back Jan Bartram, who while on international duty soon after denounced his new manager to the Copenhagen paper *Ekstra Bladet* as "a hooligan... I will not follow orders and deliberately kick people." Bartram retracted in stages. "I regret saying so much, but I wanted to give only honest answers," he whimpered a day later. "I could not sleep at night after giving the interview. I expect a very hot reception because of what I said. I think I may be fired." Upon his return to Govan, Bartram appeared in front of the press with Souness in a sweetness-and-light press conference, explaining that "it would be suicide for me to say the things I am supposed to have said." What was discussed backstage between the pair remains a secret but we can hazard a guess, for Bartram left not long after anyway.

5 Romeo Benetti on Kevin Keegan (England v ITALY, World Cup qualifier, 1977)

You would have to have a heart of stone not to feel sorry for little Kevin Keegan, the poor wretch, who has spent much of his life getting roughed up by the big boys. Take what is perhaps the signature image of seventies football: Keegan taking his leave of the 1974 Charity Shield with shirt off and face on, his top lip and nipples quivering gently in the summer breeze after being worked over by Johnny Giles and Billy Bremner, the Leeds pair taking turns to clank their fists into the Liverpool striker's indignant face. Keegan was banned for 11 matches for the privilege, time he at least put to good use by playing lots of golf and getting married.

Mind you, that wasn't even the height of it that summer. On a post-season trip to Yugoslavia with England, Keegan was spotted gooning around in Belgrade airport near the luggage carousel. He was taken by the throat by some Yugoslav officials, pinned against a wall, punched on the nose and in the stomach, and then dragged into a side room for a proper going over. FA officials eventually negotiated the release of their hapless striker, who was cashiered back into society bleeding and crying but not before smashing an earthenware coffee set he'd just purchased in the duty-free shop.

And then there's that business with the baseball bat. But let's leave the man with at least a sliver of dignity.

But before we move on, it's worth remembering the attention Italy gave England's mighty mouse during a qualifier for the 1978 World Cup at Wembley. The *Azzurri* were certainly in the mood that night, with Romeo Benetti and Claudio Gentile both going in the referee's notepad for lunges which were perfectly timed, in the comedic sense, on the heels of the dancing winger Peter Barnes. And yet it was Keegan who attracted most of the flak. To be fair, he had brought some of it on himself by loosening the teeth of the moustachioed nutcase Benetti, a challenge which led to the Juventus midfielder promising to "get" Keegan "before the finish". Also, it probably didn't help Italy's mood that Keegan had already scored the opening goal.

Benetti would honour his promise, but not before his teammate Marco Tardelli had softened Keegan up a wee bit. Chasing a ball going towards the corner flag, Keegan fell a step behind Tardelli, affording the Italian the opportunity of crumping his elbow into the striker's face. Keegan was sent to the floor spark out; the referee shrugged and took no action as the smelling salts were administered to England's groggy star. And with 10 minutes to go, the *pièce de résistance*. Keegan slid a peachy pass down the inside-right channel to split the Italian defence in two and allow Trevor

Brooking to seal a 2-0 win — and had both legs whipped from under him as Benetti arrived to clean him out while everyone else's attention was occupied by Brooking. The referee, needless to say, took no action there either, but he'd missed this one. Sneaky, spiteful, and perfectly timed. There's genius in this.

 ### Mario David on Leonel Sánchez (Chile v ITALY, World Cup, 1962)

The history of football is littered with instances of bench-emptying brouhahas. A 1997 game between Mexican also-rans Toros Neza and the Jamaica national team ended (on 19 minutes) with the sort of brawl only previously seen in the saloon bars of the Wild West. A common-or-garden trade of scything tackle and retaliatory smack in the mouth instigated a five-minute 22-man synchronised display of haymakers and highkicks, before several members of the Jamaica side nipped into the changing rooms, coming back tooled up with bricks, bottles and — deliciously — a chair. All that was missing from the scene was a staircase with a rickety wooden bannister for folk to fall through and barrelhouse piano to fall on top of and we'd have had ourselves a John Ford movie.

A more sinister rumble was played out at Boca Juniors' Bombonera stadium in 1971, upon the home side letting a two-goal lead slip in a must-win Copa Libertadores tie with Sporting Cristal of Peru. In the dying minutes, with Boca desperately pressing for a winner, the striker Robert Rogel collapsed it in the box, but failed to get the penalty decision he was after. Cue a 19-man dust-up which saw Boca captain Rubén Suñé fly-kicked in the face

(seven stitches), Cristal's Fernando Mellán toe-punted in the head (initial prognosis brain damage, although this was later downgraded to fractured skull) and the Cristal defender Orlando de la Torre's mum suffering a fatal heart attack while watching the rumpus unfold on the telly. We were also going to mention Arsenal's spats with Manchester United and Norwich City during their morally bankrupt (and therefore really rather entertaining) years under George Graham but those suddenly seem oh so tame.

But quite often the most obvious choices are made for a reason and the infamous Battle of Santiago remains the yardstick by which all Outrages Which We Secretly Swing Our Boots Up On The Desk To Enjoy are measured. David Coleman famously introduced the BBC's highlights package — no live intercontinental transmission back in 1962, pop kids, with footage having to be flown back from Chile by metal bird — by calling the match "stupid, appalling, disgusting and disgraceful", and questioning whether the World Cup could even "survive in its present form". But he was always a pompous bag of flatulent air. And in any case, he could barely disguise his excitement when actually commentating on the antics as they unfolded.

In retrospect, the game was always going to kick off. A couple of Italian journalists had written a travelogue describing Santiago as a slum full of sluttish women, the charmers, and had been chased out of the country as a result. The poor sods representing them on the football field had no choice but to stay put, however, and face the music in a group game with the hosts. AC Milan's Mario David, fresh from winning

Serie A, decided to address any potential recriminations in a proactive manner. His performance, fuelled by one long hot rush of blood, stands as one of the great indiscreet meltdowns of all time. On five minutes, he hacked the opposing midfielder Leonel Sánchez to the floor, then seconds later raked his studs across Eladio Rojas's ankles, before springing to his feet with dukes up. The brazen wantonness of the double whammy set the tone. "This looks like turning into a real battle," chirped Coleman, adding with an audible smile: "What a scene!"

The view in Italy was more circumspect. "There is a lot of electricity in this match," noted the Canale 5 commentator Nando Martellini. "The climate is very heavy." He'd called that damn straight. Within three minutes, Giorgio Ferrini launched a needless roundhouse at Honorino Landa and refused to walk. The peelers were called on to escort him off. Meanwhile David's over-enthusiasm could not be curbed. Just before half-time, he decided to kick away at the prone Sánchez in a wholly disingenuous attempt to release a ball that had been trapped under the Chilean. Bad move. Sánchez, the southpaw son of a pro boxer, jumped up and clattered David under the chin with a majestic haymaker. David was spark out. Sánchez, amazingly, was allowed to stay on the field without so much as a caution from the referee Ken Aston. As a Fifa advisor, Aston would later revolutionise refereeing with the coldly logical red and yellow card system but appears to have taken a more avant-garde, freeform approach to administering the laws of the game when on the beat himself.

It's just as well Sánchez was allowed to stay on because had he walked we would never have witnessed the foul we're about to celebrate. By way of retribution, David launched himself towards Sánchez a few minutes later, pushing his studs into the Chilean's coupon with kung-fu grace. "Ooh, that was one of the worst tackles I've ever seen," cooed Coleman. "He's bought it right in the face!" David having been sent packing, consumed by his own hot heat, the rest of the match was tame by comparison: Sánchez broke the Internazionale striker Humberto Maschio's hooter after throwing hands again; Jorge Toro rugby tackled Bruno Mora, the two rolling around on the floor like actors in a PCP-fuelled production of *Women In Love*; Sandro Salvadore and Honorino Landa went chest to chest in the very last act of the match. But it's Sánchez's sweet left hook and David's divine retribution that everyone remembers. The highlight of the 1962 World Cup by some distance. Can you replay the goals from the final in your mind's eye?

---

7 **Oscar Malbernat and Carlos Pachamé on Joop van Daele (Feyenoord v ESTUDIANTES, 1970)**

Alf Ramsey had some cheek calling out Antonio Rattin and his Argentina side for their animalistic tendencies during *that* 1966 World Cup quarter final, given the way Nobby Stiles had autographed the France midfielder Jacky Simon's leg a few days earlier. But English football's most successful old xenophobe should be congratulated for his prescience, if nothing else. Because as the sixties trundled towards their depressing denouement, everyone involved with the Argentinian club scene was busy loading up the handcart in preparation for a journey to the bottom of a very hot hole.

The first stage of their diabolical journey was embarked on in 1967, when Racing Club took on Celtic in the Intercontinental Cup. Argentina still harboured a grudge regarding the perceived injustices of the Rattin affair and were simply not interested in the fact that Celtic's homeland is not wholly in sync with their neighbours from the south. In no mood to differentiate between the English and the Scots, Racing spent the two legs of the prestige rubber kicking the two legs of Jimmy Johnstone. With the sides level after 180 minutes of Jinky being tossed around like that plastic bag in American Beauty, a third match was staged. It was described by Reuters as "a bar-room brawl with soccer skills abandoned for swinging fists, flying boots and blatant body checking". Johnstone was again hacked down and retaliated, causing a melée which resulted in Alfio Basile and Bobby Lennox being sent off.

Johnstone was among four other players dismissed during a tumultuous second half, John Hughes, Juan Carlos Rulli and Bertie Auld also walking. Auld, cooking at gas mark nine, refused to leave the field and was allowed to play on by a referee who had lost all control. Celtic, having had four men sent off, fined their players £250 each. The Racing players, who had won 1-0, were all rewarded with a new car. The game cost Jock Stein a knighthood. "His name was removed from the New Year's Honours list because of the unfortunate events in South America," said a letter sent by the Scottish Office to the prime minister Harold Wilson in 1970. "The next year

when Manchester United won the European Cup an immediate knighthood went to Matt Busby in the birthday list. Had we been able to move as quickly the previous year, Stein would have had his honour before the troubles in Argentina."

Enter Estudiantes de la Plata, who would raise the bar with their anti-fútbol. (One of their tactics was known as 'pincharratas' and involved players carrying pins which they would jab into opponents at corners and free-kicks.) Their 1968 clash with Manchester United was nothing short of explosive — Bobby Charlton getting his head broken open, George Best goaded into punching José Medina on the nose, Medina being pelted to the ground with coins as he attempted to make for the dressing-room — but their brouhaha with Milan a year later was thermonuclear.

In the second leg of that nonsense, the Milan striker Pierino Prati was flattened by the elbow of Alberto Suárez (who had once served a 30-day jail sentence for a soft-shoe shuffle on the head of a prone opponent in a league match). While Prati was receiving treatment, the Estudiantes goalkeeper Alberto Poletti sidled up behind the player and, as he tried to get up, kicked him in the back.

After Milan scored, Poletti went on a small rampage, setting about several Italians as they celebrated their goal. Suárez then punched Nestor Combin in the face — the striker nearly lost an eye — and was sent off. Combin was stretchered off and immediately arrested by bobbies who falsely claimed that the Argentina-born star had evaded national service. He was later released after several hours of frantic diplomatic chat.

Suárez meanwhile was arrested, along with Poletti and the midfielder Madero, on the order of Argentina's embarrassed president, and put in the jug for a month.

But Estudiantes' zenith came the following year, when the defender Oscar Malbernat whipped the spectacles off the nose of the Feyenoord defender Joop van Daele and passed them to his teammate Carlos Pachamé, who stamped on them. It was an act of playground brutality — kids really are the cruellest — although Van Daele had the last laugh by scoring the winner to secure the trophy.

Ajax would refuse to play Nacional of Uruguay the year after. They relented to face Independiente in 1972, but when Johan Cruyff's ankle was shredded, Europe decided enough was enough. The next few years saw the European champions Ajax, Bayern Munich, Liverpool and Nottingham Forest all turn down opportunities to compete. Forest got back on the horse in 1980 and some sort of intercontinental match has been played in some form or other ever since. But while hostilities were resumed, hostilities have never been resumed. The pundits can get as pious as they like, but it's never been anywhere near as much fun. Good old Estudiantes!

Ⓑ

Contributors

The Blizzard, Issue Seven

David Ashton is a playwright, TV and film screenwriter; creator of the BBC Radio 4 series, *McLevy*. He has written three novels, the latest being *A Trick of the Light*. Also an actor, he played Dr McDuff in *Brass*. His website is **www.david-ashton.co.uk**.

Philippe Auclair is the author of *The Enchanted Kingdom of Tony Blair* (in French) and *Cantona: the Rebel Who Would Be King*, which was named NSC Football Book of the Year. His biography of Thierry Henry has just been published. He writes for *France Football*, *Offside* and *Champions* and provides analysis and commentary for RMC Sport. He also pursues a parallel career in music under the name 'Louis Philippe'. **Twitter: @PhilippeAuclair**

Paolo Bandini is a freelance football journalist. After six years on staff at the *Guardian*, he has now relocated to the US Midwest where he continues to write and talk for a variety of publications and broadcasters on both sides of the Atlantic. **Twitter: @Paolo_Bandini**

Joachim Barbier is a football and cinema writer mostly contributing for *So Foot*. He is the author of *Football, Made in Africa* (ahead of the 2010 World Cup) and *The Country that Doesn't Like Football* (on France's lack of football culture). After focusing on football in Africa for 10 years, he has turned his attention to central and eastern Europe.

Dominic Bliss has contributed articles to a number of magazines and prestige publications, including the FA Cup Final, Football League Play-Off Finals and Uefa Super Cup programmes. He is founder and editor of the online football journal TheInsideLeft.com. **Twitter: @theinsidelefty**

Paul Brown has written for the *Guardian*, *FourFourTwo* and *When Saturday Comes*. His books include *Unofficial Football World Champions*, *Balls: Tales from Football's Nether Regions* and the forthcoming *Football and Stottie Cakes*. He is the editor of *Goal-Post: Victorian Football*. **Twitter: @paulbrownUK**

Anthony Clavane is the author of *Promised Land: A Northern Love Story*, which won the National Sporting Club's Football Book of the Year Award. His latest book is *Does Your Rabbi Know You're Here?* He writes about sport for the *Sunday Mirror*. **Twitter: @lufcpromised**

John Harding lives and works in North London and writes on a variety of topics, ranging from literary and sporting biography to cultural history and criticism. Past subjects include the footballers Billy Meredith and Alex James, boxer Jack 'Kid' Berg and poet and cartoonist Ralph Hodgson. He is also the Professional Footballer's Association's official historian. He is working on a study of the playwright Shelagh Delaney.

Henry Leach was born in 1874 and began his career as a local football reporter, before being appointed editor of the *Nottingham Evening News* while still in his early twenties. In 1898, he moved to London to write about sport for various publications including the boys' weekly *Chums*. He went on to become a leading writer on golf and the editor of *Golf Illustrated*.

Sergio Levinsky is an Argentinian sociologist and journalist. He is the author of three books and the editor of a World Cup encyclopaedia. He is a columnist for *Jornada* (Argentina), the Chinese website www.163.com and Yahoo in Japan. His website is **www. sergiolevinsky.com**.

Scott Murray writes for the *Guardian*. He is author of on-this-day football miscellany *Day of the Match*, and the preposterous but amusing *Phantom of the Open: Maurice Flitcroft, The World's Worst Golfer*.

Brian Phillips is a staff writer for Grantland and the editor of the football blog *The Run of Play*. His writing has appeared in Slate, Deadspin, *Poetry*, and The Hudson Review, among other publications. **Twitter: @runofplay**

Zac Lee Rigg is a senior editor of Goal. com USA. His favourite emotion is nostalgia. **Twitter: @zacrigg**

Septima Photos is a British-run photo agency based in Bogotá. Working in editorial and commercial photography they aim to change the world's negative pre-conceptions about Colombia. Often working with foundations to help disadvantaged children, they have a unique

philosophy as to what a photo agency can achieve. **Twitter: @Septima_Agency**

Stany Sirutis is a writer based in Bogotá. After a few years working on a novel, he's turned to freelance writing about football and other topics. He once worked in Canada as an AI tester on video-games such as Fifa and Total Club Manager. **Twitter: @RetoricaFutbol**

Zach Slaton is a freelance soccer writer, and is currently a contributor at the Sports & Leisure section of Forbes.com. His work can also be found in *Howler Magazine*, The Tomkins Times, The Transfer Price Index blog, and his own blog at abeautifulnumbersgame.com. **Twitter: @the_number_game**

Elliott Turner blogs about football at Futfanatico.com.

Jonathan Wilson is the author of *Inverting the Pyramid*, a winner of the National Sporting Club's Football Book of the Year, *Behind the Curtain*, *The Anatomy of England* and *Nobody Ever Says Thank You*. His latest book is *The Outsider: A History of the Goalkeeper*. He writes for the *Guardian*, *World Soccer*, *Foxsoccer*, *ESPN Star* and *Sports Illustrated*. **Twitter: @jonawils**

Richard Winton is the assistant sports editor of *The Herald* newspaper in Glasgow. **Twitter: @richardwinton**

Carl Worswick is a writer and journalist based in Bogotá specialising in Colombian football. He writes for the likes of *World Soccer* and *When Saturday Comes*. **Twitter @cworswick**

Blizzard Subscriptions

Subscribe to the print version of The Blizzard, *be the first to receive new issues, get exclusive Blizzard offers and access digital versions of all back-issues FREE*

Subscription Options

Set Price for Four Issues

Get a four-issue subscription to *The Blizzard* — for you or as a gift — for a flat fee including postage and packing (P&P):

UK:	£35
Europe:	£45
Non-Euorpe:	£55

Recurring Pay-What-You-Like

Set up a quarterly recurring payment for each edition of *The Blizzard*. The recommended retail price (RRP) is £12, but pay what you like, subject to a minimum fee of £6 plus P&P

See www.theblizzard.co.uk for more

Digital Subscriptions

If the cost of postage is prohibitive, or you just want an excuse to use your new iPad or Kindle, you can set up a subscription to digital versions of *The Blizzard* for just £3 per issue.

See www.theblizzard.co.uk for more

Information for Existing Subscribers

Free Digital Downloads for *Blizzard* Subscribers

Whether you have taken advantage of our set price or pay-what-you-like offer, for the duration of your subscription to *The Blizzard* you are entitled to download every issue FREE.

See www.theblizzard.co.uk for more

We very much value the commitment of our print subscribers and have a policy to make available new issues, special offers and other limited access events and benefits to print subscribers first.

About *The Blizzard*

Distribution & Back Issues
Contact Information
About Issue Seven

Buy *The Blizzard*

We want as many readers as possible for *The Blizzard*. We therefore operate as far as we are able on a pay-what-you-like basis for digital and print versions.

Digital Version (Current & Back Issues)

All issues of *The Blizzard* are available to download for Kindle, Android, iOS and PC/Mac at: *www.theblizzard.co.uk*.

- *RRP: £3*
- *Pay-what-you-like minimum: £0.01*

Printed Version (Current & Back Issues)

Purchase a physical copy of *The Blizzard* in all its luxurious, tactile, sensual glory at: *www.theblizzard.co.uk*. If you haven't felt our rough textured cover-varnish and smelled the inner genius, you haven't properly experienced its awesome true form. Read it, or leave it on your coffee table to wow visitors.

- *RRP: £12* (+P&P)
- *Pay-what-you-like min: £6* (+P&P)

Contact *The Blizzard*

All advertising, sales, press and business communication should be addressed to the Central Publishing Office:

The Blizzard
Ashmore Villa,
1, Ashmore Terrace,
Stockton Road,
Sunderland,
SR27DE

Email: info@theblizzard.co.uk
Telephone: +44 (0) 191 543 8785
Website: www.theblizzard.co.uk
Facebook: www.facebook.com/blzzrd
Twitter: @blzzrd

About Issue Seven

Editor Jonathan Wilson
Publisher The Blizzard Media Ltd
www.theblizzard.co.uk
Design Azure
www.azure-design.com

Copyright

All content is ©Copyright The Blizzard Media Ltd and may not be reproduced without explicit consent. Thanks to Jeanette G Sturis at the Kingsley Motel, Manjimup, for kind use of Warren Walker's original sketches of Dog.

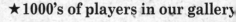